The Canon of the Mass and Liturgical Reform

The Canon of the Mass and Liturgical Reform

The Canon of the Mass and Liturgical Reform

CIPRIANO VAGAGGINI

Translation editor PETER COUGHLAN

First published as *Il canone della messa e la reforma liturgica*, by Elle di Ci, Torino-Leumann, in 1966.

First published this edition 1967

Nihil obstat: R. D. Jacobus Wroe, D.D., Ph.D., Censor Deputatus
Imprimatur: H. Gibney, Vicarius Generalis
Datum Southwarci die 29a Martii 1967

This book is set in 11/13 Imprint 101

Made and printed in Great Britain

Contents

Translator's Note

This translation was prepared by a group at the English College in Rome. Although in the Italian edition no translation of the anaphoras in the first chapter was given we have followed here the advice of Fr. A-M. Roguet, O.P., who, together with Dom Rouillard, O.S.B., has recently translated this book into French, and who suggested that a translation of the anaphoras would be useful. The translation of the present Roman canon is that of Fr. Harold Winstone, with a few minor changes.

Translations of the Fathers—including the anaphoras—are made from the Latin texts in Dom Vagaggini's Italian edition; faithfulness to these texts has been put before considerations of literary style and euphony. However, the translation of Dom Vagaggini's own suggested canon does attempt to present an English metrical version. It follows a definite syllabic pattern, which allows a wide variety of linear divisions: this form was chosen to facilitate the reading of the canon aloud. Even here it was thought preferable—where the two were in conflict—to try to render the exact sense of the original, rather than to sacrifice it for the sake of literary effect.

PETER COUGHLAN

ROME, *March*, 1967

Preface

One of these days the eucharistic prayer of the Roman Mass will change. Whether this comes about by way of radical revision of the Roman canon or by the addition of several alternative anaphoras, the change will come.

It will perhaps be only a minor tragedy if such a development catches the Catholic people—priests and laity—unprepared, but it will be one of a long series of unnecessary instances of this kind. In the English-speaking world, with some notable exceptions, discussion of the reform of the Roman canon has been negligible.

The lesson of the immediate past has not been learned. Bishops, priests, and teachers have been giving assurances for two or three decades now that liturgical changes are impossible or unlikely. Everything from the introduction of the vernacular to the Eucharist facing the people has been decried. And every such assurance has proved false.

At least one lesson should be learned, that liturgical reform has been decreed by a general Council—and the corollary is that we should listen to the prophets who have been proved right. In the English-speaking world these are the Reinholds, Hellriegels, Diekmanns, Howells, Crichtons, Ellards, and the like. Outside the English-speaking world no name stands higher in the field than Cipriano Vagaggini, the author of this study.

It is strange that in 1967, in spite of underground rumblings and clandestine celebrations, vast numbers of clergy and laity do not seriously expect the radical liturgical changes already determined by the Second Vatican Council. Some, most imprudently and unwisely, would prefer to have liturgical revisions drop from heaven or from the Holy See.

The import of this book is just the opposite: to prepare for change and to initiate discussion. It goes without saying that the author's approach is sound and scholarly.

In 1966 the National Conference of Catholic Bishops of the United States formally (and publicly) asked the Holy See to permit the Roman canon to be said or sung in English. This petition was the right of the episcopal conference under articles 54 and 40 of the conciliar *Constitution on the Liturgy*—as it was the Holy See's right under the same articles to give or to deny its consent.

The eucharistic prayer in the vernacular, however desirable, will make public something that has been overlooked except by liturgical and pastoral experts, namely, the defects of the Roman canon. The experience since 1964 provides a parallel case history.

Most of the priests who read the Latin texts and the people who perused their English translations prior to 1964 had not the remotest idea of the deficiencies of the Roman rite, especially the texts of the Roman Mass. It was only when the texts were sung or said aloud in the mother tongue that the problems became apparent.

This was evident even in the uninformed complaints concerning the English translations which were introduced provisionally. The criticism was one part stylistic and justified, one part ignorant of the meaning of the Latin, Greek, and Hebrew originals—the Latin prayers and the Hebrew and Greek scriptures. This latter criticism was not of translation but of the inconsistency and irrelevance, the imperfections and the complexities of the Roman liturgy itself.

Inevitably the use of the Roman canon in the vernacular, however brilliant the translation, will reveal unsuspected defects.

We can hope that the evidence of these defects will be considered patiently and that all the possibilities of development will be weighed calmly. The Roman eucharistic prayer has extraordinary worth; it is as good as and often better than most of the other anaphoras in widespread use. It would be arrogant and ignorant to dismiss it out of hand.

Yet the limitations and defects will call for the evolution of new forms. More importantly, the call comes from the need for contemporary and relevant expression of the paschal mystery which the Eucharist celebrates.

The simplistic solutions are already at hand: to use a relatively primitive eucharistic prayer, of which that of Hippolytus is the common favorite; to adopt oriental anaphoras, however incompatible with the sense and style of the Roman liturgy (or theology); to create a bland eucharistic prayer which might (or might not) serve ecumenical purposes.

We do not really need such solutions, even though they might well be acceptable as still additional options. We need rather the serious construction of new eucharistic prayers which reflect the progress of theological and liturgical science and which are meaningful—or can be made meaningful through study and reflection—to the twentieth-century Christian.

As these proposed versions of the eucharistic prayer are developed, they should be submitted to the widest possible public discussion and criticism. They should also be subjected to widespread and controlled experiment where they can be evaluated soundly for theological breadth, liturgical style and consistency, pastoral effectiveness, and simple intelligibility.

There has been much disapproval of clandestine liturgical celebrations with creative and uncreative innovations. Certainly these are often as naive as they are unlawful in the Church community. But the failure to welcome dialogue and liturgical evolution is just as bad, and the failure to develop official and public procedures of experiment is worse.

Father Vagaggini's book is a major contribution to the discussion. It should make a wider audience aware of the problems of the Roman canon and of possible solutions. In recommending the book, I cannot help adding a special note. Father Vagaggini's public contributions as scholar and writer are well known, but only the historian will be able to detail and evaluate his efforts at every stage in the work of the preparatory and conciliar commissions responsible for the *Constitution on the Liturgy* and in the postconciliar liturgical commission. Added to this are his personal greatness and goodness of which his liturgical studies and proposals are the sign.

FREDERICK R. MCMANUS

List of Liturgical Texts Frequently Quoted

B. Botte, *La tradition apostolique de saint Hippolyte. Essai de reconstitution* (*Liturgiew. Quellen und Forschungen*, 39), Münster i. W., 1963.

B. Botte, *Le canon de la messe romaine*, éd. critique, Louvain, 1935.

F. E. Brightman, *Liturgies Eastern and Western*, vol. I, Oxford, 1896.

J. Doresse and E. Lanne, *Un témoin archaïque de la liturgie copte de saint Basile. En annexe: Les liturgies "basiliennes" et saint Basile, par* D. B. Capelle (*Bibliothèque du Muséon*, 47), Louvain, 1960.

M. Ferotin, *Le "Liber Ordinum" en usage dans l'Eglise wisigothique et mozarabe*, Paris, 1904.

M. Ferotin, *Le "Liber mozarabicus Sacramentorum"*, Paris, 1912.

F. X. Funk, *Didascalia et Constitutiones Apostolorum*, 2 vols., Paderborn, 1905. The anaphora of the Apostolic Constitutions is to be found in vol. I, 498–514; and that of Serapion in vol. II, 172–6.

L. C. Mohlberg, *Sacramentarium veronense* (quoted: Leonine Sacramentary), Rome, 1956.

L. C. Mohlberg, *Missale francorum*, Rome, 1957.

L. C. Mohlberg, *Missale gallicanum vetus*, Rome, 1958.

L. C. Mohlberg, *Liber sacramentorum romanae aecclesiae ordinis anni circuli* (quoted: Gelasian Sacramentary), Rome, 1960.

L. C. Mohlberg, *Missale gothicum*, Rome, 1961.

A. Paredi, *Sacramentarium bergamense*, Bergamo, 1962.

E. Renaudot, *Liturgiarum orientalium collectio*, 2 vols., 2nd edition, Frankfurt, 1847.

C. H. Roberts-B. Capelle, *An Early Euchologium. The Dêr-Balizeh Papyrus Enlarged and Re-edited* (*Bibliothèque du Muséon*, 23), Louvain, 1949.

H. A. Wilson, *The Gregorian Sacramentary under Charles the Great* (*Henry Bradshaw society*, 49), London, 1915.

Glossary of Technical Terms

Anamnesis: a Greek word meaning "memorial", it was used in the narrative of the Eucharist in the New Testament (I Cor. 11: 24 ff.; Luke 22: 19). It is normally used to describe the prayer in which the Church remembers the Lord, and the redemptive acts he has accomplished. A great deal has been written, however, on the theology implied in the idea of "anamnesis".

Anaphora: normally applied to the oriental liturgies, this word is used to express the liturgical text which accompanies and expresses the offering of the Church's sacrifice to the Father. It is thus the central or essential prayer of the eucharistic liturgy. Like the word "canon" in the Roman liturgy, it refers to the consecratory prayer of the Eucharist, and extends from the dialogue of the *Sursum corda* to the great doxology. It tends to be freer and wider in its meaning than "canon", sometimes being taken to include also the communion.

Doxology: used of a prayer which ascribes glory to someone, it sometimes refers to prayers ascribing glory to Christ, but more generally of prayers ascribing glory to all the Persons of the Blessed Trinity, e.g. at the end of the canon.

Epiclesis: originally meaning merely "invocation", it normally refers to an invocation to the Father to send down the Holy Spirit in order to sanctify something or someone. The term has a wider meaning than this, however, and has been applied to many forms of invocation, e.g. the "Logos-epiclesis". When used of the Eucharist it refers to the invocation to the Father to sanctify the offerings and the people who participate in them. The epiclesis is pneumatological when we ask the Father to send the Spirit to sanctify, and it is consecratory when we ask that the bread and wine may become the body and blood of Christ.

Introduction

The Roman canon presents those engaged in liturgical reform with problems both in the text and in the actions that accompany the text. Here our concern is with the text alone.

We must approach this task with great care and reverence, especially because of the aura of mystery which surrounds the sacred action contained in the canon. We must also show due regard for its antiquity and its importance in the history of Western liturgy and spirituality. Nor must we forget that it is the only anaphora known to priests, and is intimately linked with their spiritual life. Furthermore, it has very real virtues as a liturgical document and derives added importance from the fact that the Church found herself obliged to defend this canon against the attacks of the Protestants, who took exception not so much to its liturgical and literary structure as to the traditional Catholic dogmas it enshrines. These considerations then oblige us to tackle the reform of the canon with all due care and respect.

However, such respect should not—and today cannot—deter us from beginning an objective examination of the canon's intrinsic limitations and manifest defects.

For a variety of reasons, it is now possible and indeed essential to evaluate the merits and demerits of the present Roman canon, both from the theological and liturgical aspects, and from the point of view of spiritual and pastoral needs.

The principles of liturgical reform and the Roman canon

I shall first of all give the principles formulated by the Second Vatican Council. Then we shall be able to see the form the liturgy must take if it is to meet the demands made upon it. These principles are, of course, already well known to every liturgist and pastor of souls:

1. The fundamental norm: the texts and rites must, as far as possible, nourish the faith of the people, and encourage their full, active participation; and so the faithful should normally be able to understand these texts and rites.[1]

2. The conclusion which follows inevitably from this first principle concerns the language used in the liturgy—a conclusion which the Council did not hesitate to make. And it hardly needs a prophet to predict that the obstacles put in the way of its execution will soon be overcome. This will come about not so much by means of a *fait accompli*, but for a much more important reason, namely that people are becoming more aware of the overriding principle in the liturgy, the good of souls.

3. It also follows that the rites and texts must be "distinguished by a noble simplicity; they should be short, clear, and unencumbered by useless repetitions; they should be within the people's powers of comprehension; and normally should not require much explanation".[2]

4. If for one reason or another this is not the case, then the reform of such texts and rites should be undertaken. For the liturgy "is made up of unchangeable elements divinely instituted, and of elements subject to change. The latter not only may but ought to be changed with the passing of time, if features have by chance crept in which are less harmonious with the intimate nature of the liturgy, or if existing elements have grown less functional. In this restoration, both texts and rites should be drawn up so that they express more clearly the holy things which they signify. Christian people, as far as possible, should be able to understand them with ease, and to take part in them fully, actively, and as befits a community".[3]

5. In the reform, sound traditions must be preserved, but at the same time, the way must be left open for legitimate progress. Reform must, therefore, be based on accurate research, which should be theological, historical and pastoral, while taking into

[1] *Constitution on the Liturgy*, art. 33.
[2] Ibid., art. 34.
[3] Ibid., art. 21.

consideration the general laws which underlie the structure of the liturgy and form its spirit. Of course, no innovation may be introduced except in proven cases of genuine benefit for the Church. However, once such benefit is indeed proven, we should not shirk the task of creating afresh if necessary, although it must be remembered that any new forms "must in some way grow organically from forms already existing".[4]

6. These general norms concerning the whole liturgy have been applied by the Council itself to the Mass: "The Church, therefore, earnestly desires that Christ's faithful, when present at this mystery of faith, should not be there as strangers or silent spectators. On the contrary, through a proper appreciation of the rites and prayers they should participate knowingly, devoutly and actively. They should be instructed by God's Word and be refreshed at the table of the Lord's body; they should give thanks to God; by offering the Immaculate Victim, not only through the hands of the priest, but also with him, they should learn to offer themselves too. Through Christ the Mediator, they should be drawn day by day into ever closer union with God and with each other, so that finally God may be all in all."[5]

7. "The rite of the Mass is to be revised in such a way that the intrinsic nature and purpose of its several parts, as also the connection between them can be more clearly manifested, and that devout and active participation by the faithful can be more easily accomplished. For this purpose the rites are to be simplified, while due care is taken to preserve their substance. Elements which, with the passage of time, came to be duplicated, or were added with but little advantage, are now to be discarded. Where opportunity allows or necessity demands, other elements which have suffered injury through accidents of history are now to be restored to the earlier norm of the holy Fathers."[6]

It needs only a moment's thought to realise that the present arrangement and structure of the Roman canon will not bear

---

[4] Ibid., art. 23.
[5] Ibid., art. 48.
[6] Ibid., art. 50.

comparison with these principles. And today we can no longer put off such a comparison and its consequences, since these principles are the very essence of the renewed appreciation of the liturgy which we see spreading everywhere today.

Data from comparative liturgy and from liturgical history, and the Roman canon

Modern studies in comparative liturgy have made available a wide range of information concerning the anaphora tradition of the universal Church.[7] Although much remains to be done in this field, the data already acquired shed considerable light on the exact value of the Roman canon.

Nothing could be more simple today than to compare the Roman canon with, for example, the canon of Hippolytus—a canon which is now known to be the oldest form of anaphora that has come down to us from the primitive Church. We could also

---

[7] There is no need here to refer to older works, for which see the bibliography in Cabrol, art. "Canon", in *Dict. d'arch. chrét. et de lit.*, II, 2 (1925), 1847–1905; and ibid., art. "Anaphore", I, 2 (1924), 1898–1918. Useful, if debatable in his general theories of interpretation, is H. Lietzmann, *Messe und Herrenmahl*, Bonn, 1926 (3rd ed., Berlin, 1955). For a bibliography on the oriental anaphoras, cf. J. M. Hanssens, *Institutiones liturgicae de ritibus orientalibus*, t. III, pars altera, Rome, 1932, 345–485; J. M. Sauget, *Bibliographie des liturgies orientales* (1900–1960), Rome, 1962, 17–20. The following have made notable contributions: H. Engberding, *Das Eucharistische Hochgebet der Basileiosliturgie*, Münster i. W., 1931; B. Capelle, "L'anaphore de Serapion; essai d'exégèse", in *Le Muséon*, 59 (1946), 425–43; C. H. Roberts-B. Capelle, *An Early Euchologium, The Dêr-Balizeh Papyrus Enlarged and Re-edited*, Louvain, 1949; J. Doresse-E. Lanne, *Un témoin archaïque de la liturgie copte de Saint Basile; En annexe: Les liturgies "basiliennes" et Saint Basile, par* B. Capelle, Louvain, 1960; B. Botte, *La tradition apostolique de saint Hippolyte*, Münster i. W., 1963; ibid., "Problèmes de l'anaphore syrienne des apôtres Addaï et Mari", in *L'Orient syrien*, 10 (1965), 89–106; "L'euchologe de Sérapion est-il authentique?", in *Oriens christianus*, 48 (1964), 50–6. For the Ethiopian anaphoras cf. G. M. Harden, *The Anaphoras of the Ethiopian Liturgy*, London, 1928. For the Ambrosian anaphora cf. P. Borella, "Unità et continuità del canone nei testi ambrosiani del giovedì santo e della veglia pasquale", in *Ambrosius*, 41 (1965), 79–100. For the early Spanish tradition, cf. M. Ramos, *La gran oraciòn eucaristica en la antigua misa española*, Granada, 1963. For the general meaning and structure of the anaphoras see P. Audet, "Esquisse historique du genre littéraire de la 'bénédiction' juive et de l''eucharistie' chrétienne", in *Rev. Bibl.*, 65 (1958), 371–99; B. Fraigneau-Julien, "Eléments de la structure fondamentale de l'eucharistie. Bénédiction, anamnèse et action de grâces", in *Rev. Sc. Relig.*, 34

compare it with the Alexandrine anaphora, attributed to St Basil, which is thought to be the most ancient of all known anaphoras—or at least the purest example of the so-called Antioch tradition. In comparison with the clarity, simplicity and lapidary structure of these examples, the Roman canon, it must be admitted, leaves much to be desired. On the other hand, it is perfectly clear that no other anaphora tradition can compare with the Roman, especially the ancient one, for the richness, variety and exceptional quality of its prefaces.

Finally, there are the many studies on the historical circumstances which led to the formation of the Roman canon.[8] Admittedly the details of this history are often very obscure where the primitive Latin canon is concerned, and we know little of how it developed between the fifth and seventh centuries and became the canon we have today. Nevertheless, taken together with the internal criticism of the canon itself, these historical studies provide

---

(1960), 35–61; G. Every, *Basic Liturgy, A study of the Eucharistic Prayer*, London, 1961, with a bibliography of preceding works. In the Anglican church recently there has been a serious movement for the revision of the anaphoras and the creation of new forms; see the texts in B. Wigan (ed.), *The Liturgy in English*, London, 1962; cf. also C. K. Sansbury, "Recent Revisions of the Eucharistic Prayer", in *Theology*, 59 (1956), 281–8; and ibid., 57 (1954), 163–9. A similar movement exists among the Protestant communities.

The recent studies on the epiclesis give considerable assistance in understanding more fully the nature and structure of the anaphoras. Very relevant is H. Lietzmann, *Messe und Herrenmahl*, 3rd ed., 68–122, not to mention M. Jugie, *De forma eucharistiae. De epiclesibus eucharisticis*, Rome, 1943 (cf. also "Epiclèse eucharistique", in *Dict. théol. cath.*, V-1 (1939), 194–300). The following authors have also been of use to me: C. C. Richardson, "The Origin of the Epiclesis, I", in *Angl. Theol. Rev.*, 28 (1946) 148–53; C. Kern, "En marge de l'epiclèse", in *Irenikon*, 24 (1951), 166–94; B. Botte, "L'epiclèse dans les liturgies orientales", in *Sacris Erudiri*, 6 (1954), 48–72; H. Smit, "Epiclèse en sacramentologie", in *Tijdschr. v. Lit.*, 40 (1956), 84–115; P. Dienesen, "Die Epiklese im Rahmen altkirchlicher Liturgien. Eine Studie über die eucharistische Epiklese", in *Studia Theologica*, 16 (1962), 42–107.

[8] A review of the relevant works written during the last hundred years, together with the conclusions which can now be taken for certain, and an attempted reconstruction of the primitive Roman canon can be found in B. Opfermann, "Die Erforschung des römischen Messkanons", in *Theol. und Glaube*, 44 (1954), 263–79; cf. also P. Borella, "Il canone della messa romana nella sua evoluzione storica", in *Ambrosius*, 35 (1959), suppl. [26–50]; K. Gamber, "Canonica Prex. Eine Studie über den altrömischen Mess-Kanon", in *Heiliger Dienst*, 17 (1963), 57–64, 87–94.

sufficient information to show that the canon underwent a profound change during this period, a change which, taken all in all, was most unfortunate. The text seems to have been considerably altered, or at least the development aggravated faults already latent in the text.

In any case studies made during the last hundred years have put out of court once and for all the legend that the present Roman canon is the primitive Latin canon of the Church of Rome, and it is no longer accepted that this primitive canon had been subject to merely superficial changes over the centuries. Moreover, we cannot entertain today the view that the present canon is one integral structure, or indeed that it is the best possible form of anaphora.

For example, suppose the canon were said out loud in the vernacular today, in keeping with the spirit of the liturgy and as a means of giving full spiritual benefit to the people (and this must always be the first consideration). We would soon realise just how serious are the liturgical and pastoral problems arising from the text. If only a few priests so far are aware of these issues, it is because many have had their awareness blunted by routine and a more or less mechanical recitation (even if in a general spirit of devotion) of a text in a dead language. And this routine conceals the problems fairly effectively. But how much longer can this state of affairs continue?

The time thus seems ripe for a dispassionate consideration of the whole question of the Roman canon. We ought to look at the canon from every point of view, whether it be theological, liturgical, spiritual or pastoral, and try to establish its merits and defects. Would it be possible to "correct" these defects by reforming the canon? Or should we go so far as to abolish it altogether, and replace it by a completely different canon? Or perhaps it may be better to keep it as it is and admit into the Roman liturgy, over and above the one canon, several other formularies, which could be used on different occasions. If this were to be the case, we will have to decide which canon we are to take—the anaphora of Hippolytus, for example, or perhaps an oriental anaphora.

Another alternative would be to take one or more newly composed formularies, but then the question arises whether it is in fact possible to attempt any new composition of this kind today.

Purpose of this book

My feeling is that these questions must now be taken up in earnest; otherwise clandestine private attempts will before long begin to circulate more or less indiscriminately and without check. Then chaos will ensue—and this whole problem is too closely bound up with our faith and spirituality for us to allow that to happen.

I would be happy to think that this modest essay could help to stimulate a wide public discussion of these problems. With the advance of the liturgical reform, it is becoming increasingly obvious that not only many of the rites, but also quite a few of the texts are in need of correction. In fact I think that the liturgical reform will inevitably have to face the very delicate problem of creating new texts, a task which must not be confused with reviving the ancient texts, whether these new texts are in Latin or the vernacular. This seems to me to be a simple question of fact, which is practically upon us, whether we like it or not. Certainly it is envisaged by the Council in the *Constitution on the Liturgy* (art. 23).

I would like to suggest that before any new composition is definitely adopted—especially if it concerns a canon (or canons), prefaces, prayers, hymns or responsories—that there should first be a period of trial throughout the Church at large. This would provide an opportunity for criticism and discussion by anyone who is competent and interested in such matters. After all, these texts have to be considered from many different angles, and every shade of opinion must be given a hearing.

This for me is the real crux of the matter; it is not enough to consult the philologist or artist, the historian of religion, theologian or pastor. The different experiments will provoke many varied reactions, and in my opinion this is still the best way of ensuring sound progress. In this way too we will prepare the ground for further and more mature development.

But it should be understood that the purpose of this book is above all a practical one, namely to examine objectively the virtues and defects of the Roman canon; to see if these defects can be corrected; to suggest in conclusion a second canon, and one alternative canon to accompany it.

I appreciate the need to give good critical and historical backing to this attempt. But it is not absolutely necessary to take up a definite position on all the problems still being debated. Whatever is commonly admitted by historians of the liturgy is sufficient for my purpose. Nor would the whole enterprise necessarily be vitiated, if one or other of the historical or critical assumptions were called into question at some future date.

I owe a particular debt of gratitude to my colleague Don Anselmo Lentini of Montecassino, who first introduced me to the secrets of the *cursus*, and who made some valuable suggestions during the revision of these pages, which I now present to the public.

Cipriano Vagaggini

CHAPTER I

Texts

To allow the reader to follow the general argument more easily I have thought it best for reference purposes to begin with a selection of liturgical texts, each with its own introduction.

The selection and arrangement of these texts were dictated by the practical purpose of this book. Admittedly the ideal would be to use the original language at least for the Greek texts, but for practical reasons I shall be content with the Latin. In any case, this collection makes no pretensions to absolute accuracy in philology or textual criticism.

The purpose in this chapter is to give examples of the various types of anaphora. They have been selected so as to give a fair idea of the different families of anaphora, classified according to their structure, as is the practice in the history of the liturgy.

Of the many attempts to correct the Roman canon or to write a new one, I have taken into consideration only such as have been printed and published.

I. The anaphora of Hippolytus

Our study of anaphoras begins with Hippolytus, since this would seem to give us the usual structure of an anaphora in the early Church, before the different groups began to emerge during the fourth century and later. Chapter IV of the *Apostolic Tradition* gives the anaphora of the Mass in the context of the consecration of a bishop. Here then is the Latin translation, corrected in accordance with the critical text edited in French by Botte, *La tradition apostolique de saint Hippolyte*, Münster i. W., 1963, 11–17.

Quicumque factus fuerit episcopus, omnes ei os offerant pacis, salutantes eum quia dignus effectus est. Ei vero offerant diaconi oblationem, et ipse, imponens manus in eam cum omni presbyterio, dicat gratias agens:

All should give the kiss of peace to whoever has become a bishop, honouring the dignity he has received. The deacons should give him the offering, and as he and all the priests extend their hands over it, he offers thanks, saying:

I

Dominus vobiscum.
Et omnes dicant: Et cum spiritu tuo.
Sursum corda.
Habemus ad Dominum.
Gratias agamus Domino.
Dignum et iustum est.
Et sic iam prosequatur:

I

The Lord be with you.
All reply: And with you.
Lift up your hearts.
We have raised them up to the Lord.
Let us give thanks to the Lord.
It is right and fitting.
He continues:

II

Gratias tibi referimus, Deus, per dilectum puerum tuum Iesum Christum, quem in ultimis temporibus misisti nobis salvatorem et redemptorem et angelum voluntatis tuae, qui est Verbum tuum inseparabile, per quem omnia fecisti et quem, in beneplacito tuo, misisti de caelo in matricem virginis, quique in utero conceptus incarnatus est et filius tuus ostensus est, ex Spiritu Sancto et virgine natus.

II

We give you thanks, O God, through your beloved Son, Jesus Christ, whom in these days you have sent to save and redeem us, and to show us your will. He is your Word, inseparable from you, through whom everything was made. In your goodness, you sent him from heaven to be a virgin's son. Conceived in her womb, he took flesh and was revealed as your Son, born of the virgin and the Holy Spirit.

III

Qui voluntatem tuam complens et populum sanctum tibi adquirens extendit manus cum pateretur ut a passione liberaret eos qui in te crediderunt. Qui cum traderetur voluntariae passioni, ut mortem solveret et vincula diaboli dirumperet et infernum calcaret et iustos ad lucem duceret et terminum figeret et resurrectionem manifestaret, accipiens panem gratias tibi agens

III

In carrying out your will, and forming for you a holy people, he stretched out his hands as he suffered, to free from suffering those who had faith in you. When he allowed himself to be given up to suffer, so that he could conquer death and break the bonds of sin in crushing the power of hell, and so lead the just to the light, make a covenant with them and manifest

dixit: Accipite, manducate, hoc est corpus meum quod pro vobis confringitur. Similiter et calicem dicens: Hic est sanguis meus qui pro vobis effunditur. Quando hoc facitis, in meam commemorationem hoc facite.

the resurrection, he took bread, and giving thanks to you, said: Take, eat, this is my body, which is broken for you. He did the same with the cup, saying: This is my blood which is poured out for you. When you do this, do it in memory of me.

IV

Memores igitur mortis et resurrectionis eius, offerimus tibi hunc panem et calicem, gratias tibi agentes quia nos dignos habuisti adstare coram te et tibi ut sacerdotes ministrare.

IV

Remembering therefore his death and resurrection, we offer you this bread and cup, thanking you for holding us worthy to stand in your presence and to serve you as priests.

V

Et petimus ut mittas Spiritum Sanctum tuum in oblationem sanctae Ecclesiae. In unum eos congregans des omnibus qui percipiunt ex sanctis (ita ex eis percipere) ut repleantur Spiritu Sancto ad confirmationem eorum fidei in veritate

V

We ask you to send your Holy Spirit down upon the offerings of your holy Church. Gathering together all those who receive these mysteries, grant that they may be filled with the Holy Spirit, and their faith may thus be strengthened in your truth.

VI

ut te laudemus et glorificemus per puerum tuum Iesum Christum, per quem tibi gloria et honor Patri et Filio cum Sancto Spiritu in sancta Ecclesia et nunc et in saecula saeculorum.[1]

VI

So may we praise and glorify you, through your Son Jesus Christ. Through him be honour and glory to you, the Father, Son, with the Holy Spirit, in the holy Church, now and always. Amen.

---

[1] To have a precise idea of the value of these and other prayer formulas which can be found in Hippolytus, it is necessary to bear in mind what he himself says in Chapter 9 (ed. Botte, 29): "Let the bishop give thanks, as we said above. It is not at all necessary that he should pronounce the same words as we have given, as if he were making an effort to say them by heart while giving thanks to God; but rather let each one pray according to his ability. If someone is able to pray at solemn length and to say a solemn prayer, it is in order. But if someone, when he is praying, limits the length of his prayer, he should not be prevented, providing his prayer conforms to the faith."

II. The early Roman canon: a suggested reconstruction of the canon between 378 and 416 A.D.

Naturally this reconstruction is merely hypothetical, but I think it will serve some purpose by giving us an idea of the early text.

The text is that of Righetti (*Storia liturgica III*, Milan, 1949, n. 274, 385–7), as corrected by Opfermann ("Die Erforschüng des römischen Messkanons", in *Theol. und Glaube*, 44 (1955), 277–8).

I have based this reconstruction on the following principles:

1. We know that a Latin canon was in existence about 370–374 A.D., which was almost certainly Roman, and in this canon there was a passage which spoke of Melchisedech as *sacerdos summus* (Ambrosiaster, *Quaestiones Veteris ac Novi Testamenti*, 109, 21; CSEL, 50, 268). This corresponds to the text of the canon given in *De Sacramentis*. In 416 A.D. there could be found in the Roman canon the prayers of intercession for those who had made the offering, and these prayers came after the *Commendatio Oblationis* (*Epistula Innocentii Papae I ad Episcopum Eugubinum*; PL, 20, 553–4). In these prayers *publice recitantur offerentium nomina* (Jerome, *In Hier. II, 11*: PL, 24, 784, written after 415).

2. In *De Sacramentis* (IV 5, 21; 6, 26; 6, 27; VI 24; ed. Botte SC 25 bis, Paris, 1961, 114–6; 152, written about 378) there is the text which was in use in Milan at that time. Now the least we can say is that the text is very similar to the text used in Rome. It includes:

— a prayer that God may accept the oblation (*Fac nobis hanc oblationem ascriptam, ratam, rationabilem acceptabilem quod figura est corporis et sanguinis Domini nostri Iesu Christi. Qui pridie . . .*);

—the *Qui pridie* with the narration of the institution;

—the anamnesis with the offering (*Ergo memores . . . offerimus . . .*); a prayer that the oblation will be accepted on the heavenly altar, and Melchisedech is mentioned;

—the doxology.

Further the *De Sacramentis* states, without actually giving the text, that in the parts preceding the passage which is set out in full, by the priest's prayers "*laudes Deo deferuntur, oratio petitur pro populo, pro regibus, pro ceteris*". This must surely be understood as referring to the preface and the intercessions which come before the institution.

3. The *De Sacramentis* does not give the text of the preface, *Commendatio oblationis* or intercessions. To supply the defect two texts in particular are available:

(*a*) The text of the anonymous Arian of the fourth century edited by Mai, and more recently by Mohlberg in his edition of the Leonine Sacramentary (p. 202, 9–25). Now this fragment actually contains the text of a preface from a Catholic canon, which is Latin, of Italian origin, and belongs to our period (even though there is nothing to guarantee it as Roman). This fragment further gives a *Commendatio oblationis* without being interrupted by the *Sanctus*. The last words of the fragment mark the passage from the *Commendatio oblationis* to the intercessions (. . . . *ante conspectum tuae divinae pietatis per Iesum Christum Dominum et Deum nostrum per quem petimus et rogamus* . . . the fragment finishes here).

(*b*) A Mozarabic *Post pridie*, which, in the part that concerns us, is clearly an intercession. (*Lib. Sacr.* n. 1440; cf. also *Lib. Ord.* 321–2). Liturgists are agreed that this text is on the whole of Roman origin. Now the opening words of this text coincide with the final words just before the Arian fragment interrupts its quotation (*Per quem petimus et rogamus, omnipotens Pater, ut* . . .). Further the closing words of the Mozarabic text have a literary link with the words which begin the long fragment of *De Sacramentis*, which then carries on to the end of the canon.

In this way we have three fragments whose content and structure link them together very neatly. Even the end of the Mozarabic text and the beginning of the quotation of *De Sacramentis* are clearly the same text with slight variations. In this case, for our reconstruction of the Roman canon, I think the readings of the Mozarabic text are to be preferred to the readings of *De*

Sacramentis, because Pope Gelasius (492–6) provides a guarantee that the Roman canon at least in his day contained the words "*imago et similitudo corporis et sanguinis*" of Christ (*Adv. Eutych.* III 14, Thiel, *Epist. rom. Pont.* I 541). In this instance the reading of the Mozarabic text is the correct one, and it certainly demonstrates how rash it is to identify without more ado the text of *De Sacramentis* with the authentic ancient Roman canon.

Naturally all this does not prove that we are here dealing with one original text spread over three separate fragments, and much less can it be taken for granted that this original text is the genuine ancient Roman canon. A more likely suggestion is that we have here fragments of three different canons, which nevertheless were only variations of one basic framework, and this framework was substantially the same in Rome, Milan and other parts of Italy from 370 to 416. And so the structure of the common framework should be apparent if we join the three fragments together.

At all events, the three fragments, when joined, give us the text of a canon which appears to be complete. But then there remains the question whether we can be sure that there is no essential part missing in the structure of this composite canon. For example, such a text has no *Sanctus*. However, there is a solution to that difficulty, since we do know that the *Sanctus* of the Mass is not mentioned in Italy until the middle of the fifth century (cf. Righetti, *Storia Liturgica*, III, Milan, 1949, 298–9).

More complex, however, is the problem of the epiclesis, since it has a twofold function as consecratory prayer and as a prayer for a fruitful communion. We may ask whether there was an epiclesis in the early Roman canon, and whether it had this double function. If it did exist, we still do not know if it mentioned the Holy Spirit explicitly, nor do we know its precise place in the text. The canon obtained by putting the three fragments together does not seem to contain any epiclesis at all. And there are other unanswered questions too in this matter of the epiclesis (cf. Righetti, loc. cit., 320–2, note 232). In the following reconstruction I have put in brackets the words which refer to the epiclesis coming before and after the institution.

I

Dominus vobiscum.
Et cum spiritu tuo.
Sursum corda.
Habemus ad Dominum.
Gratias agamus Domino Deo nostro.
Dignum et iustum est.[2]

I

The Lord be with you.
And with you.
Let us lift up our hearts.
We have raised them up to the Lord.
Let us give thanks to the Lord our God.
It is right and fitting.

II

Dignum et iustum est, aequum et iustum est nos tibi super omnia gratias agere, Domine, Sancte Pater, omnipotens aeterne Deus, qui incomparabili tuae bonitatis honestate lucem in tenebris fulgere dignatus es mittens nobis Iesum Christum suspitatorem animarum nostrarum, qui nostrae salutis causa humiliando se ad mortem usque subiecit, ut nos ea quae Adam amiserat immortalitate restitutos efficeret sibi heredes et filios.

II

It is right and fitting, good and just, that we should always give thanks to you for all things.

Lord, holy Father, almighty eternal God, who in your incomparable goodness were pleased to make light shine in darkness when you sent Jesus Christ to us as protector of our souls.

For our salvation he humbled himself, and subjected himself to death, so as to restore to us that immortality which Adam had lost, and to make us God's heirs and sons.

III

Cuius benignitatis agere gratias tuae tantae magnanimitati quibusque laudibus nec sufficere possumus petentes de tua magna et flexibili pietate accepto ferre sacrificium istud, quod tibi offerimus stantes ante conspectum tuae divinae pietatis per Iesum Christum Dominum et Deum nostrum.

III

For such goodness and generosity we can never praise and thank you sufficiently, and so we ask you in your great love and compassion kindly to accept this sacrifice which we offer you in the presence of your divine goodness, through Jesus Christ our Lord and God.

IV

Per quem petimus et rogamus,[3] omnipotens Pater ut accepta habeas

IV

Through him we humbly ask and pray you, almighty Father, to

---

[2] Introductory dialogue, taken very largely from the anaphora of Hippolytus.

[3] The anonymous Arian has provided the preface, the prayer that the sacrifice be accepted, the *Commendatio oblationis*, and the transition to the intercessions (from *Dignum et justum est* to *Per quem petimus et rogamus*). There follows then the fragment from the Mozarabic text, which takes up the words *Per quem petimus et rogamus*, and continues as far as *ac redemptoris nostri*, except for the words in brackets.

et benedicere digneris haec munera et haec sacrificia inlibata quae tibi in primis offerimus pro tua sancta ecclesia catholica, quam pacificare digneris per totum orbem terrarum diffusam (una cum beatissimo papa nostro illo et omnibus orthodoxis atque apostolicae fidei cultoribus).

Memorare etiam, quaesumus Domine, servorum tuorum, qui tibi in honore sanctorum tuorum N.N. reddunt vota sua Deo vivo ac vero pro remissione suorum omnium delictorum.

accept and to bless these gifts, these pure offerings. We offer them to you, first of all, for your holy catholic Church: be pleased to give peace to her, spread over all the earth (We offer them to you at the same time, for our blessed bishop, N., and for all the bishops faithful to the true doctrine, who are the guardians of the apostolic faith).

Remember also, Lord, your servants who address their prayers to you, the living and true God, in honour of your saints, N.N., for the forgiveness of their sins.

V

(Emitte, Domine, Spiritum tuum Sanctum de caelis[4]) quorum (et horum) oblationem benedictam, ratam rationabilemque facere digneris, quae est imago et similitudo corporis et sanguinis Iesu Christi filii tui ac redemptoris nostri.

V

(Send, Lord, your Holy Spirit from heaven) and mercifully bless and accept this offering which is the image and likeness of the body and blood of Jesus Christ your Son, our redeemer.

VI

Qui pridie[5] quam pateretur in sanctis manibus suis accepit panem, respexit in caelum ad te, Sancte Pater, omnipotens aeterne Deus, gratias agens benedixit fregit fractumque apostolis et discipulis suis tradidit dicens: accipite et edite ex hox omnes hoc est enim corpus meum quod pro vobis confringetur.

VI

For on the day before he suffered, he took bread into his holy and blessed hands, looked up to heaven, to you, holy Father, almighty eternal God, and giving thanks, blessed and broke it and gave it to his apostles and disciples, saying "Take and eat this, all of you, for this is my body that will be broken for you."

---

[4] *Emitte de caelis*: inserted for the sake of the idea; but these words are not in the Mozarabic text.

[5] From *Qui pridie* to the end is taken from the fragment in *De Sacramentis* except for the words in brackets. Before the *Qui pridie* the fragment has: *fac nobis oblationem ascriptam, ratam, rationabilem, acceptabilem quod figura est corporis et sanguinis Domini nostri Iesu Christi*; these words are merely a variant reading on the Mozarabic text: *quorum oblationem redemptoris nostri.*

Similiter etiam calicem postquam caenatum est pridie quam pateretur accepit respexit in caelum ad te sancte Pater, omnipotens aeterne Deus gratias agens benedixit, apostolis suis et discipulis tradidit dicens: accipite et bibite ex hoc omnes hic est enim sanguis meus, qui pro vobis et pro multis effundetur in remissionem peccatorum. Quotiescumque hoc feceritis toties commemorationem meam facietis donec iterum adveniam.

In the same way, on the day before he suffered, after he had eaten, he took the cup into his holy and blessed hands, looked up to heaven, to you, holy Father, almighty eternal God, and giving thanks, blessed and gave it to his apostles and disciples, saying "Take and drink of this, all of you, for this is my blood which shall be poured out for you and for everyone to take away all sins. Each time that you do this, you will do it in memory of me until I return."

VII

Ergo memores gloriosissimae eius passionis et ab inferis resurrectionis et in caelos ascensionis offerimus tibi hanc immaculatam hostiam incruentam hostiam hunc panem sanctum et calicem vitae aeternae.

VII

That is why, mindful of his most glorious passion and of his resurrection from the dead and ascension into heaven, we offer you this spotless victim, this unbloody victim, this holy bread and cup of eternal life.

VIII

Et petimus et precamur ut hanc oblationem suscipias in sublimi altari tuo, per manus angelorum tuorum, sicut suscipere dignatus es munera pueri tui iusti Abel et sacrificium patriarchae nostri Abrahae et quod tibi obtulit summus sacerdos tuus Melchisedech.

VIII

And we ask and pray you to accept this offering carried by your angels to your heavenly altar, as you wished also to accept the gifts of your just servant Abel, the sacrifice of Abraham, father of our race, and the offering of your high priest Melchisedech.

IX

(Obsecrantes ut per gratiam Spiritus Sancti in munere tuae caritatis firmemur, et quod ex tua hac benedictione acceperimus, aeternitatis gloria consequamur.)[6]

IX

(We ask you that through the grace of the Holy Spirit the gift of your love may be confirmed in us, and that we may possess in eternal glory what we already receive from your goodness.)

---

[6] The words in brackets: *obsecrantes . . . consequamur*, are the text put together by Righetti out of fragments from the *Missale Gothicum* and Fulgentius.

X

Per Dominum nostrum Iesum Christum, in quo tibi est, cum quo tibi est honor, laus, gloria, magnificentia, potestas, cum Spiritu Sancto a saeculis et nunc et semper et in omnia saecula saeculorum. Amen.

X

Through our Lord, Jesus Christ, in whom and with whom honour, praise, glory, might, and power are yours with the Holy Spirit, from the beginning, now and always, for ever and ever. Amen.

III. The present Roman canon

The text is from L. Eizenhöfer, *Canon Missae Romanae, pars prior, traditio textus*, Rome, 1954. In the notes, I have put after the letter B the principal variant readings found in the text published by Botte, *Le canon de la messe romaine. Edition critique, introduction et notes*, Louvain, 1935.

I

Dominus vobiscum.
Et cum spiritu tuo.
Sursum corda.
Habemus ad dominum.
Gratias agamus domino deo nostro.
Dignum et iustum est.

I

The Lord be with you.
And with you.
Lift up your hearts.
We have raised them up to the Lord.
Let us give thanks to the Lord, our God.
It is right and fitting.

II

Vere dignum et iustum est aequum et salutare nos tibi semper et ubique gratias agere, domine, sancte pater, omnipotens aeterne deus, per Christum dominum nostrum. Per quem maiestatem tuam laudant angeli, adorant dominationes, tremunt potestates, caeli caelorumque virtutes ac beata seraphim socia exsultatione concelebrant. Cum quibus et nostras voces ut admitti iubeas deprecamur supplici confessione dicentes:

Sanctus sanctus sanctus dominus deus sabaoth. Pleni sunt caeli et terra gloria tua. Hosanna in excelsis. Benedictus qui venit in

II

It is indeed right and fitting, our duty and our salvation, to give thanks to you always and everywhere, Lord, holy Father, almighty and eternal God, through Christ our Lord. It is through him, that angels praise your sovereign glory, the dominions adore it, the powers are held in awe; through him that the heavenly and the celestial virtues, together with the blessed seraphim, join in one exultant hymn of praise. We pray you, let our voices blend with theirs, as we also humbly praise you, singing:

Holy, holy, holy, Lord God of all. Your glory fills all heaven and

nomine domini. Hosanna in excelsis.[7]

earth. Hosanna in the heights of heaven. Blessed is he who comes in the name of the Lord. Hosanna in the heights of heaven.

III

Te igitur, clementissime pater, per Iesum Christum filium tuum dominum nostrum supplices rogamus ac petimus, uti accepta habeas et benedicas haec dona, haec munera, haec sancta sacrificia illibata, in primis quae tibi offerimus pro ecclesia tua sancta catholica, quam pacificare custodire adunare et regere digneris toto orbe terrarum, una cum famulo tuo papa nostro N. et antistite nostro N. et omnibus orthodoxis atque catholicae et apostolicae fidei cultoribus.[8]

III

Most merciful Father, we humbly pray and beseech you through Jesus Christ your Son, our Lord, to accept and bless these gifts, these offerings, this holy, unblemished sacrifice. First and foremost we make you this offering for your holy catholic Church. Grant her peace and protection, unity and guidance, throughout the world, together with your servant our pope, N., our bishop, N., and with all who faithfully teach the catholic, apostolic faith.

IV

Memento, domine, famulorum famularumque tuarum N. et N. et omnium circumstantium,[9] quorum tibi fides cognita est et nota devotio, pro quibus tibi offerimus vel[10] qui tibi offerunt hoc sacrificium laudis pro se suisque omnibus, pro redemptione animarum suarum, pro spe salutis et incolumitatis suae tibique[11] reddunt vota sua aeterno deo vivo et vero.

IV

Remember, Lord, your servants, men and women, N. and N., and all who are gathered here around your altar. You know their faith; you have witnessed the offering they have made of themselves. On their behalf we offer you—as they are offering you—this sacrifice of praise for themselves and all who are dear to them, for the redeeming of their souls, for the security and salvation they hope for; as they fervently pray to you, the eternal living and true God.

V

Communicantes et memoriam venerantes in primis gloriosae

V

In the unity of holy fellowship, we honour the memory of all

[7] After: *sabaoth*, B omits: *Pleni sunt . . . domini. Hosanna in excelsis.*
[8] After: *papa nostro*, B omits: *et antistite . . . cultoribus.*
[9] Instead of: *circumstantium*, B has: *circum adstantium.*
[10] B omits: *pro quibus tibi offerimus vel.*
[11] Instead of: *tibique*, B has: *tibi.*

semper virginis Mariae genitricis dei et domini nostri Iesu Christi, sed et beati Ioseph eiusdem virginis sponsi,[12] et beatorum apostolorum ac martyrum tuorum Petri et Pauli Andreae Iacobi Ioannis Thomae Iacobi Philippi Bartholomei Matthaei Simonis et Thaddaei Lini Cleti Clementis Xysti Cornelii Cypriani Laurentii Chrysogoni Ioannis et Pauli Cosmae et Damiani et omnium sanctorum tuorum, quorum meritis precibusque concedas, ut in omnibus protectionis tuae muniamur auxilio: per eundem Christum dominum nostrum. Amen.[13]

your saints; the memory, first of all, of the glorious, ever-virgin Mary, Mother of our God and Lord Jesus Christ; the memory of her husband St Joseph, and of your blessed apostles and martyrs, Peter and Paul, Andrew, James, John, Thomas, James, Philip, Bartholomew, Matthew, Simon and Jude, Linus, Cletus, Clement, Sixtus, Cornelius, Cyprian, Lawrence, Chrysogonus, John and Paul, Cosmas and Damian and of all your saints. Through their merits and prayers, give us always the help of your protection; through the same Christ our Lord. Amen.

VI

Hanc igitur oblationem servitutis nostrae sed et cunctae familiae tuae, quaesumus, domine, ut placatus accipias diesque nostros in tua pace disponas atque ab aeterna damnatione nos eripi et in electorum tuorum iubeas grege numerari: per Christum dominum nostrum. Amen.[14]

VI

Graciously accept then, Lord, this offering which we your servants and your whole family make to you. Order our days in your peace, save us from everlasting doom, and number us among your chosen people; through Christ our Lord. Amen.

VII

Quam oblationem tu, deus, in omnibus, quaesumus, benedictam adscriptam ratam rationabilem acceptabilemque facere digneris, ut nobis corpus et sanguis fiat dilectissimi filii tui domini[15] nostri Iesu Christi.

VII

Be pleased, O God, to bless this offering, to give it your full approval, to make it perfect and worthy of your acceptance, so that it may become for us the body and blood of your beloved Son, our Lord Jesus Christ.

VIII

Qui pridie quam pateretur accepit panem in sanctas ac venera-

VIII

The day before he suffered, he took bread into his holy, worshipful

---

[12] *Sed et beati Ioseph eiusdem virginis sponsi*: recent addition by Pope John XXIII.

[13] *Per eundem . . . Amen*: B omits *eundem* and *Amen*.

[14] B omits: *Amen*.

[15] *Domini*: B adds: *dei*.

biles manus suas et[16] elevatis oculis in caelum ad te deum patrem suum omnipotentem tibi gratias agens benedixit fregit deditque[17] discipulis suis dicens: Accipite et manducate ex hoc omnes, hoc est enim corpus mcum.

Simili modo postquam cenatum est accipiens et hunc praeclarum calicem in sanctas ac venerabiles manus suas item tibi gratias agens benedixit deditque[18] discipulis suis dicens: Accipite et bibite ex eo omnes, hic est enim calix sanguinis mei novi et aeterni testamenti, mysterium fidei, qui pro vobis et pro multis effundetur in remissionem peccatorum.

Haec quotiescumque feceritis in mei memoriam facietis.

hands, and with eyes lifted up to heaven, to you God, his almighty Father, giving thanks to you, he blessed, broke and gave it to his disciples, saying: "Take this, all of you, and eat, for this is my body."

So too, when the meal was over, he took this noble cup in his holy, worshipful hands, and, again giving thanks to you, he blessed it and gave it to his disciples, saying: "Take it, all of you, and drink, for this is the cup of my blood, of the new and eternal covenant—the mystery of faith—which shall be shed for you and for the many for the forgiveness of sins."

As often as you do these things, you shall do them in memory of me.

IX

Unde et memores, domine, nos servi tui[19] sed et plebs tua sancta Christi filii tui domini[20] nostri tam beatae passionis necnon et ab inferis resurrectionis sed et in caelos gloriosae ascensionis offerimus praeclarae maiestati tuae de tuis donis ac datis hostiam puram, hostiam sanctam, hostiam immaculatam, panem sanctum vitae aeternae et calicem salutis perpetuae.

IX

We do indeed, Lord, remember the blessed passion of the same Christ your Son, our Lord, his resurrection from the dead and his ascension to glory in heaven, and we, your servants, with your holy people offer to your resplendent majesty, from the gifts which you yourself have given to us, the perfect sacrifice, the holy sacrifice, the unblemished sacrifice, the holy bread and the cup of everlasting salvation.

X

Supra quae propitio ac sereno vultu respicere digneris et accepta habere, sicuti accepta habere dignatus es munera pueri tui iusti

X

Look on these offerings with favour and contentment. Accept them as you graciously accepted the offerings of your just servant, Abel,

[16] B omits: *et.*

[17] Instead of: *deditque,* B has: *dedit.*

[18] Instead of: *deditque,* B has: *dedit.*

[19] Instead of: *servi tui,* B has: *tui servi.*

[20] After: *domini,* B adds: *dei.*

Abel et sacrificium patriarchae nostri Abrahae et quod tibi obtulit summus sacerdos tuus Melchisedech, sanctum sacrificium, immaculatam hostiam.

the sacrifice of our father Abraham, and that of your high priest Melchisedech—a holy sacrifice, an unblemished victim.

XI

Supplices te rogamus, omnipotens deus, iube haec perferri per manus sancti angeli tui in sublime altare tuum in conspectu divinae maiestatis tuae, ut quotquot ex hac altaris participatione sacrosanctum filii tui corpus et sanguinem sumpserimus, omni benedictione caelesti et gratia repleamur: per eundem[21] Christum dominum nostrum. Amen.[22]

XI

We humbly beseech you, almighty God, to command that these offerings be carried by your holy Angel to your altar in heaven, in the sight of your divine majesty. May we, who receive your Son's most sacred body and blood at this altar here, be filled with every heavenly blessing and grace; through the same Christ our Lord. Amen.

XII

Memento etiam, domine, famulorum famularumque tuarum N. et N. qui nos praecesserunt cum signo fidei et dormiunt in somno pacis. Ipsis, domine, et omnibus in Christo quiescentibus locum refrigerii lucis et pacis ut indulgeas deprecamur: per eundem[23] Christum dominum nostrum. Amen.[24]

XII

Remember also, Lord, your servants, men and women, N. and N., who have gone before us sealed with the sign of faith, and are now sleeping the sleep of peace. To them, Lord, and to all that rest in Christ, grant, we pray you, a place of refreshment, light and peace; through the same Christ our Lord. Amen.

XIII

Nobis quoque peccatoribus famulis tuis de multitudine miserationum tuarum sperantibus partem aliquam et societatem donare digneris cum tuis sanctis apostolis et martyribus, cum Ioanne Stephano Matthia Barnaba Ignatio Alexandro Marcellino Petro

XIII

And to us sinners too, your servants who trust in your countless mercies, grant some place and fellowship with your holy apostles and martyrs: John, Stephen, Matthias, Barnabas, Ignatius, Alexander, Marcellinus, Peter, Felicity, Perpetua, Agatha, Lucy, Agnes,

---

[21] B omits: *eundem.*
[22] B omits: *Amen.*
[23] B omits: *eundem.*
[24] B omits: *Amen.*

Felicitate Perpetua Agatha Lucia Agnete Caecilia Anastasia et omnibus sanctis tuis, intra quorum nos consortium non aestimator meriti sed veniae, quaesumus, largitor admitte: per Christum dominum nostrum.

Cecily, Anastasia, and all your saints.

We pray you, let us share their company—not because we ourselves have merited this, but because you have freely pardoned us; through Christ our Lord. Amen.

XIV

Per quem haec omnia domine semper bona creas sanctificas vivificas benedicis et praestas nobis. Per ipsum et cum ipso et in ipso est tibi deo patri omnipotenti in unitate spiritus sancti omnis honor et gloria per omnia saecula saeculorum. Amen.

XIV

It is through him, Lord, that you are ever creating, hallowing, vivifying and blessing all these good things, and giving them to us.

Through him and with him and in him is given to you, God the almighty Father, in the unity of the Holy Spirit, all honour and glory, for ever and ever. Amen.

IV. The great prayer of the consecration of the oils for Maundy Thursday in the Gelasian Sacramentary

Cf. Mohlberg, *Liber Sacramentorum*, 62. This text is printed here as an example of the great prayers, in which, as was the ancient Roman custom, some object is consecrated during a hymn of praise and thanksgiving. (The hymn refers to the wonders which God has accomplished in the history of salvation in connection with the object being consecrated.) This text is also an example of an epicletic prayer to God to send the Holy Spirit, who by his presence will consecrate the object, and so grant to those who use it the spiritual benefits of salvation. There is every reason to think that this text has come down to us intact from the purest euchological tradition of Rome, as opposed to the history of some other similar texts (in particular, the blessing for the water of the baptismal font).

I

Dominus vobiscum.
Respondetur: Et cum spiritu tuo.

I

The Lord be with you.
Reply: And with you.

Sursum corda.
Respondetur: Habemus ad Dominum.

Gratias agamus Domino Deo nostro.
Respondetur: Dignum et iustum est.

Let us lift up our hearts.
Reply: We have raised them up to the Lord.

Let us give thanks to the Lord our God.
Reply: It is right and fitting.

II

Vere dignum et iustum est, aequum et salutare nos tibi semper hic et ubique gratias agere, Domine, Sancte Pater, omnipotens aeterne Deus. Qui in principio inter cetera bonitatis et pietatis tuae munera, terram producere fructifera ligna iussisti, inter quae huius pinguissimi liquoris ministrae oleae nascerentur, quarum fructus sacro chrismati deserviret. Nam David prophetico spiritu gratiae tuae sacramenta praenoscens vultus nostros in oleo exhilarandos esse cantavit. Et cum mundi crimina diluvio quondam expiarentur effuso, in similitudinem futuri muneris columba demonstrans per olivae ramum pacem terris redditam nunciavit. Quod in novissimis temporibus manifestis est effectibus declaratum cum baptismatis aquis omnium criminum commissa delentibus, haec olei unctio vultus nostros iucundos efficiat ac serenos. Inde etiam Moysi famulo tuo mandata dedisti, ut Aaron fratrem suum prius aqua lotum per infusionem huius unguenti constitueret sacerdotem. Accessit ad hoc amplior honor, cum Filius tuus, Dominus noster Iesus Christus, lavari a Ioanne undis iordanicis exigisset, et Spiritu Sancto in columbae similitudine desuper misso unigenitum tuum, in quo tibi optime complacuisse testi-

II

It is indeed fitting and right, our duty and salvation, always and everywhere to give thanks to you, Lord, Holy Father, almighty and eternal God. You it was who in the beginning, among other gifts of your goodness, ordered the earth to produce fruit trees, among which were the olive trees that give us the fruit we use for the rich oil of holy chrism. David, knowing by prophetic inspiration the sacraments of your grace, sang of the oil which was to gladden our countenances. And when the sins of the world were swept away in the flood, a dove, prefiguring by an olive branch (the grace to come), announced that peace had returned to the earth. That is what has been brought about in this last age of the world, when the waters of baptism have wiped out all sins and this anointing with oil has filled man with joy and peace. Again, that is why you told Moses to wash his brother Aaron with water, and then to consecrate him high priest by this anointing. A greater honour still was added to this when your Son, our Lord Jesus Christ, asked to be washed in the waters of the Jordan, that you might send down from heaven the Holy Spirit in the form of a dove for you to speak and give witness that this was your only Son in whom you were

monio subsequentis vocis ostenderis, hoc illud esse manifestissime conprobaris, quod eum oleo laetitiae prae consortibus suis unguendum David propheta cecinisset.

well pleased. In this way you showed in a most striking way what David had sung: that he would be anointed with the oil of gladness before all his companions.

III

Te igitur deprecamur, Domine, Sancte Pater, omnipotens aeterne Deus, per Iesum Christum Filium tuum Dominum nostrum, ut huius creaturae pinguedinem sanctificare tua benedictione digneris et ei Sancti Spiritus immiscere virtutem per potentiam Christi tui, a cuius sancto nomine chrisma nomen accepit, unde unxisti sacerdotes, reges, prophetas et martyres tuos, ut sit his qui renati fuerint ex aqua et Spiritu Sancto chrisma salutis, eosque aeternae vitae participes et caelestis gloriae facias esse consortes: per eundem Dominum nostrum Iesum Christum Filium tuum.

III

We therefore pray you, Lord, holy Father, almighty and eternal God through Jesus Christ your Son, our Lord, be pleased to sanctify with your blessing the fat of this creature. Pour into it the might of the Holy Spirit through the power of your Son the Christ, from whose holy name this chrism has taken its name, this chrism with which you have anointed the priests, kings, prophets and martyrs, in order that it may be, for those reborn by water and the Holy Spirit, the chrism of salvation, making them sharers in eternal life and co-heirs of heavenly glory. Through Jesus Christ, your Son, our Lord.

V. The Palaeo-Hispanic anaphora

(I have included an example of the variable parts taken from the Mass of the Third Sunday after the Easter Octave.)

Anaphoras in the West can be divided into two principal kinds, the Roman and the Gallico-Spanish. We do not know the text of the fixed parts of the Gallican anaphora, so I have given here the Palaeo-Hispanic anaphora. The readings of the fixed parts belong to the B tradition (*Missale Mixtum*, PL, 85, 543 ff.), which seems to be better than the A tradition (the latter is to be found in *Missa Omnimoda*, in *Lib. Ord.*, 229–43). The text of the *Missale Mixtum*, as corrected by Dom G. Pinell, is printed here. The variable parts are taken from *Lib. Sacr.*, n. 714–18. Before the anaphora itself, I have placed the intercessions and the peace rite, since in this tradition they are inserted between the offertory and the anaphora.

INTERCESSIONES ET RITUS PACIS

ORATIO PRO ECCLESIA:

Ecclesiam sanctam catholicam in orationibus in mente habeamus, ut eam Dominus fide spe et charitate propitius ampliare dignetur. Omnes lapsos captivos infirmos atque peregrinos in mente habeamus, ut eos Dominus propitius respicere redimere sanare et confortare dignetur.

℟. Praesta aeterne, omnipotens Deus.

ALIA:

Deus sine principio, qui fecisti aeterna, principiis perpetua condidisti, sine conditione perpetuus: te fusis ex affectu mentis precibus imploramus, ut concessa nobis in praesenti saeculo venia, dignos misericordiae aeternae nos facias illudque nobis, dum misereris, indulgeas, unde in nobis propter quod semper miserearis, invenias.

℟. Amen.

Per misericordiam tuam, Deus noster, in cuius conspectu sanctorum apostolorum et martyrum, confessorum atque virginum nomina recitantur.

℟. Amen.

Offerunt Deo Domino oblationem Sacerdotes nostri Papa romensis et reliqui, pro se, pro omni clero et plebibus sibimet consignatis et pro universa fraternitate. Item offerunt universi

PRAYERS OF INTERCESSION AND THE RITE OF PEACE

PRAYER FOR THE CHURCH:

Let us remember in our prayers the holy Catholic Church, that God in his goodness may be pleased to increase her faith, her hope and her love. Let us remember all sinners and captives, the sick and pilgrims, in order that in his goodness, the Lord may look on them, redeem them, heal them and strengthen them.

℟. Graciously hear us, eternal and almighty God.

ANOTHER PRAYER:

O God without beginning, who created all that is eternal, who created beings that are perpetual in their origin, but who yourself are perpetual in an absolute way; we implore you with all our heart: in giving us your pardon in this present world, make us worthy to enjoy your mercy eternally, and grant that you may always find in us the dispositions to receive your forgiveness.

℟. Amen.

Through your mercy, our God, before whom are proclaimed the names of the holy apostles and martyrs, the confessors and virgins.

℟. Amen.

Our bishops, the Pope of Rome and the others, offer this oblation to the Lord God for themselves, for all the clergy and the people entrusted to them, and for all the brethren. All the priests, deacons,

presbyteri, diaconi, clerici ac populi circumadstantes, in honore sanctorum pro se et suis.

clergy and people here present offer it also in honour of the saints, for themselves and for theirs.

℟. Offerunt pro se et pro universa fraternitate.

℟. They offer it for themselves and for all the brethren.

Facientes commemorationem beatissimorum apostolorum, gloriosae sanctae Mariae Virginis, Zacariae, Ioannis, Stephani, Petri et Pauli, Ioannis, Iacobi, Andreae, Fructuosi, Saturnini, Eulogii, Vincentii, Felicis, Aciscli, Eulaliae, Engratiae, Iustinae, Leocadiae.

We honour the memory of the holy apostles, of the glorious Virgin Mary, of Zachary, John, Stephen, Peter and Paul, John, James, Andrew, Fructuosus, Saturninus, Eulogius, Vincent, Felix, Acisclus, Eulalia, Engratia, Justina, Leocadia.

℟. Et omnium martyrum.

℟. And of all the martyrs.

Item confessorum Hilarii, Athanasii, Martini, Ambrosii, Augustini, Fulgentii, Leandri, Isidori, Eugenii, Hildephonsi, Iuliani.

We honour the memory likewise of the confessors Hilary, Athanasius, Fulgentius, Leander, Isidore, Eugene, Hildephonsus, Julian.

℟. Et omnium confessorum.

℟. And of all the confessors.

Offert Ecclesia Dei sancta catholica pro spiritibus et animabus omnium fidelium defunctorum, ut eos Dominus inter agmina beatorum propitius collocare dignetur.

The holy and catholic Church of God offers the sacrifice for the souls of all the faithful departed, that the Lord may in his goodness number them among the ranks of the blessed.

℟. Praesta aeterne, omnipotens Deus.

℟. Graciously hear us, almighty and eternal God.

Post nomina oratio (*variabilis*).

Prayer after the names (*variable*):

Facito nos, omnipotens Deus, ut carnali devicta concupiscentia, veraciter gloriemur in cruce tua. Per illam et viventium probra et defunctorum abdicentur exitia: per eam acceptentur oblationes fidelium: per eam confusa ad Christum redeat infidelitas perfidorum. Quo nos, qui te resurrexisse fideliter credimus, ita ex nostris tibi actibus placeamus, ut per hoc sacrificium placabilem te nobis ostendas et viventibus pacem et sepultis optatam conferas mansionem.

℟. Amen.

Almighty God, grant that we may overcome the desires of the flesh and find our true glory in your cross. By your cross, may the faults of the living be blotted out and the sufferings of the dead taken away; by your cross receive the offerings of your faithful, and may the faithless, ashamed, return to Christ. May we, who firmly believe in your resurrection be able to please you by our acts, so that, thanks to this sacrifice, you may show us your mercy granting peace to the living and the desired rest to the departed.

℟. Amen.

Quia tu es vita vivorum, sanitas infirmorum et requies omnium fidelium defunctorum, in aeterna saecula saeculorum.

℟. Amen.

For you are the life of the living, the health of the sick and the repose of all the faithful departed for ever and ever.

℟. Amen.

AD PACEM ORATIO (*variabilis*).

Super corpus benevoli Redemptoris spirituales aquilae volitantes, et resurgentis Domini claritatem rediante fidei obtutu cernentes, debitas tibi offerimus, Pater clementissime, gratias: et ideo deprecamur ut huius delectabilis mensae ad caelestes epulas invitati, dono pacis aeternae in hoc paschali mereamur convivio recreari.

℟. Amen.

PRAYER FOR PEACE (*variable*):

Flying like spiritual eagles over the body of our kind Redeemer, and contemplating in the light of faith the splendour of the risen Lord, we offer you, most merciful Father, the thanks which is your right: we also ask that, invited to the feast of this heavenly table, we may also be renewed in this paschal banquet with the gift of eternal peace.

℟. Amen.

Gratia Dei Patris omnipotentis, pax ac dilectio Domini nostri Iesu Christi et communicatio Spiritus Sancti sit semper cum omnibus vobis.

℟. Et cum hominibus bonae voluntatis.

Diaconus: Quomodo adstatis pacem facite.

May the grace of God the Father almighty, the peace and love of our Lord Jesus Christ and the gift of the Holy Spirit be with you all for ever.

℟. And with all men of good will.

The deacon: Give one another the kiss of peace.

ANTIPHONA AD PACEM:

Pacem meam do vobis, pacem meam commendo vobis; non sicut mundus dat pacem, do vobis. ℣. Novum mandatum do vobis, ut diligatis invicem. ℟. Pacem meam . . . ℣. Gloria et honor Patri et Filio et Spiritui Sancto in saecula saeculorum, Amen. ℟. Pacem meam . . .

ANTIPHON FOR PEACE:

I give you my peace, I entrust my peace to you; I do not give peace as the world gives it. ℣. I give to you a new commandment, that you should love one another. ℟. I give you . . . ℣. Glory and honour to the Father, to the Son and to the Holy Spirit for ever and ever, Amen. ℟. I give you . . .

ANAFORA

I

Introibo ad altare Dei mei.

℟. Ad Deum qui laetificat iuventutem meam.

ANAPHORA

I

I will go to the altar of God.

℟. The God of my gladness and joy.

Aures ad Dominum.
℟. Habemus ad Dominum.
Sursum corda.
℟. Levemus ad Dominum.

Deo ac Domino nostro Iesu Christo, Filio Dei, qui est in caelis, dignas laudes dignasque gratias referamus.
℟. Dignum et iustum est.

II

INLATIO (*variabilis*):

Dignum et iustum est, vere preclarum atque sublime est, nos confessione pectoris, vocis organo, oris officio, innumerabilium tuorum, Deus, munerum dona preferre et amaritudinem nostrarum faucium beati eloquii sapore condire. Sed angustum est ad tam immensa preconia pectus hominis, et quo te quisque interius aspexerit maior semper adcrescis, quia semper novus, semper antiquus es.

Misisti in hunc mundum Filium tuum lege nascendo, qui prius quam nasceretur in utero virginali, tecum ante secula, cuncta formavit. Viderunt eum elementa nascentem, quae cum disponerentur viderant ordinantem. Teneram eius populi mirantur aetatem, quorum patres antiquam iam tunc intellexere virtutem.

Quod si grande est pulchrumque mysterium res illa cum nascitur, quanto magis miraculi est res illa cum moritur! Capta enim mors est corporis fraude, et dum carne contectum Deum non agnovit interius latentem, sub esca hamum fauce suscepit, et in cruce clavis fixa congemuit. O quam praeclara, Domine, aviditatem draconis antiqui arte lusisti! ut dum et osten-

Listen to the Lord.
℟. We open ourselves to the Lord.
Lift up your hearts.
℟. Let us lift them up to the Lord.

To our God and Lord Jesus Christ, Son of God who is in the heavens, let us sing our praises and thanksgiving.
℟. That is right and fitting.

II

PREFACE (*variable*):

It is right and fitting, truly glorious and sublime, to recall in our hearts, voices and mouths, O God, your gifts and kindnesses which pass all counting, and to flavour the insipidity of our voices with the savour of your holy word. But man's heart is too small for the praise of such magnitude, and the more each one contemplates you in the depths of his being, the greater you become in his eyes, because you are always ancient and always new.

You sent your Son into this world, born under the Law. He was in the Virgin's womb before his birth, was with you before all time and created all things. The elements of the world that saw him born were those same elements that had seen him putting them in their first order. Peoples were astonished at his tender age—those whose ancestors had known his ancient power.

If his birth was so great and beautiful a mystery, how much more wonderful yet was his death! Death in fact was deceived by his incarnation; not recognising God hidden in the flesh which clothed him, he bit upon the hook that was

deris corporis praedam, ipse configeretur in ligno. Et spolians carne Verbum liber ad inferos pergis, confractisque portarum claustris vinctos laxas e vinculis: et inter mortuos liber tenebras nova luce perfundis.

Non subiacebat Maiestas tua, Domine, (huic necessitati) ut ista patereris, sed nos eramus necessitas tua.—Perierat enim, Domine, vita nostra, nisi Filii tui morte fuisset inventa. Misisti super nostrorum criminum cautionem unigeniti Filii tui, et delesti eam iure victoris. Vulneribus eius sanasti vulnera nostra, ut nos redimeres per Filium tuum absque divinitatis iniuria, ipsumque pretium hominis idem Deus factus est.

Quid ergo faciemus nunc tam magno talique redempti pretio? Quae nostra opera compensabit hoc pretium? Qualiter serviemus tali Domino, a quo nobis est promissa libertas et offertur hereditas? Operare in nobis, Domine, quod tibi placeat: et ut te possidere possimus, ipse nos posside. Non discedimus a te, vivificabis nos et nomen tuum invocabimus: Nomen illud quod est super omne nomen, quod conlaudant Angeli et Archangeli, ita dicentes:

hidden under the bait, and fastened by nails to the cross, began to weep and groan. Lord, with what wonderful skill you baffled the greed of the ancient dragon—so that when you seemed to him a prey upon the cross, it was then that he himself was nailed to the wood. Shedding your flesh, you, the Word, enter the underworld with complete freedom. You break open the doors which encircle it and free the captives from their chains. Free among the dead, you fill the darkness with new light.

In no way was your majesty, Lord, obliged to undergo this suffering, but we were your necessity. In fact, Lord, our life would have been lost, if by the death of your Son it had not been found again. Against the debt of our sins you produced the surety of your only Son, and you have cancelled it by right of the victor. By his wounds you have healed our wounds, and you have redeemed us through your only Son, without in any way injuring the rights of the Godhead: God himself has made himself man's ransom.

What shall we do then, now that we have been redeemed with such a ransom and one of such magnitude? What work of ours can compensate this price? In what way can we serve such a Lord, who has promised us liberty and offers us his inheritance? Realise in us Lord whatever pleases you, and in order that we may possess you, take possession of us yourself. We shall not stray far from you, you will give us life and we shall invoke your name, that name which is above all names, and which the angels and archangels praise saying:

℟. Sanctus, Sanctus, Sanctus, Dominus Deus Sabaoth. Pleni sunt caeli et terra gloria maiestatis tuae. Hosanna Filio David. Benedictus qui venit in nomine Domini. Hosanna in excelsis. Agios, Agios, Agios, Kyrie o Theos.

℟. Holy, holy, holy, the Lord, God of the universe! Heaven and earth are filled with the glory of your majesty. Hosanna to the Son of David, Blessed is he that comes in the name of the Lord. Hosanna in the highest heaven. *Agios, agios, agios. Kyrie o Theos.*

III

POST SANCTUS (*variabilis*)

Vere sanctus, vere benedictus Dominus noster Iesus Christus Filius tuus. Qui solus verbo virtutis cuncta moderans et omnia crucis destina portans, vectes ferreos conminuit portarumque aerearum claustra perfregit, tartaris profunda descendit, sedentibus in umbra mortis ignotae lucis claritate resplenduit: et sol iustitiae de tumulo corpore suscitato procedens, radiis suis tenebras nostras mirabiliter inlustravit: Christus Dominus ac Redemptor aeternus.[25]

III

AFTER THE SANCTUS (*variable*)

Truly holy and truly blessed is our Lord Jesus Christ, your Son. He alone, by the power of his word governs the universe, bears and sustains all things through his cross. He shattered the doors of iron and smashed the gates of bronze; he descended into the depths of hell, and for those who sat in the shades of death he shone forth with the splendour of unknown light. At last, he, the sun of justice, came out of the tomb in his risen body, and, in a marvellous way dispersed the darkness with the rays of his brightness, he, the Lord Christ and eternal Redeemer.

IV

MISSA SECRETA (*invariabilis*)

Qui pridie quam pateretur,[26] accepit panem et gratias agens,

IV

SECRET MASS (*fixed*)

On the day before he suffered, he took bread, and, giving thanks,

[25] The formula *Christus Dominus ac Redemptor aeternus* is the fixed conclusion for the variable prayers *Post Sanctus*; for an example, cf. the *Post Sanctus* for Christmas in the *Missale Mixtum*, PL, 85, 189. There is a logical connection with the *Qui pridie*, and the two belong together. It is clear that the narration of the institution which follows began in the ancient Spanish tradition with the words *Qui pridie*, for the prayer which comes after the institution is always referred to as the *Post pridie oratio*. There are textual difficulties in the opening words of this narration, and I rather think that they have originated at a time when it had been forgotten that the formula *Christus Dominus ac Redemptor noster* was in fact the obligatory ending of every prayer *Post Sanctus*.

[26] *Qui pridie quam pateretur*: the *Missale Mixtum* and the *Missa Omnimoda* of the *Lib. Ord.* have: *Dominus noster Iesus Christus in qua nocte tradebatur.* The *Missale F* of Toledo (cf. *Lib. Sacr.*, p. XXV) has: *Quoniam Dominus Iesus in qua nocte tradebatur.*

benedixit ac fregit deditque discipulis suis dicens: Accipite et manducate: hoc est corpus meum quod pro vobis tradetur. Quotiescumque manducaveritis, hoc facite in meam commemorationem.

℟. Amen.

Similiter et calicem postquam caenavit dicens: Hic est calix novi testamenti in meo sanguine, qui pro vobis et pro multis effundetur in remissionem peccatorum. Quotiescumque biberitis, hoc facite in meam commemorationem.

℟. Amen.

Quotiescumque manducaveritis panem hunc et calicem biberitis, mortem Domini annuntiabitis donec veniat in claritate de caelis.

℟. Sic credimus, Domine Iesu.

blessed and broke it and gave it to his disciples saying: Take and eat, this is my body which is given for you. Whenever you eat it, do this as a memorial of me.

℟. Amen.

Likewise after the meal, he took the chalice, saying: This is the cup of the new covenant in my blood, which will be poured out for you and for the many in forgiveness of sins. Whenever you drink it, do so as a memorial of me.

℟. Amen.

Every time you eat this bread or drink this cup, you will be proclaiming the death of the Lord until he comes from heaven in glory.

℟. We believe it, Lord Jesus.

V

Post pridie (*variabilis*)

Confitemur, Domine, confitemur et credimus pro nostro scelere te corporaliter mortis subisse supplicium, et pro omnium salute prostrato mortis interitu triumphantibus Angelis celestem Patris ex qua veneras ad mansionem reversum. Pro quod te, Deus omnipotens, rogamus et petimus, ut oblata in conspectu tuo nostrae servitutis libamina ipse tibi acceptabilia facias, et accepta discurrente sancto Angelo tuo nobis sanctificata distribuas: ut dum corda nostra corporis et sanguinis Filii tui Domini nostri conmixtione purificas, petitiones nostras in odorem suavitatis accipias.[27]

V

After the Pridie (*variable*)

We acknowledge, Lord, we acknowledge and believe that it was for our faults that you underwent the pains of death in your body, and that afterwards, for the salvation of all, having conquered death, you returned amongst the triumphant angels to the heavenly dwelling place of your Father from which you had come. That is why, almighty God, we ask and pray you willingly to accept these offerings which we, your servants, bring before you. Deign, too, through your holy Angel, to distribute these gifts to us which you have accepted and sanctified, so that while you purify our hearts

[27] This *Post pridie* is a true epiclesis, even if of a rather special kind (cf. H. Lietzmann, *Messe und Herrenmahl*, 3rd ed., Berlin, pp. 109–10). It is well known that many of the Mozarabic *Post pridie* prayers have an epiclesis, of what we might call the classical type, e.g. the *Post pridie* of Christmas Day (*Missale Mixtum*, PL, 85, 189): *Haec, Domine, dona tua et praecepta servantes: in altare*

℟. Amen.

in uniting us to the body and blood of your Son our Saviour, you may also receive our prayers in the odour of sweetness. ℟. Amen.

VI

DOXOLOGIA (*invariabilis*)

Praesta, Pater ingenite, per Unigenitum tuum Dominum nostrum Iesum Christum, per quem tu haec omnia nobis indignis servis tuis valde bona creas, sanctificas, vivificas, benedicis ac praestas nobis, ut sint benedicta a te Deo nostro, in saecula saeculorum.

℟. Amen.

VI

DOXOLOGY (*fixed*)

Grant this, uncreated Father, through your only Son, our Lord Jesus Christ. Through him, you do not cease, for us your unworthy servants, to create, sanctify, vivify and bless these good things so as to make a gift to us, so that they may be blessed by you, our God, for ever and ever.

℟. Amen.

VI. The Greek Alexandrine anaphora of St Basil

I have chosen this anaphora as being typical of the Antioch type. In general, the oriental anaphoras can be divided into three principal types, the Antioch, East-Syrian, and Egyptian. The Antioch tradition embraces many different anaphoras:

1. The Alexandrine anaphoras of St Basil in Greek and in Coptic; and the anaphoras of St Gregory in Greek (Renaudot, I, 25–37) and Coptic (E. Hammerschmidt, *Die koptische Gregorios-anaphora*, Berlin, 1957).

2. The Jerusalem anaphora of St James in Greek (Brightman, 49–58; Mercier, "*La liturgie de St Jacques*", in *Patri. Orient.*, XXVI (1946), 198–222, gives a Latin translation) and in Syriac (*Anaphorae Syriacae*, II, 2, Rome, 1953, 142–170).

3. The anaphora of the Apostolic Constitutions VIII (F. X. Funk, I, 498–514).

4. The Byzantine anaphoras of St Basil and St John Chrysostom

tuum panis ac vini holocausta proponimus. Rogantes profusissimam tuae misericordiae pietatem: ut in eodem Spiritu quo te in carne virginitas incorrupta concepit, has hostias Trinitas indivisa sanctificet: ut cum a nobis fuerint non minori trepidatione quam veneratione percepta, quidquid contra animam male vivit intereat: quidquid interierat nullatenus reviviscat.

(Brightman, 309–44, gives the text of the ninth century; the modern text can be found in the same author, 352–411).

5. The Armenian anaphoras: the common anaphora (Brightman, 434–47); the anaphora of St James (Baumstark, *Oriens christianus*, n.s. 7 (1918), 13–17); the anaphora of Catholikos Sahak (Perhat, ibid., 3 (1913), 18–25); and the anaphora of St Gregory Nazianzene (Perhat, ibid., 1 (1911), 206–12).

6. The seventy West-Syrian anaphoras (the critical edition is now being prepared for publication: *Anaphorae Syriacae*, Rome, 1939. For a further bibliography cf. Sauget, *Bibliographie des liturgies orientales*, Rome, 1962, 111–14).

H. Engberding (*Das Eucharistiche Hochgebet der Basileiosliturgie*, Münster i. W., 1931) has demonstrated that the Greek Alexandrine anaphora of St Basil is earlier than the Byzantine anaphora likewise named after St Basil. And then Capelle ("Les liturgies 'basiliennes' et saint Basile", in Doresse-Lanne, 45–74) has pointed out how in all probability St Basil of Caesarea made use of the Alexandrine anaphora. This has been corrected and further developed in the Byzantine anaphora, whose author is none other than St Basil again. On the other hand, at one time some liturgists regarded the anaphora in Book VIII of the *Apostolic Constitutions* as the most primitive and fairly typical of the age. But now it is thought to be neither primitive, nor particularly typical of those times, nor indeed of much doctrinal value. Thus we may reasonably take the Greek Alexandrine anaphora of St Basil as the earliest and purest example of the Western Antioch type.

There exists also a Coptic recension of this anaphora (Renaudot, I, 13–19), and Doresse-Lanne (loc. cit.) have published a long fragment from this recension. Taken overall, it is certainly an earlier version of the text than the Greek published by Renaudot. For this reason, I have given in the notes after the letters CDL the more important variant readings from Doresse-Lanne.

Up to the institution, I follow the text established by Engberding (loc. cit.); then I have used Renaudot (I, 64–71), although I have slightly altered the Latin translation. The parts assigned to the deacon and people and the other rubrics are as given by Renaudot, and it should not be presumed that they all necessarily indicate usages of the fourth century. They are lacking in Engberding's critical edition and likewise in the fragment edited by Doresse-Lanne.

I

Sursum habeamus corda.
Habemus ad Dominum.
Gratias agamus Domino.
Dignum et iustum est.

I

Let us lift up our hearts.
We have lifted them to the Lord.
Let us give thanks to God.
It is right and fitting.

II

Dignum et iustum: dignum et iustum: vere dignum est et iustum.

Tu qui es, Dominator, Domine, Deus veritatis, qui existis ante saecula et regnas in saecula; qui in excelsis habitas et humilia respicis; qui fecisti caelum et terram et mare et omnia quae in eis sunt: Pater Domini et Dei et Salvatoris nostri Iesu Christi, per quem omnia fecisti visibilia et invisibilia; qui sedes super thronum sanctae gloriae tuae, qui ab omni sancta virtute adoraris;

II

It is right and fitting: right and fitting; it is truly right and fitting. It is you who are the supreme ruler, Lord, God of truth, who exist before the ages and reign through the ages; who live on high and regard the humble, who have made heaven and earth and sea and all that is in them: Father of our Lord and Saviour Jesus Christ, through whom you have made all things, visible and invisible: who are seated upon the throne of your glory and adored by every holy power;

(*Diaconus:* Qui sedetis surgite)

(*Deacon:* Let those who are seated rise.)

cui adstant Angeli et Archangeli, Principatus et Potestates, Throni, Dominationes et Virtutes.

before you stand the angels and archangels, the princes and powers, the thrones, the dominations and hosts of heaven.

(*Diaconus:* Ad orientem aspicite)

(*Deacon:* Face towards the East.)

Tibi circum astant Cherubim multis oculis praediti, Seraphim sex alis instructi, semper laudantes, clamantes et dicentes:

Before you stand ranged the many-eyed cherubim, the six-winged seraphim ceaselessly praising, proclaiming and announcing:

(*Diaconus:* Attendamus-

Populus: Sanctus, Sanctus, Sanctus, Dominus Sabaoth.)

(*Deacon:* Be attentive!

People: Holy, holy, holy, Lord God of Hosts.)

III

Sanctus, Sanctus, Sanctus es vere, Domine Deus noster. Qui plasmasti nos et posuisti nos in paradiso voluptatis. Cum vero transgressi essemus mandatum tuum per deceptionem serpentis et excidissemus vita aeterna, expulsique essemus ex paradiso voluptatis, non abiecisti nos usque in finem, sed assidue visitasti nos per sanctos tuos prophetas. Et novissime diebus istis nobis sedentibus in tenebris et umbra mortis illuxisti per unigenitum Filium tuum Dominum Deum et Salvatorem nostrum Iesum Christum.

Qui ex Spiritu Sancto et ex sancta virgine Maria incarnatus et factus homo demonstravit nobis vias salutis, concedens nobis supernam regenerationem ex aqua et Spiritu et fecit nos sibi populum adquisitum, sanctificavit nos Spiritu Sancto.

Qui dilexit suos qui erant in mundo, deditque seipsum redemptionem regnanti super nos morti, in qua detinebamur venumdati sub peccato. Cumque descendisset per crucem ad inferos, rexurrexit ex mortuis tertia die; et cum ascendisset in caelum, sedit ad dexteram tuam, Pater, definiens diem retributionis in quo manifestatus iudicabit orbem in iustitia et reddet unicuique secundum opus eius.

(*Populus:* Secundum misericordiam tuam et non etc.)

III

You are indeed holy, holy, holy, Lord our God. Who shaped us and established us in a paradise of delights. When we transgressed your commandment by the serpent's fraud, and had lost eternal life and had been banished from the paradise of delights, you did not abandon us forever, but carefully visited us through your holy prophets. And in these last days, when we sat in darkness and the shadow of death, you enlightened us through your only begotten Son, our Lord God and Saviour Jesus Christ.

He was born of the Holy Spirit, incarnate of the holy Virgin Mary and made man, and showed us the way of salvation, granting us eternal regeneration by water and the Spirit, and made us his own people, sanctified by the Holy Spirit.

He loved his own who were in the world and gave himself as a ransom for us, when we lay under the domination of death, poisoned by sin. He descended into hell from the cross and rose on the third day from the dead and ascending into heaven he sat at your right hand, Father, appointing the day of wrath in which he will be manifest, judging the world in justice, and will render to each according to his works.

(*People:* According to your mercy and not . . . etc.)

IV

Reliquit autem nobis hoc magnum pietatis mysterium. Cum enim traditurus foret seipsum in mortem pro mundi vita,

(*Populus:* Credimus)

IV

He left us this great mystery of love.

When he was about to hand himself over to death that the world should live,

accepit panem, in sanctas, immaculatas et beatas manus suas; suspexit in excelsa caelorum ad te, Patrem suum, Deum nostrum et Deum universorum: gratias egit,[28]

(*Populus:* Amen)
benedixit,
(*Populus:* Amen)
sanctificavit,
(*Populus:* Amen)
fregit, dedit sanctis suis discipulis et apostolis dicens: Accipite, manducate:[29] hoc est corpus meum quod pro vobis et multis frangitur et[30] distribuitur in remissionem peccatorum. Hoc facite in meam commemorationem.

Similiter et calicem postquam cenavit, miscuit ex vino et aqua, gratias egit[31]

(*Populus:* Amen)
benedixit,
(*Populus:* Amen)
sanctificavit,
(*Populus:* Amen)
gustavit,[32] iterum dedit sanctis suis discipulis et apostolis dicens: Accipite, bibite ex eo omnes: hic est sanguis meus, Novi Testamenti,[33] qui pro vobis et multis effunditur in remissionem peccatorum.

Hoc facite in meam commemorationem. Quotiescumque enim manducaveritis panem hunc et calicem hunc bibetis, mortem meam annuntiatis et resurrectionem ascensionemque meam confitemini,[34] donec veniam.

(*People:* We believe.)
he took bread in his holy, immaculate and blessed hands, looked up to heaven on high to you, his Father, our God, and God of all things: he gave thanks,

(*People:* Amen)
blessed,
(*People:* Amen)
sanctified,
(*People:* Amen)
broke, and gave it to his holy disciples and apostles saying: Take, eat: this is my body, which is broken for you and for many and shared among you for the remission of sins. Do this in memory of me.

Similarly, after he had eaten, he took a chalice, mixed water and wine, gave thanks,

(*People:* Amen)
blessed,
(*People:* Amen)
sanctified,
(*People:* Amen)
tasted it and again gave it to his holy disciples and apostles saying: Take and drink of this, all of you: this is my blood, of the New Covenant, which is shed for you and for many, for the remission of sins.

Do this in memory of me. As often as you shall eat this bread and drink this cup you announce my death and proclaim my resurrection and ascension, until I come.

---

[28] CDL omits: *in sanctas . . . gratias egit.*
[29] CDL adds: *ex hoc omnes.*
[30] CDL omits: *frangitur et.*
[31] CDL omits: *gratias egit.*
[32] CDL omits: *gustavit.*
[33] CDL omits: *Novi Testamenti.*
[34] CDL omits: *et resurrectionem ascensionemque meam confitemini.*

(*Populus:* Amen, Amen, Amen, mortem tuam Domine, etc.)

V

Memores igitur nos quoque sanctarum ipsius passionum et resurrectionis a mortuis atque in caelos adscensionis sessionisque ad dexteram tui Dei et Patris, gloriosique ac timendi reditus, tua ex tuis donis offerimus tibi. De omnibus, per omnia et in omnibus.

(*Populus:* Te laudamus: tibi benedicimus.)

(Inclinate capita vestra cum timore.)

VI

Et rogamus et deprecamur te, amator hominum, bone, Domine,[35] nos peccatores et indigni servi tui et adoramus te, ut beneplacito bonitatis tuae veniat Spiritus tuus Sanctus super nos servos tuos et super proposita haec dona tua sanctificetque et ostendat ea sancta sanctorum.

(*Diaconus:* attendamus. - *Populus:* Amen)

(*Sacerdos: alta voce:*)

Et faciat panem quidem istum fieri sanctum corpus ipsius Domini Dei et Salvatoris nostri Iesu Christi in remissionem peccatorum et in vitam aeternam iis qui ex illo participant.

(*Populus:* Amen)

Et calicem hunc, pretiosum sanguinem Novi Testamenti ipsius Domini Dei et Salvatoris nostri Iesu Christi in remissionem pecca-

(*People:* Amen. Amen. Amen. Your death, O Lord . . . etc.)

V

Remembering his holy passion, resurrection from the dead, his ascension into heaven and installation at your right hand, God and Father, and his glorious and fearful return, we offer you this, from your own gifts. Among all things, through all things and in all things.

(*People:* We praise you. We bless you.)

(Bow your heads in awe.)

VI

We sinners and your unworthy servants adore you, lover of men, the Lord, the Good, and we pray and beseech you that, in your merciful goodness, your Holy Spirit may come upon us your servants and upon these offered gifts and sanctify them and make them holy nourishment for your holy people.

(*Deacon:* Be attentive! *People:* Amen)

(*Priest: in a loud voice:*)

And may he make this bread become the holy body of our Lord God and Saviour Jesus Christ for the remission of sins and the eternal life of those who partake of it.

(*People:* Amen)

And this chalice, the precious blood of the New Covenant of our Lord God and Saviour Jesus Christ, for the remission of sins and

---

[35] CDL instead of: *tua ex tuis . . . bone Domine,* has: *proposuimus tibi et coram te tua de tuis donis: hunc panem et hunc calicem et te rogamus, Deus noster, nos isti peccatores.*

torum et in vitam aeternam iis qui ex illo participant.[36]

(*Populus:* Amen. Kyrie eleison, *ter*).

Et fac nos dignos Domine participandi sanctis mysteriis tuis ad sanctificationem animae, corporis et spiritus, ut efficiamur unum corpus et unus spiritus et inveniamus partem consequamurque hereditatem[37] cum omnibus sanctis tuis qui a saeculo tibi placuerunt.

the eternal life of those who partake of it.

(*People:* Amen. Kyrie eleison, *three times.*)

And make us worthy, Lord, of participating in your holy mysteries for the sanctification of soul, body and spirit, so that we may be made one body and one spirit, and take our place and succeed to the inheritance with all the saints who have pleased you in ages past.

VII

Memento, Domine,[38] sanctae, unicae, catholicae tuae Ecclesiae et pacatam fac eam quam adquisivisti pretioso sanguine Christi tui.

VII

Remember, Lord, your holy, one, catholic Church, which you have bought by the precious blood of your anointed, and keep her at peace.

---

[36] CDL omits: *et faciat panem quidem . . . Novi Testamenti ipsius Domini Dei et Salvatoris nostri Iesu Christi in remissionem peccatorum et in vitam aeternam iis qui ex illo participant.*

[37] CDL omits: *consequamurque hereditatem.*

[38] CDL from here until the end of the anaphora has the following text: *Memento etiam, Domine, tuae unius sanctae catholicae apostolicae Ecclesiae; pacem da ei quam salvasti per pretiosum sanguinem Christi.*

Et omnium episcoporum orthodoxorum qui in ea sunt. In primis memento servi tui Benjamin et socii ejus in ministerio Colluthi sancti episcopi, et illorum qui cum eis dispensant verbum veritatis. Da eis pascere ecclesias sanctas, greges tuos orthodoxos in pace.

Presbyterorum et omnis diaconiae qui ministrat et omnis qui est in virginitate et puritate totiusque populi tui fidelis, memento, Domine, et miserere eorum omnium.

Memento etiam, Domine, huius loci et habitantium in eo in fide Dei.

Etiam bonae temperantiae aëris memento, Domine, et fructum terrae.

Et eorum qui tibi haec dona obtulerunt et eorum pro quibus ea obtulerunt, memento, Domine, et da eis omnibus mercedem caelorum.

Quoniam autem, Domine, praeceptum est Filii tui unigeniti ut communicemus memoriae sanctorum tuorum, memento dignare patrum nostrorum qui tibi a saeculo placuerunt: patriacharum, prophetarum, apostolorum, martyrum, confessorum, praedicatorum, evangelistarum, omnisque iusti qui in fide consummatus est: praecipue vero virginis in omni tempore sanctae et gloriosae Mariae Dei genitricis et miserere nostrum omnium precibus eius et salva nos propter nomen sanctum tuum quod invocatum est super nos.

Similiter memento omnium qui in sacerdotio obdormierunt et omnium ex ordine laicorum: et requiem da eis in sinibus Abrahae, Isaac et Iacob in loco viridi ad aquam refrigerii, loco unde fugerunt dolor cordis, tristitia et gemitus. (*Nomina enuntiate.*) *Da illis requiem apud te.*

Nos autem hic habitantes conserva in fide tua et duc nos in regnum tuum, pacemque tuam nobis omni tempore concede per Iesum Christum et Spiritum Sanctum.

In primis memento, Domine, sancti Patris nostri Archiepiscopi Abba N. Papae et Patriarchae Alexandriae, quem dignare praestare in pace salvum, gloriosum, sanum, longaevum, recte dispensantem verbum veritatis, et pascentem gregem tuum in pace.

Remember first of all, Lord, our holy father Archbishop Abba N., Pope and Patriarch of Alexandria; grant of your mercy to keep him in peace, safe, glorious, in good health, with length of days, rightly spreading the word of truth, and feeding your flock in peace.

Memento, Domine, orthodoxorum presbyterorum, omnisque ordinis diaconici et ministerii omniumque virginitatem servantium et omnis fidelissimi populi tui.

Remember, Lord, orthodox priests, the whole order of deacons and ministers, all those observing chastity and all your faithful people.

Memento nostri, Domine, ut omnium nostrum miserearis simul et semel.

Remember us, Lord, and all we do, and have mercy upon us now and forever.

(*Populus:* Miserere nostri Deus, Pater, Dominator.)

(*People:* Have mercy on us O God, Father, Lord.)

Miserere nostri Deus, Dominator (*ter*).

Have mercy on us God, Lord (*three times*).

(*Populus:* Kyrie eleison: *ter.*)

(*People:* Kyrie eleison: *three times.*)

Memento etiam, Domine, salutis urbis nostrae huius, et eorum qui in fide Dei habitant in ea.

Remember also, Lord, the well-being of this our city, and of those who live here in the faith of God.

Memento, Domine, aëris et fructuum terrae. Memento, Domine, pluviarum et sementum terrae. Memento, Domine exundationis aquarum fluvialium iuxta mensuram. Laetifica etiam et renova faciem terrae: sulcos eius inebria, multiplica genimina eius. Praesta nobis illam, qualis esse debet ad sementem et ad messem: benedicendoque nunc benedic. Vitam nostram guberna. Benedic coronae anni benignitatis tuae, propter pauperes populi tui, propter viduam et orphanum, propter peregrinum et advenam, et propter nos omnes sperantes in te, et invocantes nomen tuum sanctum: oculi enim omnium in te sperant, et tu das escam illorum in tempore opportuno. Fac nobiscum secundum bonitatem tuam qui das escam

Remember, Lord, the weather and the harvest of the soil. Remember, Lord, the rains and the seeds of the earth. Remember, Lord, to let the waters flow in accordance with the measure of each month. Renew the face of the earth and make it thrill with joy, fill its furrows to overflowing, multiply its seed. Grant us what we need for the sowing and the harvest, and bless it with your blessing. Govern our lives. Bless the new year in your mercy, for the sake of the poor among your people, for the sake of widows and orphans, for the sake of strangers and travellers, and for our sakes, who hope in you and call upon your holy name. The eyes of all look to you in hope and you give them food at the right time. You give food to

omni carni. Imple gaudio et laetitia corda nostra, ut in omnibus semper omnem sufficientiam habentes, abundemus in omne opus bonum ad faciendam voluntatem tuam sanctam.

(*Populus:* Kyrie eleison.)

Memento, Domine eorum qui pretiosa haec dona tibi offerunt et eorum propter quos et per quos ea intulerunt, mercedemque caelestem illis omnibus tribue.

Quoniam, Domine, praeceptum est unigeniti Filii tui, memoriae sanctorum nos communicare, etiam meminisse dignare, Domine, eorum qui a saeculo tibi placuerunt sanctorum Patrum, Patriarcharum, Apostolorum, Prophetarum, Praedicatorum, Evangelistarum, Martyrym, Confessorum, et omnis spiritus iusti qui in fide Christi consummatus est. Praecipue vero sanctissimae, gloriosissimae, immaculatae, benedictionibus, cumulatae, Dominae nostrae Deiparae et semper Virginis Mariae. Sancti gloriosi prophetae, precursoris baptistae et martyris Joannis. Sancti Stephani primi diaconorum et primi martyrum. Et Sancti beatique Patris nostri Marci Apostoli et evangelistae: et sancti Patris nostri Thaumaturgi Basilii. Sancti N. cuius memoriam hodierna die celebramus et omnis chori sanctorum tuorum, quorum precibus et intercessionibus etiam nostri miserere et salva nos propter nomen tuum sanctum quod invocatum est super nos.

(*Diaconus legit dypticha: sacerdos legit secreto*)

Similiter memento Domine et omnium ex ordine sacerdotali qui

all living things—deal with us according to your merciful goodness. Fill our hearts with gladness and joy, so that having a sufficiency of everything we need, we may abound in all good works in fulfilling your holy will.

(*People:* Kyrie eleison.)

Be mindful, Lord, of those who offer you these precious gifts, and of those for whom and through whom they offer them, and grant them all a heavenly reward.

Since, Lord, it is a command of your only Son that we should play our part in the communion of the saints, graciously be mindful, Lord, of those who pleased you in ages past, the fathers, patriarchs, apostles, prophets, preachers, evangelists, martyrs, confessors and souls of the just who have died in the faith of Christ. Especially be mindful of our most holy, most glorious, immaculate, most blessed Lady, Mother of God and ever-virgin Mary; of your holy and glorious prophet, John the Baptist, precursor and martyr: of St Stephen, first deacon and first martyr: of our holy father St Mark, apostle and evangelist, of our holy father Basil, the wonder-worker: of Saint N. whose memory we celebrate today, and of all your choir of saints. By their prayers and intercession have mercy on us and save us for the sake of your holy name which is invoked upon us.

(*The deacon reads the dyptych: the priest reads it secretly*)

Similarly, be mindful, Lord, of all those of the priestly order who

pridem quieverunt et eorum qui erant in statu laicorum. Praesta omnium animas requiescere in sinibus sanctorum Patrum nostrorum Abraham Isaac et Iacob. Induc et congrega eos in locum viridem super aquam requietis, in paradiso voluptatis unde fugerunt dolor, tristitia et gemitus, in splendore sanctorum tuorum.

have gone to rest, and those of the lay state. Grant that the souls of all may repose in the bosoms of our holy fathers Abraham, Isaac, and Jacob. Guide and gather us in green pastures by the waters of repose, in that paradise of delights from which pain, sadness and mourning are banished, in the splendour of your saints.

(*Et post dypticha sacerdos dicit:*)

(*After the dyptych the priest says*)

Illis quidem Domine, quorum animas accepisti, illic quietem tribue, eosque in regnum caelorum transferre dignare.

Grant, Lord, to those whose souls you have received there to find repose, and mercifully transfer them to the kingdom of heaven.

Nos vero hic peregre habitantes, conserva in fide tua, et deduc nos ad regnum concedens nobis tuam pacem omni tempore.

Keep us in faith, Lord, who live here in exile, and lead us to the kingdom, granting us your peace at all times.

VIII

ut in hoc sicut et in omnibus, glorificetur, exaltetur, laudetur, benedicatur et sanctificetur sanctissimum, gloriosum et benedictum nomen tuum cum Christo Iesu et Sancto Spiritu.

(*Populus:* Sicut erat [et est et erit in generationem et generationem et in omnibus saeculis saeculorum. Amen.])

VIII

So that in this, as in all things, your most holy, most glorious and blessed name may be glorified, exalted, praised, blessed and sanctified, with Christ Jesus and the Holy Spirit.

(*People:* As it was [is and will be from age to age and forever, Amen.])

VII. The anaphora of Theodore of Mopsuestia

An example of the anaphoras in the Edessa or East-Syrian tradition.

The East-Syrian anaphoras are quite different in structure both from the Antioch tradition and more especially from the West-Syrian type. This is marked by the reversed positions of the epiclesis and the intercessions. The West-Syrian has this order: dialogue; thanksgiving; institution; anamnesis; epiclesis; intercessions; doxology. In the East-Syrian however we

find: dialogue; thanksgiving; institution; anamnesis; intercessions; epiclesis; doxology.

Examples of this type are the anaphora of Addaï and Mari (Renaudot, II, 583–6); the so-called anaphora of Nestorius (ibid., 621–8); and the anaphora of Theodore of Mopsuestia. The Maronite anaphora of St Peter (Italian version, Rome, 1943) belongs to the same family as that of Addaï and Mari (for further bibliography, cf. Sauget, *Bibliographie des liturgies orientales*, Rome, 1962, 123–5).

This anaphora of Addaï and Mari is certainly the most interesting because of several passages of an exceptionally archaic nature. Some scholars have concluded from this that it is perhaps the primitive form, possibly belonging to the time of Hippolytus (cf. Botte, "L'anaphore chaldéenne des Apôtres", in *Orient. Christ. period.*, 15 (1949), 259–76). But the manuscripts in which the text has been preserved date only from the sixteenth century. Thus the text has given rise to many serious difficulties concerning its original form (cf. Botte, "Problèmes de l'anaphore syrienne des Apôtres Addaï et Mari", in *L'Orient syrien*, 10 (1965), 89–106). In particular, it is difficult to explain why the text in its present state does not contain the narration of the institution. And it is questionable whether the *Sanctus*, or for that matter the order of the prayers, is at all primitive. These questions, then, are so difficult, and the answers suggested are so hypothetical, that it would be foolish to take Addaï and Mari as an example of the East-Syrian tradition. For these reasons I have preferred the anaphora of Theodore, relatively late though it is (6th–7th centuries). Granted that its theology is certainly well developed, nevertheless it seems to have kept many features of Addaï and Mari, while at the same time it does have a more reasonable arrangement.

The text is from Renaudot, II, 611–615.

I

Gratia Domini nostri Iesu Christi et caritas Dei Patris et communicatio Spiritus Sancti sit

I

The grace of our Lord Jesus Christ, the love of God the Father, and the gift of the Holy Spirit be

cum omnibus nobis, nunc et semper et in saecula saeculorum.

Sursum in excelsis sublimibus, in regione timenda gloriae, ubi non cessant Cherubim alas suas agitare, neque desinunt iubili et laudes suaves santificationum Seraphim, ibi sint mentes vestrae.

Sunt apud te, Deus.

Oblatio viva et rationabilis primitiarum nostrarum, victimaque non immolata et acceptabilis Filii generis nostri, pro omnibus creaturis universim, Deo omnium Domino offertur.

Dignum et iustum est.

(*Diaconus:* Pax nobiscum.)

with all of us, now and for evermore.

May your minds be raised aloft, to the sublime heights, to the awe-inspiring region of glory where the wings of the cherubim never cease to move and the seraphim never cease from singing the sweet praises of your holiness.

They are with you, O God.

The living and worthy offering of our first fruits, the acceptable and unbloody victim, the Son of our race, is offered for the creatures of the universe to God, the Lord of all.

That is right and fitting.

(*Deacon:* Peace be with us.)

II

Dignum est Domine quotidie, et iustum omni tempore, aequumque horis omnibus gratias agere nomini tuo sancto, et adorare maiestatem tuam in omni regione et loco: te Deus Pater veritatis qui existis ab aeterno et Filium tuum unigenitum Dominum nostrum Iesum Christum et Spiritum Sanctum in saecula saeculorum: quia tu es Dominus et conditor omnium visibilium et invisibilium: qui per Filium tuum unigenitum Deum Verbum, qui est lux gloriae tuae et splendor ex te imagoque substantiae tuae, creasti et constituisti caelum et terram et omnia quae in eis sunt. Et per Spiritum Sanctum tuum veritatis, qui ex te est, Pater, omnes naturae rationales, visibiles et invisibiles, confortantur, sanctificantur, dignaeque fiunt referendi laudes divinitati tuae adorandae.

Qui coram te, Pater, vere et coram Filio tuo unigenito Domino nostro Iesu Christo, et coram

II

It is right, Lord, every day, and fitting at all times, and good at every hour to give thanks to your holy name and to adore your divine majesty in every region and place: you, O God, Father in very truth, who exist from eternity, and your only Son our Lord Jesus Christ, with the Holy Spirit for ever and ever: for you are Lord and creator of all things, seen and unseen: who through your only Son, God and Word, who is the reflection of your glory, the splendour which radiates from you, and the image of your substance, have created and established heaven and earth with all they contain. And through your Holy Spirit of truth, who comes from you, Father, all rational natures, seen and unseen, are strengthened, sanctified and made worthy to offer praise to your adorable godhead.

In truth, Father, there stands before you and before your only

Spiritu Sancto consistunt millena milia sublimium spirituum et decies milies decem milia angelorum sanctorum, quorum vitae voluptas est in constanti tua voluntate ut nomen tuum magnum et sanctum laudatione perpetua sanctificent. Dignum etiam fecisti Domine per gratiam tuam genus nostrum infirmum hominum mortalium ut cum coetibus omnibus sublimium maiestati tuae omnibus dominanti laudem et honorem referrent, cum illis qui semper coram maxima sanctitate tua iubilant ad celebrandam gloriam Trinitatis tuae gloriosae, (*Canon*) vociferantes, glorificantes indesinenter, clamantesque unus ad alterum, dicentes et respondentes: Sanctus, Sanctus (*Sacerdos dicit hanc orationem:* Sanctus, Sanctus, Sanctus Dominus potens).

begotten Son our Lord Jesus Christ and before the Holy Spirit thousands upon thousands of sublime spirits, and ten thousand times ten thousand holy angels, whose bliss in life lies in hallowing, by never-ceasing praise, your name, great and holy. Through your grace, Lord, you have once more made our frail race of mortals worthy to give praise and honour, with all the choirs of these sublime beings, to your majesty which controls all things; with those who rejoice without pause before your supreme holiness, in celebration of the glory of your glorious Trinity, exclaiming, glorifying perpetually, crying out one to another, saying and replying: Holy, holy (*The priest says this prayer:* Holy, holy, holy the all-powerful Lord).

III

(*Sacerdos prosequitur tacite hanc orationem inclinationis*)

Vere Domine sanctus et laudandus in aeternum. Sanctus es Deus Pater verus solus, sanctus quoque est Spiritus Sanctus, natura divina non facta, omnium conditor, qui naturaliter et omnino vere sanctus est: et sanctum nomen eius et sancta inhabitatio eius, qui etiam vere sanctificat omnes quicumque digni sunt suscipere donum gratiae eius. Et referimus tibi laudem, gloriam, gratiarum actionem et adorationem, Patri et Filio et Spiritui Sancto, nunc semper et in saecula saeculorum.

Adoramus te Domine et gratias agimus tibi et glorificamus te propter omnia tua beneficia erga

III

(*The priest says this prayer of supplication in a low voice*)

Truly holy and worthy of praise, Lord for all eternity. You are holy, God our Father, unique and true, and holy is the Holy Spirit, of divine nature, not created, the founder of all things, who is by nature truly and absolutely holy: holy is his name and holy his dwelling place, he who sanctifies all those who are worthy to receive the gift of his grace. And we give praise, glory, thanksgiving and adoration to you, Father and Son and Holy Spirit, now and for ever age after age.

We adore you, Lord, give you our thanks and glorify you for all your gifts to us: for you created us

nos: quia creasti nos ex nihilo, dignosque fecisti nos honore magno libertatis et intelligentiae: qui perpetuo et erga unumquemque curam habes conservandae vitae nostrae.

Coram nomine magno tuo et tremendo genua flectimus et adoramus; nobiscumque laudant et gratias agunt coetus omnes sublimium quod propter gratiam tuam ineffabilem erga nos homines et propter nostram salutem unigenitus tuus Verbum, cum imago Dei esset, non rapinam arbitratus est esse se aequalem Deo, sed seipsum exinanivit et similitudinem servi accepit, descenditque de caelo, induitque humanitatem nostram, corpus mortale et animam rationalem, intelligentem et immortalem ex Virgine sancta per virtutem Spiritus Sancti: et per illud perfecit et complevit omnem dispensationem hanc magnam et mirabilem, quae dudum praeparata erat per praescientiam tuam ante constitutionem mundi. Eam quoque complevisti postmodum temporibus ultimis per Filium tuum unigenitum Dominum nostrum Iesum Christum in quo habitat omnis plenitudo divinitatis corporaliter: ipseque est caput Ecclesiae et primogenitus ex mortuis: et ipse est perfectio omnium a quo perficiuntur. Ipse per Spiritum aeternum se ipsum obtulit immaculatum Deo et sanctificavit nos per oblationem corporis sui semel factam et pacificavit per sanguinem crucis suae quae in caelis et quae in terris sunt. Qui traditus est propter peccata nostra et resurrexit ut iustificaret nos.

out of nothing, and made us worthy by honouring us with the gift of liberty and understanding: you who are solicitous at every instant to preserve in being the life of every one of us.

In the presence of your great and awesome name, we kneel and adore: and with us give praise and thanks all the choirs of the sublime spirits, because through your inexpressible favour to us, mankind, and for our salvation, your only Son, the Word, although he was the image of God, did not cling to his rank of equality with God, but emptied himself and took upon himself the likeness of a slave, descended from heaven, put on our humanity, a mortal body and a rational soul endowed with intelligence and immortality, through the holy Virgin by the power of the Holy Spirit: he thus accomplished and completed the whole of this great and admirable dispensation which had been prepared in your foreknowledge before the foundation of the world. You have again fulfilled it in most recent times through your only Son, Jesus Christ, our Lord, in whom dwells corporeally all the fullness of the Godhead: it is he who is the head of the Church and the first-born from among the dead, and he himself is the perfection of all things, because it is through him that they achieve perfection. He offered himself without spot to God, through the eternal Spirit and sanctified us through the oblation of his body, made once and for all. Through the blood of his cross he has brought peace to heaven and earth. He was delivered up for our sins and he rose again for our justification.

IV

Qui cum Apostolis suis ea nocte qua traditus est celebravit mysterium hoc magnum, tremendum, sanctum et divinum: accipiens panem benedixit et fregit deditque discipulis suis et dixit: Hoc est corpus meum quod pro vobis frangitur in remissionem peccatorum.

Similiter et calicem: gratias egit et dedit illis dixitque: Hic est sanguis meus novi testamenti, qui pro multis effunditur in remissionem peccatorum.

Accipite igitur vos omnes, edite ex hoc pane et bibite ex hoc calice et ita facite quotiescumque congregabimini in mei memoriam.

IV

On the night when he was betrayed, with his apostles he celebrated this mystery, great, awesome, holy and divine: taking bread he blessed it and broke it and gave it to his disciples saying: this is my body which is broken for you so that sins may be forgiven.

Likewise with the chalice: he offered thanks, gave it to them and said: this is the blood of the new covenant which is shed for many so that sins may be forgiven. Take, all of you, and eat of this bread and drink of this chalice, and do this whenever you assemble in memory of me.

V

Sicut praeceptum nobis est ita congregati sumus, nos servi tui humiles, imbecilli et infirmi, ut cum bona venia gratiae tuae, celebremus mysterium magnum, tremendum, sanctum et divinum, per quod facta salus est magna universo humano generi nostro. (*Canon*) Referimusque simul laudem, honorem, confessionem et adorationem Patri et Filio et Spiritui Sancto nunc et semper.

(*Sacerdos signat mysteria. Diaconus dicit:* Mentibus vestris orate etc. *Sacerdos dicit hanc orationem:* Domine potens.)

Adoramus te Domine et gratias agimus tibi et glorificamus te, quod nos, licet indignos propter peccata nostra, ad te accedere fecisti per miserationes tuas multas: et renovasti nos et sanctificasti per gratiam Spiritus Sancti, dignosque praestitisti nos administrandi coram

V

We are now assembled just as he prescribed, we, your servants, humble, poor and helpless, to celebrate by your favour the great, awesome, holy and divine mystery by which the salvation of all our human race has been accomplished. (*Canon*) At the same time we offer praise, honour, faith and adoration to the Father, to the Son and to the Holy Spirit, now and for evermore.

(*The deacon says:* Pray in your hearts, etc. *The priest says this prayer:* The all-powerful Lord...)

We adore you, Lord, and give you thanks and glorify you because, although unworthy on account of our sins, you have given us access to yourself through your countless mercies: and you have renewed us and sanctified us by the grace of the Holy Spirit, and made us worthy

te ministerium hoc tremendum et divinum ad salutem vitae nostrae: simulque confitemur coram te, cum gratiarum actione maxima, ob salutem magnam quae nobis omnibus praestita est, per Filium tuum dilectum Iesum Christum Dominum nostrum. Offerimusque coram Trinitate tua gloriosa, corde contrito et spiritu humilitatis sacrificium hoc vivum et sanctum, quod mysterium est Agni Dei qui tollit peccata mundi, rogantes te et deprecantes coram te, ut complaceat Domine divinitas tua adoranda et per misericordiam tuam suscipiatur oblatio haec pura et sancta per quam placatus et reconciliatus es, pro peccatis mundi.

to carry out this awe-inspiring and divine mystery in your presence, for the salvation of our life: at the same time we profess our faith before you with great thanksgiving for the salvation granted to us by your well-loved Son, Jesus Christ, our Lord. In the presence of your glorious Trinity, and with a humble heart and penitent spirit, we offer this living and holy sacrifice, which is the mystery of the Lamb of God who takes away the sins of the world, asking and praying in your presence, Lord, that your adorable divinity may find it pleasing and that through your mercy this pure and holy oblation, by which you are appeased and reconciled, may be accepted for the sins of the world.

VI

Nunc etiam Domine ecce offertur haec oblatio coram nomine tuo magno et tremendo, pro universa Ecclesia tua sancta catholica: ut habitet in medio eius tranquillitas tua et pax tua cunctis diebus saeculi: et removeantur procul ab ea persecutiones, tumultus, contentiones, schismata et divisiones, omnesque invicem adhaereamus per unanimem concordiam cum corde puro et caritate perfecta.

Et pro omnibus patribus nostris Episcopis et chorepiscopis, sacerdotibus et diaconis qui sunt in hoc ministerio veritatis: ut stent et ministrent coram te pure, splendide et sancte placeantque voluntati tuae ita ut mereantur consequi a te gradus bonos sublimes in revelatione Domini nostri Iesu Christi.

Pro omnibus etiam filiis Ecclesiae sanctae catholicae qui hic sunt

VI

Now once again, O Lord, this oblation is offered in the presence of your great and awesome name, for all your holy and catholic Church: so that your tranquility and peace may dwell in her midst for all time; and that she may remain far removed from persecutions, agitations, schisms and division, and that we may all be united among ourselves in unanimous agreement, with pure hearts and in perfect love.

And for all our father bishops, priests and deacons, who are in this ministry of truth: in order that they may hold firm and fulfil their ministry in your presence in a pure, radiant and holy manner, and so please your will that they may deserve to obtain from you sublime blessings in the revelation of our Lord Jesus Christ.

et in quacumque regione: ut proficiant in adoratione maiestatis tuae, in fide vera et in operibus bonis et laudibus ad salutem vitae suae.

Et pro servo tuo peccatore et culparum reo: ut per gratiam tuam Domine parcas peccatis meis et auferas delicta mea quae sciens vel nesciens commisi coram te.

Et pro illis omnibus pro quibus offeretur haec oblatio: ut inveniant coram te miserationes et gratiam et vivant.

Et pro fructibus terrae atque aëris temperie: ut benedicatur corona anni benignitatis tuae per gratiam tuam.

Et pro omni genere hominum qui in peccato aut errore versantur: ut per gratiam tuam dignos illos efficias cognitione veritatis et adoratione maiestatis tuae: ut cognoscant quoque te tamquam Dominum ab aeterno et a saeculo, naturam divinam non factam, conditorem omnium, Pater, Fili et Spiritus Sancte; quodque propter nos homines et propter nostram salutem, Filius Dei, Deus Verbum, induit hominem perfectum, Dominus noster Iesus Christus: perfectusque et iustificatus est per virtutem Dei et per Spiritum Sanctum et ipse est mediator Dei et hominum et largitor vitae in saecula saeculorum illis qui per eum accedunt ad Deum Patrem: sui sint laudes et benedictiones in saecula saeculorum.

Domine Deus noster suscipe a nobis per gratiam tuam sacrificium hoc gratiarum actionis, fructus scilicet rationales labiorum nostrorum, ut sint coram te memoria bona iustorum antiquorum, prophetarum sanctorum, Apostolorum

And for all the sons of the holy Catholic Church who are here and in every land: that they may advance in adoration of your majesty, in true faith, good works and praises for the salvation of their lives.

And for your servant, sinful and guilty: so that by your grace, Lord, you may pardon my sins and forgive the offences which I have committed in your presence knowingly or in ignorance.

And for all those for whom this sacrifice is offered: so that they may find mercies and graces in your presence, and live.

And for the fruits of the earth and the calmness of the air: so that the year may be blessed in your grace and kindness.

And for the whole race of men who are to be found in sin or error: so that by your grace you may make them worthy to know the truth and adore your majesty: so that they may come to the knowledge of you as Lord from all eternity, divine nature, not created, creator of all things, Father, Son and Holy Spirit: and so that they may know that for us men, for our salvation, the Son of God, the Word of God, put on the perfect man, he who is our Lord Jesus Christ: he was made perfect and justified by the power of God and by the Holy Spirit, and he is the mediator between God and man, he who gives life age after age to those who through him have access to God the Father: to whom be praises and blessings for evermore.

Lord our God, receive from us, by your grace, this sacrifice of thanksgiving, the worthy fruits of our lips so that they may become in

beatorum, martyrum et confessorum, episcoporum, doctorum, sacerdotum, diaconorum et omnium filiorum Ecclesiae sanctae catholicae, eorum qui in fide vera transierunt ex hoc mundo: ut per gratiam tuam, Domine, veniam illis concedas, omnium peccatorum et delictorum quae in hoc mundo, in corpore mortali et cum anima mutationi obnoxia, peccaverunt aut offenderunt coram te, quia nemo est qui non peccet.

your presence a happy memorial of just men of former times, of holy prophets, of the blessed apostles, martyrs and confessors, bishops, doctors, priests, deacons and of all the sons of the holy Catholic Church, of those who have departed this world in the true faith, so that by your grace, Lord, you may grant them the forgiveness of all the sins and errors they have committed in sinning and offending you in this world, mortal and subject to change, for there is nobody who does not sin.

VII

Rogamus te, Domine, deprecamur et obsecramus te ut complaceat divinitas tua adoranda, per clementiam tuam

(*Diaconus:* Cum silentio et timore)

et veniat super nos et super oblationem hanc gratia Spiritus Sancti, habitetque et illabatur super panem hunc et super calicem hunc benedicatque et sanctificet et obsignet illos, in nomine Patris et Filii et Spiritus Sancti: fiatque panis, per virtutem nominis tui, panis, inquam, iste, corpus sanctum Domini nostri Iesu Christi: et calix iste sanguis Domini nostri Iesu Christi: ut quicumque cum vera fide ederit ex hoc pane et biberit ex hoc calice fiant illi Domine ad veniam delictorum et remissionem peccatorum, ad spem magnam resurrectionis a mortuis, ad salutem animae et corporis et ad vitam novam in regno caelorum.

Dignos etiam fac nos omnes per gratiam Domini nostri Iesu Christi ut cum omnibus illis qui placuerunt voluntati tuae et secundum praecepta tua vitam instituerunt

VII

We ask, beg and beseech you Lord, that your adorable divinity be pleased, and that by your goodness

(*Deacon:* In silence and fear)

the grace of the Holy Spirit may come down upon us and upon this oblation, that he may stay and descend on this bread and on this chalice, bless them, sanctify them and sign them with his seal in the name of the Father and of the Son and of the Holy Spirit: and that the bread may become by the power of your name—this bread I mean—the holy body of our Lord Jesus Christ, and this cup, the blood of our Lord Jesus Christ: so that to all those who eat of this bread and drink of this cup in true faith, there will be given the pardon of sins and the forgiveness of offences, the great hope of the resurrection from the dead, the salvation of body and soul, and the new life in the kingdom of heaven.

And make us all worthy, by the grace of our Lord Jesus Christ, so that with all those who have been

laetemur in regno caelorum, fruentes bonis futuris quae non transeunt.

pleasing to your will and directed their lives according to your commandments, we may rejoice in the kingdom of heaven in the possession of those goods which will not pass away.

VIII

Et hic et illic nos omnes simul et aequaliter confitebimur, adorabimus et laudabimus Patrem et Filium et Spiritum Sanctum nunc et semper et in saecula saeculorum.

VIII

And here below and there on high we will all equally and in unison profess our faith, adore and praise the Father, the Son and the Holy Spirit now and for ever age after age.

VIII. The Greek Alexandrine anaphora of St Mark

I have taken this as a sample of the Egyptian anaphoras. The strictly Egyptian type of anaphora can be classed under two heads:

1. Some, but not all, of the Abyssinian anaphoras (cf. G. M. Harden, *The Anaphoras of the Ethiopian Liturgy*, London, 1928; E. Hammerschmidt, *Studies in the Ethiopic Anaphoras*, Berlin, 1961. For a further bibliography see Sauget, *Bibliographie des liturgies orientales*, Rome, 1962, pp. 94–6).

2. A number of Egyptian anaphoras. This includes the anaphora of Serapion (Funk, II, 172–7); the anaphora of St Mark both in Greek and in the Coptic recension (named after St Cyril, cf. Renaudot, I, 40–8); the fragment of Dêr-Balizeh (ed. Roberts-Capelle); the Louvain Coptic fragment 27 (Lefort, in *Le Muséon*, 53 (1940), 22–4); and the fragment contained in an ostracon (W. E. Crum, *Coptic Ostraca*, London, 1902, 2).

It has been shown that the present text of Serapion is not in the least typical, containing as it does ideas of doubtful orthodoxy. Therefore it is probably not authentic (Capelle, "L'anaphore de Sérapion, essai d'exégèse", in *Le Muséon*, 59 (1946), 425–43; Botte, "L'Euchologe de Sérapion est-il authentique?" in *Oriens christianus*, 48 (1964), 50–6), and could not be taken as a reliable example of the Egyptian tradition. Dêr-Balizeh contains: a

collection of three prayers of intercession, with a further prayer before the *Sanctus*; the *Sanctus*; the first epiclesis before the narration of the institution; the narration itself; and the final section of a prayer for a fruitful communion. The Louvain fragment contains the first epiclesis before the narration of the institution, and part of the institution itself. The ostracon has part of the prayer before the *Sanctus*.

And so, in fact, only the anaphora of Mark is complete. The *textus receptus* of the Greek recension is from a manuscript of the twelfth century from Rossano, *Vat. gr. 1970* (Brightman, 125–34; Renaudot, I, 131–42, including a Latin version). In the first section, from the beginning of the anaphora to the end of the intercession, it is possible to recognise a shortened version of the Strasbourg papyrus of the 4th–5th centuries (M. Andrieu-P. Collomp, in *Rev. Sc. Relig.*, 8 (1928), 500–1; reproduced by Gamber, in *Ostkirchliche Studien*, 8 (1959), 34–5).

The concluding part, from the first epiclesis to the end, constitutes the Manchester papyrus (C. H. Roberts, "Catalogue of the Greek and Latin Papyri", in *Bulletin of the John Rylands Library*, III (1938), 25–8). The text of this papyrus in some places is more primitive than the *textus receptus*. I have given here the *textus receptus*, as translated by Renaudot. But I have not included the intercessions from this very diffuse text. In their place, the text of the Strasbourg papyrus has been set out in the notes. For the second epiclesis I have added in the notes the text of the Manchester papyrus.

Even so, it is not certain that the anaphora of St Mark is fully representative of the pure Egyptian tradition. Influence from Syria on its composition cannot be excluded. "The influence of the anaphora of St James on the anaphora of St Mark is quite noticeable. And the same is true of the sacramental rites, where there are prayers of Syriac origin. Therefore there must have been considerable influence from Syria in Egypt" (Botte, in A. B. Martimort (ed.), *L'Eglise en Prière*, Paris, 1961, p. 25). Most important of all however, we must establish whether the second epiclesis, which follows the institution and is found also in Mark,

had in fact its consecratory character in primitive times in Egypt, or whether this is a later development under Syrian influence.

Our doubts are all the stronger after the discovery of the Dêr-Balizeh and Louvain fragments. In these texts, the epiclesis before the institution has clear and well-developed consecratory characteristics, as clear and well-developed as in the Syriac epiclcses which come after the institution. Now admittedly the Louvain fragment contains none of the second epiclesis and Dêr-Balizeh has only the last part. Nevertheless, as Capelle has said in reference to the missing sections: "The one thing that we can be certain about is that the formula used was not an epiclesis of consecration. For such an epiclesis can be found already before the narration of the institution, and is formulated in such explicit and unequivocal terms that its repetition after the anamnesis is impossible" (Roberts-Capelle, 52).

Dom Capelle must surely be right here. Therefore, we must conclude that Dêr-Balizeh and the Louvain fragment separate the two ideas contained in an epiclesis, and put the prayer for consecration before the institution, and the prayer for a fruitful communion after the anamnesis, as is the practice of the Roman canon (*Quam oblationem; Supplices . . . ut quotquot . . .*). Is it possible that Dêr-Balizeh and the Louvain fragment here reflect the early Egyptian tradition?

Whatever the answer to this question I have given here the text of Dêr-Balizeh (Roberts-Capelle, 24–30):

. . . Sanctus, sanctus, sanctus Dominus Sabaoth. Plenum est caelum et terra gloria tua.

Reple et nos gloria quae est a te et mittere dignare Spiritum Sanctum tuum super creaturas istas et fac panem quidem corpus Domini et Salvatoris nostri Iesu Christi, calicem autem sanguinem novi testamenti ipsius Domini nostri et Dei et Salvatoris nostri Iesu Christi. Et sicut panis iste dispersus super montes et colles et paratus et com-

. . . Holy, holy, holy Lord of all! Heaven and earth are full of your glory.

Fill us too with your glory, and deign to send your Holy Spirit upon these offerings which you have created, and make this bread the body of our Lord and Saviour Jesus Christ, and this cup the blood of the new covenant of our same Lord, God and Saviour, Jesus Christ. And as this bread scattered on the mountains and hills has been

mixtus factus est unum corpus . . . sicut vinum istud ortum ex sancta vite David, et aqua ex agno immaculato et mixta facta est unum mysterium: ita collige catholicam Ecclesiam Iesu Christi.

Ipse enim Dominus noster Iesus Christus, nocte qua semetipsum tradidit . . .

. . . mortem tuam annuntiamus et resurrectionem tuam confitemur et deprecamur . . . et concede nobis servis tuis ad confortationem Spiritus Sancti (*in nobis*) ad augmentum fidei ad spem futurae aeternae vitae.

per Dominum nostrum Iesum Christum cum quo tibi, Patri est gloria cum Sancto Spiritu, in saecula. Amen.

gathered to become one body . . . just as this wine from David's holy branch and this water from the spotless lamb have been mixed so as to become a single sacrament: so gather together the catholic Church of Jesus Christ.

For our Lord Jesus Christ, on the night in which he gave himself up . . .

(*Beginning and last part of the prayer which follows the anamnesis:*)

. . . your death we announce; your resurrection we proclaim . . . and we pray . . . grant us your servants the power of the Holy Spirit that our faith may grow to the hope of the eternal life that is to come.

Through our Lord Jesus Christ, with whom glory is given to you Father with the Holy Spirit forever. Amen.

I

Dominus vobiscum omnibus.
Et cum spiritu tuo.
Sursum corda.
Habemus ad Dominum.
Gratias agamus Domino.
Dignum et iustum.

I

The Lord be with you all.
And with you.
Let us lift up our hearts.
We have raised them up to the Lord.
Let us give thanks to the Lord.
That is right and fitting.

II

Vere quippe dignum et iustum est sanctumque ac conveniens atque nostris animabus perutile, qui es, o Dominator Domine, Deus Pater omnipotens, te laudare, te celebrare, tibi gratias agere, tibi palam confiteri nocte et die incessabili ore, numquam silentibus labiis et corde numquam tacito:

II

It is indeed right and fitting, holy and just, and most wholesome for our souls, to praise you who are the Master and Lord, God the almighty Father, and to thank and rejoice in you, to speak and to sing of you, in the day and in the night, our lips never quiet and our hearts never silent. For it is you who

tibi qui fecisti caelum et quae caeli ambitu continentur, terram et quae in terra sunt, maria, fontes, flumina, lacus et omnia quae in eis sunt; tibi qui fecisti hominem ad imaginem et similitudinem tuam, cui paradisi quoque delicias largitus es; et transgressus non aspernatus es neque deseruisti, o Bone, sed denuo per legem revocasti, per prophetas instituisti, denique reformasti et renovasti per hoc tremendum et vivificum et caeleste mysterium. Omnia autem fecisti per tuam sapientiam, lucem veram, unigenitum Filium tuum, Dominum, Deum et Salvatorem nostrum Iesum Christum.

made the heavens and all they contain, the earth and all that is in it, the sea, the torrents, the rivers, the lakes and all that is in them. It is you who made man in your own image and likeness and bestowed on him the delights of paradise; when he had sinned you did not scorn and abandon him, but in your loving kindness called him again through your law and instructed him by your prophets. At last, you restored and renewed him by this most wonderful, heavenly and life-giving sacrament. All this you accomplished through him who is your wisdom, the true light, your only Son, our Lord, God, and Saviour, Jesus Christ.

III

Per quem tibi, cum ipso et Spiritu Sancto offerimus rationabile et incruentum obsequium hoc, quod offerunt tibi Domine, omnes gentes ab ortu solis usque ad occasum, a septentrione ad meridiem: quia magnum nomen tuum in omnibus gentibus et in omni loco incensum offertur nomini sancto tuo et sacrificium purum epithysia et oblatio.

III

It is through him that we offer to you, as also to him and to the Holy Spirit, this spiritual and unbloody sacrifice which all the nations offer you Lord, from the East to the West, from the North to the South. Because great is your renown among all the nations, and in every place a sacrifice of incense is offered to your name, a pure sacrifice, a fragrant offering.

IV

Et rogamus et deprecamur te, humani generis amator bone, memento, Domine, sanctae soliusque catholicae et apostolicae Ecclesiae, quae a finibus terrae ad eiusdem fines ultimos diffunditur, omnium populorum et omnium gregum tuorum.

Pacem, quae ex caelo est largire nostris omnium cordibus, et vitae huius pacem nobis dona.

IV

We ask and pray you Lord that you who are the true lover of mankind may be mindful of the one, holy, catholic and apostolic Church, which stretches from one end of the earth to the other; remember, Lord, all your peoples and all your flocks.

Fill all our hearts with that peace which comes from heaven, and give us peace in this life.

(*A long series of prayers of intercession are inserted here for various intentions. For the most part they are rather wordy and without much order, with repetitions which show that the text is certainly later than that of the Strasbourg papyrus. So we give here in the footnote, the Latin translation of this passage of the papyrus.*[39])

(*Diaconus:* Qui sedetis surgite)

Solve vinctos, eripe eos qui sunt in necessitatibus, esurientes satia, pusillanimes consolare, errantes converte; in tenebris sedentes illumina; lapsos erige; instabiles confirma; aegrotos sana; omnes dirige in viam salutis eosdemque in sanctum ovile tuum congrega, nos autem ab iniquitatibus nostris libera, protector noster et defensor per omnia factus.

(*Deacon:* Let those who are seated rise)

Free the prisoners, come to the aid of those who are in need, nourish those who are hungry, comfort the anguished, convert those who are in error; enlighten those who are seated in darkness, lift up those who have fallen, give courage to those who hesitate, heal the sick; lead all in the way of salvation and gather them all into your sheepfold; cleanse us from our sins, you who in all things are our protector and guardian.

V

(*Diaconus:* Ad orientem aspicite)

Tu es supra omne imperium et omnem potentiam et virtutem et dominationem et omne nomen quod nominatur non solum in hoc saeculo sed etiam in futuro. Tibi adstant milia milium et decies

V

(*Deacon:* Look towards the East)

You are above all kingdoms, powers, empires and dominations, and above every name that can be named, not only in this world but in the world to come. You have around you thousand upon

[39] The Strasbourg papyrus has the following intercessions (text from Gamber): *Regem terrae* [*in pace conserva; da ei*] *pacifica* [*sentire*] *erga nos et erga sanctum nomen tuum. In omni pace conserva pro nobis gubernatorem . . ., ordines militares, senatus, concilia, introitus et exitus* (*eorum*).

Fratres nostros peregre profectos in omni loco dirige: ipse comes navigationis et itineris eorum esse dignare; suis eos restitue sanos.

Mitte pluvias tuas: laetifica faciem terrae; semina tua conserva ut fructificent et perveniant ad messem; fructus incorruptos et sanos conserva: propter pauperes populi tui, propter nos omnes qui invocamus nomen tuum, propter omnes qui sperant in te.

Eorum qui obdormierunt animabus requiem concede. Memento eorum quorum hodie memoriam facimus et quorum nomina dicimus aut non dicimus.

Memento etiam Domine, ubique degentium orthodoxorum sanctorum patrum nostrorum et episcoporum: et da nobis partem et sortem habere cum pulchra Ecclesia sanctorum tuorum prophetarum, apostolorum et martyrum. Eorum intercessione recipe orationem istam super altare tuum caeleste et dignare [. . .] *recipiens* [. . .] *ante oculos tuos, largire eis dona spiritualia, per Dominum et Salvatorem nostrum. Per quem tibi gloria in saecula saeculorum.*

milies centena milium sanctorum Angelorum et Archangelorum exercitus. Tibi adstant honoratissima tua duo animalia, nimirum multocula Cherubim et sex ala habentes Seraphim, qui duabus quidem alis facies tegunt, duabus pedes, ac duabus volant, et clamant alter ad alterum, incessabilibus vocibus et numquam tacentibus theologiis, triumphalem et ter sanctum hymnum canentia, clamantia, glorificantia et dicentia magnificae tuae gloriae:

Sanctus, Sanctus, Sanctus Dominus Deus Sabaoth. Plenum est caelum et terra gloria sancta tua.

(*Elevat vocem*): Omni quidem tempore omnia te sanctificant; at cum omnibus qui te glorificant suscipe, Dominator Domine, sanctificationem nostram qui te laudamus cum eis et dicimus:

(*Populus*): Sanctus, Sanctus, Sanctus Dominus Deus Sabaoth. Plenum est caelum et terra gloria tua.

VI

Plenum est vere caelum et terra gloria tua per manifestationem Domini et Dei et Salvatoris nostri Iesu Christi. Reple, Deus, hoc quoque sacrificium benedictione quae est a te per adventum Sanctissimi Spiritus tui.

VII

Quoniam ipse Dominus et Deus et summus Rex noster Iesus Christus, nocte qua tradebat seipsum pro peccatis nostris et pro omnibus perferebat mortem in carne, recumbens cum sanctis suis discipulis et Apostolis, panem accepit in sanctas et immaculatas et intemeratas manus suas, suspexit

thousand of holy angels and all the armies of archangels. You have before you those most noble beings: the cherubim with the innumerable eyes, and the six-winged seraphim, who use two wings to cover their faces, two to cover their feet, and two to fly. They cry one to another, never ceasing to speak and to utter your sacred praises, singing that triumphal and thrice holy hymn, proclaiming, glorifying and exalting the splendour of your glory:

Holy! holy! holy! Lord God of all! Heaven and earth are full of your glory.

(*He raises his voice*): All things glorify you at all times, but grant that together with all those who glorify you, you may also receive the praise we offer to you, our Lord and Master, we who praise you with them and say:

(*People*): Holy! holy! holy! Lord, God of all! Heaven and earth are full of your glory.

VI

Truly, heaven and earth are full of your glory through the coming of our Lord, God and Saviour, Jesus Christ. Fill, O God, this sacrifice with that blessing which comes from you by the coming of your most Holy Spirit.

VII

Our Lord and God and sovereign king Jesus Christ, on the night in which he gave himself for our sins and suffered death in his flesh for all men, when he was eating with his apostles and disciples, took bread into his holy and spotless hands, lifted his eyes to you, his Father, our God and the God of

ad te, Patrem suum, Deumque nostrum et universorum, gratias egit, benedixit, sanctificavit, fregit, distribuit sanctis et beatis discipulis suis et apostolis dicens:	all, gave thanks, blessed, sanctified, broke it and gave it to his holy and blessed apostles and disciples saying:
(*alta voce*)	(*in a loud voice*)
Accipite, manducate,	Take and eat.
(*Diaconus:* extendite)	(*Deacon:* Stretch out your hands)
(*alta voce*)	(*in a loud voice*)
Hoc est corpus meum, quod pro vobis frangitur et distribuitur in remissionem peccatorum.	This is my body, which is broken for you and is shared among you for the forgiveness of sins.
(*Populus:* Amen)	(*People:* Amen)
Similiter et calicem postquam cenavit accepit et miscuit vino et aqua, suspexit in caelum ad te, Patrem suum Deumque nostrum et universorum, gratias egit, benedixit, sanctificavit, implevit Spiritu Sancto distribuit sanctis ac beatis suis discipulis et Apostolis dicens:	Likewise, when he had finished the meal, he took the cup, filled it with wine and water, lifted his eyes to you, his Father, our God and the God of all, gave thanks, blessed, sanctified, filled it with the Holy Spirit and gave it to his holy and blessed apostles and disciples saying:
(*alta voce*)	(*in a loud voice*)
Bibite ex eo omnes:	Drink some of this all of you.
(*Diaconus:* Iterum extendite)	(*Deacon:* Stretch out your hand again)
Hic est sanguis meus, novi testamenti, qui pro vobis et pro multis effunditur et distribuitur in remissionem peccatorum.	This is my blood, the blood of the new covenant, which is poured out for you and for all men for the forgiveness of sins.
(*Populus:* Amen)	(*People:* Amen)
Hoc facite in meam commemorationem. Quotiescumque enim manducabitis panem hunc, bibebitis vero et calicem hunc, mortem meam annuntiatis resurrectionem meam et ascensionem confitemini donec veniam.	Do this in memory of me. In fact, whenever you eat this bread or drink this cup, you will proclaim my death and my resurrection and announce my ascension, until the time when I return.
VIII	**VIII**
Mortem, Dominator Domine omnipotens, caelestis Rex, unigeniti tui Filii, Domini autem et	That is why, Master and all powerful Lord, King of heaven, in proclaiming the death of your only

Dei et Salvatoris nostri Iesu Christi, annuntiantes; et triduanum beatamque eius a mortuis resurrectionem et ascensionem in caelum ac sessionem a dextris tui, Dei et Patris, confitentes; et expectantes secundum et terribilem ac tremendum eius adventum, in quo venturus est iudicare vivos et mortuos in iustitia et reddere unicuique secundum opera eius:

—parce nobis, Domine Deus noster—[40]

tibi de tuis donis proposuimus coram te.

Son, our Lord, God and Saviour Jesus Christ; in acknowledging his blessed resurrection from the dead on the third day, his ascension into heaven and his sitting at the right hand of you, God, his Father; and in waiting for his glorious and terrible second coming, when he will come to judge the living and the dead with justice and will give to each man according to his works,

—spare us, Lord our God—

we place before you these gifts which come from you.

IX

Et rogamus et obsecramus te, generis humani amator bone, emitte ex alto sancto tuo, ex praeparato habitaculo tuo, ex incircumscriptis sinibus tuis, ipsum Paraclitum, Spiritum veritatis sanctum, Dominum,[41] vivificantem, qui in lege et prophetis et apostolis locutus est, qui ubique adest et omnia replet, qui operatur propria potentia, non tamquam minister, in quibus ipse vult, sanctificationem, pro beneplacito suo: simplex quoad naturam, diversas habens operationes, divinorum charismatum fons, tibi consubstantialis, ex te procedens, sedens tecum in throno regni tui et unigeniti Filii tui Domini, Dei et Salvatoris nostri Iesu Christi.

Respice super nos et emitte super hos panes et super istos calices Spiritum tuum Sanctum ut

IX

We ask and pray you, you who are the true lover of mankind, to send from your heavenly sanctuary, from your celestial dwelling and unutterable dwelling place, the Paraclete himself, the Holy Spirit of truth, who is Lord and giver of life, who has spoken through the law, through the prophets, and through the apostles. He is present everywhere and fills all things, and he brings about by his own power and not as a minister, the sanctification of those whom he chooses of his own free will. He is simple in essence, but has many different operations; he is the source of divine gifts and consubstantial with you; he proceeds from you and sits with you on the throne of your kingdom, which is also the kingdom of your only Son, our Lord, God and Saviour, Jesus Christ.

[40] *Parce . . . noster*: this text is not in the Manchester papyrus.

[41] *Dominum . . . et faciat panem.* The Manchester papyrus has at this point a much shorter and more primitive text: . . . *veritatis sanctum super haec praesentia dona, super hunc panem et super hunc calicem, et faciat* (*facias*?) *panem . . .*

ea sanctificet ac perficiat, tamquam Deus omnipotens

(*alta voce*)

et faciat panem quidem corpus

(*Populus:* Amen)

(*alta voce*)

calicem autem sanguinem novi testamenti ipsius Domini et Dei et Salvatoris nostri et Summi Regis, Iesu Christi.

(*Diaconus:* Diaconi descendite.)

Ut fiat omnibus nobis qui ex eis participamus, in fidem, in sobrietatem, in medelam, in sapientiam, in sanctificationem, in renovationem animae, corporis et spiritus, in communionem beatitudinis vitae aeternae et immortalitatis, in glorificationem sanctissimi tui nominis, in remissionem peccatorum.

Look on us and send upon these loaves and cups your Holy Spirit, that, being God almighty, he may sanctify and consecrate them,

(*in a loud voice*)

and make of this bread the body

(*People:* Amen)

(*in a loud voice*)

and of this cup the blood of the new covenant of our Lord, God, Saviour, and sovereign King, Jesus Christ.

(*Deacon:* Deacons, come down.)

May we who participate in it find there faith, soberness, healing, wisdom, holiness, renewal of our souls, bodies and spirits, a share in happiness, eternal life and immortality, the glorifying of your holy name and the remission of sins.

X

Ut in hoc quoque, sicut in universo, glorificetur et laudetur et sanctificetur sanctissimum et honoratum et glorificatum nomen tuum, cum Iesu Christo et Spiritu Sancto.

(*Populus:* Sicut erat et est [et erit in generationem et generationem et in omnibus saeculis saeculorum. Amen]).

X

And in this time as in all times, may your most holy, venerable and glorious name be glorified and praised with Jesus Christ and the Holy Spirit.

(*People:* As it was, is, [and shall be from generation to generation and for ever and ever. Amen]).

IX. The Roman Canon; corrected by Hans Küng

H. Küng, "Das Eucharistiegebet. Konzil und Erneuerung der römischen Liturgie", in *Wort und Wahrheit*, 18 (1963), 102–7. The proposed text is on 103–4:

I

Dominus vobiscum.
Et cum spiritu tuo.
Sursum corda.

I

The Lord be with you.
And with you.
Lift up your hearts.

Habemus ad Dominum.
Gratias agamus Domino Deo nostro.
Dignum et iustum est.

We have raised them up to the Lord.
Let us give thanks to the Lord our God.
It is right and fitting.

II

Vere dignum et iustum est aequum et salutare nos tibi semper et ubique gratias agere, Domine, Sancte Pater, omnipotens aeterne Deus, per Christum Dominum nostrum. Per quem maiestatem tuam laudant Angeli, adorant dominationes, tremunt potestates, caeli caelorumque virtutes ac beata Seraphim socia exultatione concelebrant. Cum quibus et nostras voces ut admitti iubeas deprecamur, supplici confessione dicentes:
Sanctus, Sanctus, Sanctus
Dominus Deus Sabaoth.
Pleni sunt caeli et terra gloria tua.
Hosanna in excelsis.
Benedictus qui venit in nomine Domini.
Hosanna in excelsis.

II

It is indeed right and fitting to give thanks to you always and everywhere, Lord, holy Father, almighty and eternal God, through Christ our Lord. It is through him that the angels praise your majesty, the dominions adore it, the powers are held in awe; through him that the heavenly and the celestial virtues, together with the Seraphim, join in one exultant hymn of praise. We pray you, let our voices blend with theirs, as we humbly praise you, singing:
Holy, Holy, Holy, Lord God of all.
Your glory fills all heaven and earth.
Hosanna in the heights of heaven.
Blessed is he who comes in the name of the Lord.
Hosanna in the heights of heaven.

III

Te [igitur] clementissime Pater, per Iesum Christum, Filium tuum, Dominum nostrum, supplices rogamus ac petimus, ut accepta habeas et benedicas haec dona, haec munera, haec sancta sacrificia illibata.

III

Most merciful father, we humbly ask and pray that through Jesus Christ, your Son, our Lord, you will accept and bless these gifts, these offerings, this holy unblemished sacrifice.

IV

Hanc oblationem, tu Deus, in omnibus, quaesumus, benedictam, adscriptam, ratam, rationabilem acceptabilemque facere digneris, ut nobis corpus et sanguis fiat dilectissimi Filii tui, Domini nostri Iesu Christi.

IV

We pray you, O God, graciously bless and approve this sacrifice. Make it fit and worthy to be offered to you, so that it may become the body and blood of your beloved Son, our Lord, Jesus Christ.

V

Qui pridie quam pateretur accepit panem in sanctas ac venerabiles manus suas, et elevatis oculis in caelum ad te, Deum, Patrem suum omnipotentem, tibi gratias agens, benedixit, fregit deditque discipulis suis dicens: Accipite et manducate ex hoc omnes, hoc est enim corpus meum.

Simili modo, postquam cenatum est, accipiens et hunc praeclarum calicem in sanctas ac venerabiles manus suas, item tibi gratias agens, benedixit, deditque discipulis suis dicens: Accipite et bibite ex eo omnes: Hic est enim calix sanguinis mei novi et aeterni testamenti, qui pro vobis et pro multis effundetur in remissionem peccatorum.

Haec quotiescumque feceritis in mei memoriam facietis.

V

On the day before he suffered, he took bread into his holy and blessed hands, and looking up to heaven, to you, God, his almighty Father, he thanked you, blessed and broke it, and gave it to his disciples, saying: Take and eat this, all of you, for this is my body.

So too, at the end of the meal, he took this precious cup into his holy and blessed hands, and giving thanks to you, he blessed and gave it to his disciples, saying: Take and drink this, all of you; for this is the cup of my blood, of the new, everlasting covenant; for you and for all men it will be poured out for the forgiveness of sins.

Whenever you do this, you will do it in memory of me.

VI

Unde et memores, Domine, nos servi tui, sed et plebs tua sancta, Christi, Filii tui, Domini nostri, tam beatae passionis necnon et ab inferis resurrectionis, sed et in caelos gloriosae ascensionis, offerimus praeclarae maiestati tuae, de tuis donis ac datis, hostiam puram, hostiam sanctam, hostiam immaculatam, panem sanctum vitae aeternae et calicem salutis perpetuae.

VI

In memory therefore, Lord, of the passion and resurrection from the dead of Christ, your Son, our Lord, and of his glorious ascension into heaven, we your servants, and your holy people, offer to your sovereign majesty, from the gifts which you yourself have given us, a sacrifice pure, holy, and unblemished, the sacred bread of eternal life, and cup of everlasting salvation.

VII

Supra quae propitio ac sereno vultu respicere digneris et accepta habere sicuti accepta habere dignatus es munera pueri tui iusti Abel et sacrificium patriarchae nostri Abrahae et quod tibi obtulit summus sacerdos tuus Melchisedech, sanctum sacrificium, immaculatam hostiam

VII

Look on these offerings with favour and contentment. Accept them as you graciously accepted the offerings of your just servant Abel, the sacrifice of our father Abraham, and that of your high priest Melchisedech—a holy sacrifice, a victim without blemish.

VIII

Supplices te rogamus, omnipotens Deus, iube haec perferri per manus sancti angeli tui in sublime altare tuum, in conspectu divinae maiestatis tuae, ut quotquot ex hac altaris participatione sacrosanctum Filii tui corpus et sanguinem sumpserimus, omni benedictione caelesti et gratia repleamur per Christum Dominum nostrum.

VIII

We humbly beseech you, almighty God, have these offerings brought up by your Angel to your altar in heaven, before your divine majesty. So may we, in receiving the sacred body and blood of your Son, here at this altar, be filled with every heavenly grace and blessing through Christ our Lord.

IX

Per quem haec omnia, Domine, semper bona creas, sanctificas, vivificas, benedicis et praestas nobis, per ipsum et cum ipso et in ipso est tibi Deo Patri omnipotenti, in unitate Spiritus Sancti, omnis honor et gloria per omnia saecula saeculorum. Amen.

IX

It is through him, Lord, that you continue always to create, sanctify, vivify, and bless all these good things, and give them to us. Through him, with him, and in him, all glory and honour is given to you, God the almighty Father, in the unity of the Holy Spirit, for ever and ever. Amen.

X. The Roman Canon; corrected by Karl Amon

K. Amon, "Gratias Agere. Zur Reform des Messcanons", in *Liturgisches Jahrbuch*, 15 (1965), 79–98. The text is on 95–8, and also gives the actions which, in the author's opinion, ought to accompany the words.

PREX EUCHARISTICA

I

GRATIARUM ACTIO

Vere dignum et iustum est, aequum et salutare, nos tibi semper et ubique gratias agere, Domine, Sancte Pater, omnipotens aeterne Deus: Cuius bonitas hominem condidit, iustitia damnavit, misericordia redemit,[42] per Christum Dominum nostrum.

EUCHARISTIC PRAYER

I

THANKSGIVING

It is indeed right and just to give thanks to you always and everywhere, Lord, holy Father, almighty and eternal God: through your goodness man was formed, in your justice he was condemned, and by your mercy he is redeemed, through Christ our Lord.

[42] *Cuius bonitas . . . redemit*: words in the Ambrosian liturgy for Thursday in the fourth week in Lent.

Qui oblatione sui corporis, remotis sacrificiis carnalium victimarum, se ipsum per Spiritum Sanctum tibi pro salute nostra offerens, idem sacerdos et sacer Agnus exhibuit.[43]

Qui[44] ascendens super omnes caelos sedensque ad dexteram tuam, promissum Spiritum sanctum hodierna die in filios adoptionis effudit:[45] Spiritum veritatis qui a te procedit et ipsum clarificat.[46] Qui principio nascentis Ecclesiae cunctis gentibus imbuendis et deitatis scientiam inderet, et linguarum diversitatem in unius fidei confessione sociaret.[47] Quapropter profusis gaudiis totus in orbe terrarum mundus exultat. Sed et supernae virtutes atque angelicae potestates hymnum gloriae tuae concinunt, sine fine dicentes:[48]

Sanctus, Sanctus, Sanctus, Dominus Deus Sabaoth. Pleni sunt caeli et terra gloria tua. Hosanna in excelsis. Benedictus qui venit in nomine Domini. Hosanna in excelsis.

Vere sanctus, vere benedictus Dominus noster Iesus Christus manens in caelis, manifestatus in terris.[49]

For now the sacrifice of animal victims ceases, as by the sacrifice of his body, in offering himself to you, through the Holy Spirit for our salvation, he showed himself to be both sacrificing priest and sacrificial lamb.

He has ascended above the heavens, and seated at your right hand, pours out this day upon your adopted sons the Holy Spirit which he promised; the Spirit of truth who proceeds from you and glorifies the son. This Spirit, at the birth of the Church, conferred on all the peoples to be baptised knowledge of God, and unified in one confession of faith all their different languages. Because of this, the whole world is filled with joy, and all the earth joins with the angels of heaven in one exultant hymn to your glory, singing unceasingly:

Holy, Holy, Holy, Lord God of all.
Your glory fills all heaven and earth.
Hosanna in the heights of heaven.
Blessed is he who comes in the name of the Lord.
Hosanna in the heights of heaven.

Our Lord Jesus Christ is truly holy, truly blessed in heaven and revealed on earth.

---

[43] *Qui oblationem . . . Agnus exhibuit*: preface *aliis diebus de resurrectione* in the Gregorian Sacramentary, in Muratori, *Liturgia romana vetus II*, Venice, 1748, 277–8. (*Per spiritum sanctum*: cf. Heb. 9: 14.)

[44] At this point the movable prefaces are inserted. The preface from Pentecost is given by way of example.

[45] *Qui . . . effudit*: from the present preface for Pentecost.

[46] *Spiritum veritatis . . . clarificat*: text inserted by the author; compare John 15: 26; 16: 14.

[47] *Qui principio . . . sociaret*: according to Amon, these words are from the Gregorian Sacramentary, Monday of Pentecost, Muratori, op. cit.; in fact they are from the Gelasian Sacramentary, ed. Mohlberg, n. 641.

[48] *Quapropter . . . dicentes*: this is still the preface of Pentecost.

[49] *Vere sanctus . . . in terris*: from the *Missale Gothicum*, ed. Mohlberg, n. 4, p. 4. The words *Filius tuus* have been omitted, perhaps owing to a misprint.

Qui pridie quam pateretur, accepit panem in sanctas ac venerabiles manus suas, et elevatis oculis in caelum ad te, Deum, Patrem suum omnipotentem, tibi gratias agens, benedixit, fregit, deditque discipulis suis dicens: Accipite et manducate ex hoc omnes: Hoc est enim corpus meum.

Simili modo, postquam cenatum est, accipiens et hunc praeclarum calicem in sanctas ac venerabiles manus suas: item tibi gratias agens, benedixit, deditque discipulis suis dicens: Accipite et bibite ex eo omnes: Hic est enim calix sanguinis mei, novi et aeterni testamenti: mysterium fidei: qui pro vobis et pro multis effundetur in remissionem peccatorum. Haec quotiescumque feceritis in mei memoriam facietis.

On the day before he suffered, he took bread into his holy and blessed hands, and looking up to heaven, to you, God, his almighty Father, he thanked you, blessed and broke it, and gave it to his disciples, saying: Take and eat this, all of you, for this is my body.

So too, at the end of the meal, he took this precious cup into his holy and blessed hands: again giving thanks to you, he blessed and gave it to his disciples, saying: Take and drink this, all of you; for this is the cup of my blood, of the new, everlasting covenant; for you and for all men it will be poured out for the forgiveness of sins.

Whenever you do this, you will do it in memory of me.

II

ANAMNESIS

Unde et memores, Domine, nos servi tui, sed et plebs tua sancta, eiusdem Christi Filii tui, Domini nostri, tam beatae passionis, nec non et ab inferis resurrectionis, sed et in caelos gloriosae ascensionis:

II

ANAMNESIS

We, your servants and your holy people, remember then, Lord, the holy passion and resurrection from the dead of Christ, your Son, our Lord, and his glorious ascension into heaven.

III

OBLATIO

Offerimus praeclarae maiestati tuae de tuis donis ac datis hostiam puram, hostiam sanctam, hostiam immaculatam: panem sanctum vitae aeternae et calicem salutis perpetuae.

III

OFFERING

We offer to your sovereign majesty, from the gifts which you yourself have given us, a sacrifice pure, holy and unblemished, the sacred bread of eternal life and cup of everlasting salvation.

IV

COMMUNIO SANCTORUM

Communicantes, et diem sacratissimum Pentecostes celebrantes, quo Spiritus Sanctus Apostolis

IV

COMMUNION OF SAINTS

In one fellowship, as we celebrate the day of Pentecost, on which the Holy Spirit was revealed

innumeris linguis apparuit:[50] sed et memoriam venerantes, in primis gloriosae semper virginis Mariae, genitricis Dei et Domini nostri Iesu Christi, et beati Ioannis Baptistae, et beati Ioseph, eiusdem virginis sponsi, sed et beatorum Apostolorum ac martyrum tuorum: Petri et Pauli, Andreae, Iacobi, Ioannis, Thomae, Iacobi, Philippi, Bartholomei, Simonis et Thaddaei: Xysti, Polycarpi, Ignatii et Cypriani, Hippolyti et Pionii, Stephani, Laurenti et Iustini, Blandinae, Perpetuae et Felicitatis: et omnium sanctorum tuorum.

in the apostles as they spoke in many languages, we honour the memory, first, of the glorious virgin Mary, mother of our God and Lord Jesus Christ, and also that of blessed John the Baptist, blessed Joseph, the virgin's spouse, and all your holy apostles and martyrs: Peter and Paul, Andrew, James, Philip, Bartholomew, Simon, Thaddeus; Sixtus, Polycarp, Ignatius and Cyprian, Hippolytus and Pionius, Stephen, Lawrence and Justin, Blandina, Perpetua and Felicity, and of all your saints.

V

Precatio pro acceptatione sacrificii

—*Diebus dominicis:*

Quam oblationem tu, Deus, in omnibus, quaesumus, benedictam, adscriptam, ratam, rationabilem, acceptabilemque facere digneris, et perferri iubeas per manus sancti Angeli tui in sublime altare tuum, in conspectu divinae maiestatis tuae.

—*Infra hebdomadam*, loco *Quam oblationem*, dicitur:

Te igitur, clementissime Pater, per Iesum Christum, Filium tuum, Dominum nostrum, supplices rogamus ac petimus, uti accepta habeas et benedicas haec dona, haec munera, haec sancta sacrificia illibata. Supra quae propitio ac sereno vultu respicere digneris, et accepta habere sicuti accepta habere dignatus es munera pueri tui iusti Abel et sacrificium patriarchae nostri Abrahae: et quod tibi obtulit summus

V

Prayer for the acceptance of the sacrifice

—*On Sundays:*

We pray you, O God, graciously bless and approve this sacrifice. Make it fit and worthy to be offered to you. Have your angels bring it to your altar in heaven, before your divine majesty.

During the week, instead of this prayer is said:

Most merciful father, we humbly ask and pray that, through Jesus Christ your Son, our Lord, you will accept and bless these gifts, these offerings, this holy, unblemished sacrifice. Look on these offerings with favour and content. Accept them as you graciously accepted the offerings of your just servant Abel, the sacrifice of our father Abraham, and that of your high priest Melchisedech, a holy

[50] *Et diem . . . apparuit*: this is the *Communicantes* proper to Pentecost.

sacerdos tuus Melchisedech, sanctum sacrificium immaculatam hostiam.

sacrifice, a victim without blemish.

—In missis peculiaribus

(post baptismum et confirmationem, in collatione sacrorum ordinum, in consecratione virginum, in missa pro sponsis et in missis defunctorum, omissa precatione *Quam oblationem* vel *Te igitur*, dicitur precatio *Hanc igitur*, ut suo loco habetur.)

On special occasions:

(After baptism and confirmation, at ordinations and the taking of vows, in nuptial Masses or Masses for the dead, instead of one of these prayers the appropriate *Hanc Igitur* is said.)

VI

PRECATIO PRO OMNIBUS COMMUNICANTIBUS

Supplices te rogamus, omnipotens Deus: ut quotquot ex hac altaris participatione sacrosanctum Filii tui corpus et sanguinem sumpserimus, omni benedictione caelesti et gratia repleamur: ut te laudemus et glorificemus per dilectum Filium tuum Iesum Christum.[51]

—Rerum benedictio:

Si aliqua res benedicenda allata sit, celebrans manus iungit et versus rem benedicendam dicit:

Per quem haec omnia, Domine, semper bona creas, sanctificas, vivificas, benedicis et praestas nobis.

VI

PRAYER FOR ALL RECEIVING HOLY COMMUNION

We humbly pray, Almighty God, that in receiving the sacred body and blood of your Son, here at this altar, we may be filled with every heavenly grace and blessing; so may we praise and glorify you through your beloved Son, Jesus Christ.

Blessing of objects:

If there is anything to be blessed, the celebrant joins his hands and facing towards what is to be blessed, says:

It is through him, Lord, that you continue always to create, sanctify, vivify, and bless all these good things, and give them to us.

VII

DOXOLOGIA FINALIS ET ELEVATIO

Per ipsum, et cum ipso, et in ipso, est tibi Deo Patri omnipotenti, in unitate Spiritus Sancti, omnis honor et gloria, per omnia saecula saeculorum. *R.* Amen.

VII

FINAL DOXOLOGY AND ELEVATION

Through him, with him, and in him, all glory and honour is given to you, God the almighty Father, in the unity of the Holy Spirit, for ever and ever. Amen.

---

[51] *Ut te laudemus . . . tuum Iesum Christum*: the final doxology belonging to the anaphora of Hippolytus.

CHAPTER II

The Principal Merits and Defects of the Present Roman Canon

In setting out the merits of the Roman canon, it does not seem sufficient merely to point out the value or beauty of this or that particular phrase or thought, phrases in fact which can be found in abundance in scripture and tradition. It is necessary, rather, to inspect the character of the whole: to see what it is that gives the present Roman canon its special colour and value, considering it against the background of the anaphora tradition of the entire Church.[1]

I. Merits

(1) *Its antiquity and traditional character in the West*

This is without doubt the soundest argument for the position enjoyed by the present Roman canon in the Western Church. Since the second half of the fourth century, when the Church of Rome finally adopted the Latin language for liturgical use and began to employ fixed forms of prayer, it has never known, so far as we can gather from history, more than a single canon at any one time. The canon used today is the result of the changes that the primitive Latin canon of the Roman Church underwent between the fifth and seventh centuries; since the time of Gregory the Great it has undergone no further changes of any real importance.

[1] Liturgists have shown themselves for the most part reluctant to accept a number of assertions made by T. Schnitzler (*Die Messe in der Betrachtung*, Freiburg im Breisgau, 3rd ed., 1960) regarding the merits of the present Roman canon. Perhaps it is because the author has paid too little attention to this criterion.

This canon was introduced into England during the seventh century and a century later into the kingdom of the Franks; into Spain in the eleventh century and into the Celtic countries between the ninth and twelfth centuries.

Even though from the high Middle Ages at least the Milanese Church has been acquainted with a canon for Holy Thursday that is Gallican in type, its normal canon is substantially that of Rome. When was it adopted? Leaving aside the question of the relationship that exists between the canon of the Ambrosian *De Sacramentis* and the Roman canon, the opinions of liturgists range from the fifth to the ninth centuries.

Thus the canon used by the Church of the city of Rome from the period between the fifth and seventh centuries (and possibly before), has been the only canon of the entire Western Church since the eleventh or twelfth century; in many countries it had already been adopted long before. This fact alone makes the suggestion that this canon should be simply abandoned a foolhardy one.

(2) *The prefaces of the Roman tradition*

The whole of the anaphora is essentially a hymn of rejoicing, thanksgiving and supplication, but these characteristics ought to be particularly evident in the first part of the great prayer, the *eucharistia* par excellence. The second part is more directly sacrificial, containing as it must the institution, the anamnesis (the epiclesis too in my opinion), the offertory, the plea for a fruitful communion and the final doxology.

In contrast to the East, it is customary throughout the West to vary the first part of the anaphora in accordance with the feast. This is in a special way a hymn of rejoicing and praise for the gifts of creation and providence and for the wonders that God has actually done for us in saving us; above all for what he has done for us in his Son, Jesus Christ. These are the elements that go to make up the prefaces of the Roman tradition and the *inlationes* or *immolationes* or *contestationes* of the Palaeo-Hispanic and the Gallican traditions.

The system of altering the hymn of rejoicing according to the feast makes it considerably easier to emphazise the ideas and themes of the feast or saint being commemorated. A particular aspect of the economy of salvation can be developed each time, the aspect which suits the day's feast, although the canon remains the same.

Such flexibility is not possible in the system adopted by the Eastern tradition, where the anaphora forms a complete unit. Its first part is always the same, with no particular reference made to the feast being celebrated. It presents instead an overall and unchanging view of the whole economy of salvation, even though this is developed in greater detail in the Antioch tradition than in that of Edessa or of Egypt.

Each system has its advantages and its disadvantages. The Western system has the advantage of variety and is able to give closer attention, within the one anaphora, to the particular character of each individual feast. A distinct disadvantage, however, is that it never presents a synthesis of the whole economy of salvation. If a Catholic of the Latin rite wished to share this same panorama of salvation history, he would have to work his way through all the prefaces of the year.

The Eastern Catholic, on the other hand, is presented with a wide view of the history of salvation every time he looks at the anaphora. This has its drawbacks: you cannot here place special emphasis on details of the whole story. If at Christmas or Easter, for example, on Ascension Day or at Pentecost, you want to find specific reference to the feast of the day, you will have to turn to the other parts of the Mass—not the anaphora. There is, too, the danger of monotony. Almost all the Eastern Churches have sought a partial solution to this in allowing more than one anaphora so that a change is possible on certain occasions or at certain times of the year.

However, the movable prefaces are an integral part of the Roman canon. The Roman anaphora tradition is well known for the extraordinary richness of its prefaces, both in their number and in their quality. This is particularly true of the oldest tradition, as can be seen from the Leonine Sacramentary. Though this abundance was unfortunately diminished from as long ago as the time of Gregory the Great, it is certain that it will be restored by the liturgical reforms at present under consideration. In fact it may well be increased by recourse to what is valuable in the traditions of Gaul, Spain and Milan. It is unthinkable that the treasures of the Roman prefaces, increased by the finest flowerings of the Gallican, Spanish and Ambrosian traditions, could ever be put aside.

As far as we are concerned, this means that the Roman liturgy must retain a canon with variable prefaces, and that *no single anaphora* with a fixed preface, whether it is on the Eastern pattern or a new composition, will provide a satisfactory solution.

The variable prefaces express the great mysteries of salvation, but it would be impossible simply to add them to an Eastern anaphora or to another of the same type, or even to the anaphora of Hippolytus: there would be too much repetition. The movable preface would in fact develop a particular point in the pattern of salvation which would then be taken up again, even if in a briefer way, in the more complete presentation of the economy called for by this sort of anaphora. In an anaphora that follows the Eastern pattern there must be some treatment of at least the incarnation, the suffering and death of our Saviour, the resurrection, the ascension and, I think, Pentecost as well.

(3) *The theology of the offering of the gifts*

As distinct from all the other anaphora traditions, it is characteristic of the present Roman canon that, from the *Te igitur* onwards, it is directed towards the offering of our gifts, their acceptance by God and their consecration.

It appears above all as a great prayer of blessing (though very special as compared with other blessings). Blessings are called down upon the gifts offered on the altar in which we are soon afterwards to share. In this connection it is useful to compare the canon with the great prayer for blessing the oils and the water for the baptismal font in the early Roman tradition. From this we can see that the general picture presented by the modern Roman canon is one of offering and sanctification of the gifts offered, and judging by the results obtained in endeavours to reconstruct the original canon, everything leads one to believe that this character is itself primitive.

I am fully aware that the Roman canon insists so strongly on this point and returns to it so often that it falls into the error of excess. In my own opinion, however, the intrinsic value and genuine depth of this theology is undeniable, even if little understood today.

The offering of bread and wine which we make to God in the Mass has, to put it briefly, a meaning that is at the same time cosmic, anthropological and sacramental. Bread and wine are chosen from among the gifts God has given us and are offered to him as a symbol of the offering of ourselves, of what we possess and of the whole of material creation. In this offering we pray God to accept them, to bless them and to transform them through his Spirit into the body and blood of Christ, asking him to give them back to us transformed in such a way that through them we may, in the Spirit, be united to Christ and to one another, sharing in fact in the divine nature.

The very idea of sacrifice is seen against this background in the Roman canon. This is not to exclude the offering of Christ and of ourselves; on the contrary, full account is taken of it, but with the offering of the gifts before and after the consecration as the starting point.

It is basically the theme of the *sacrum commercium* which is symbolised and made concrete in the offering of the gifts, at first unconsecrated and then consecrated which, after their consecration, we receive again in the communion, transformed into the body and blood of the Lord.

It is certain that at the end of the Roman canon, with the words *Per quem haec omnia* . . ., food of various sorts was blessed. And it is very likely that the formula *Per quem* . . . was introduced into the canon by this custom. It is just as certain that this food was not blessed during every Mass, and yet the formula used to be said at every Mass, and had been for at least some time. This, in my opinion, is proved by the fact that the *Per ipsum, cum ipso* . . . which was certainly said at every Mass necessarily requires the *Per quem* . . . from a grammatical point of view, given the text as it stands. The *Per ipsum* always presupposes the *Per quem.* This, to my mind, shows that the words *Haec omnia* in the present canon, whatever may have been their origin, do not exclude the unconsecrated gifts; they are actually expressly included along with the gifts which have been consecrated. It certainly was not possible to retain the formula *Per quem haec omnia* even when the blessing of food was left out except by meaning it in the sense already referred to: by using it, that is, as a *resumé* of the idea of offering the gifts discussed above.[2] This idea is also expressed in the *Te igitur*, in the *Quam oblationem* and again (with different shades of emphasis and in connection with the idea of offering and its acceptance) in the *Hanc igitur*, the *Unde et memores*, the *Supra quae* and the *Supplices*.

(4) *Stylistic merits*

The specifically Roman character of the style, even in the canon as it now is (if we except perhaps the excessive length of the two lists of saints), has often been remarked upon by specialists.[3] It can be seen in the terminology, steeped though this is in biblical and specifically Christian language; in a certain fondness for an abundance of concepts expressed in groups of two or three together, and in the juridical precision of the language, recalling that of the sacred formulae of ancient Rome. But what constitutes the chief merit of the language of the Roman canon, especially if we include, as we should, a consideration of the prefaces, is without doubt its theological precision and its sobriety of expres-

---

[2] A substantially similar opinion is expressed by J. A. Jungmann, *Missarum Sollemnia* (Eng. abridged ed. *The Mass of the Roman Rite*, London, 1961, 453–7, esp. 456).

[3] See J. Brinktrine, *Die heilige Messe*, Paderborn, 1939, 245–7; A. Baumstark, "Antikrömischer Gebetstil im Messkanon", in *Miscellania liturgica in honorem L. C. Mohlberg*, Rome, I, 1948, 301–31; C. Callewaert, "Histoire positive du canon romain", in *Sacris Erudiri*, 2 (1949), 95–110; C. Mohrmann, "Quelques observations sur l'évolution stylistique du canon de la messe romaine", in *Vigiliae Christianae*, 4 (1950), 1–19.

sion, besides its comparative brevity. This is very noticeable if the Roman canon, even in its modern state, and the prefaces from the Roman anaphora tradition are compared with the Gallican, or more especially with the Palaeo-Hispanic anaphoras. The latter particularly, when put beside the Roman, give the impression of cloying luxuriance. Elements of great value are scattered here and there, but are often suffocated in the enormous weight of superfluous words, or disappear in the maze of the more superficial features, or are lost by reason of the sheer length of many of these compositions. The same holds true when the Roman canon is contrasted with many Eastern anaphoras; it has a number of advantages, both spiritual and pastoral, that stem from the soberness of its tone and its comparative brevity. Of course, this is not to deny that where style, sobriety and length are concerned different groups of peoples will have differing needs. All that need be said is that there is no reason for abandoning the path followed down the centuries by the Roman liturgy.

II. Defects

These defects are undeniable and of no small importance. The present Roman canon sins in a number of ways against those requirements of good liturgical composition and sound liturgical sense that were emphasized by the Second Vatican Council.[4] To understand this fact better one has to bear in mind a series of data which has been brought to light by comparative liturgical study.

(*a*) Every anaphora contains, and must always contain, in addition to the introductory dialogue and the concluding doxology: (1) The hymn of joyful thanksgiving for the works that have brought us salvation, especially in Christ the Lord. (2) The narration of the institution of the Eucharist.[5] (3) The anamnesis-

---

[4] See above, Introduction, pp. 17–20.

[5] It is now known that there is insufficient proof to say that the Nestorian anaphora of the holy apostles Addaï and Mari did not have the institution narrative. See B. Botte, "Problèmes de l'anaphore syrienne des Apôtres Addaï et Mari", in *L'Orient Syrien*, 10 (1965), 89–106.

offertory. (4) The committing of the sacrifice to God with the prayer that he will accept it.

(*b*) I fail to see how one can deny that all known anaphoras contain a more or less developed epiclesis.[6] By "epiclesis" I mean here the expression, in the form of a prayer to God, of two requests: (*a*) to fill, bless and consecrate the offerings—this is the consecratory aspect of the epiclesis; (*b*) to grant that those who receive these newly-consecrated gifts in communion may receive them with real spiritual profit; this is the aspect of the epiclesis that seeks a fruitful communion. I think that in all known anaphoras both ideas are more or less clearly expressed.[7]

---

[6] The phrase "more or less developed" is important. If there is any doubt about the existence of an epiclesis in certain anaphoras, particularly in the modern Roman liturgy, it is possibly because before asking oneself whether, in a given anaphora, there is such an epiclesis, and before examining the evidence, one already has in mind an epiclesis of a certain type, perhaps a very developed type. An instance of a highly developed sort of epiclesis is given by the Antioch tradition, which contains a clear request for the transformation of the gifts into the body and blood of Christ and an explicit reference to this taking place through the work of the Holy Spirit. For this see Lietzmann, *Messe und Herrenmahl*, Berlin, 3rd. ed. 1955, 68–122. For the presence of an epiclesis in all liturgies see S. Salaville, "Epiclèse eucharistique", in *Dict. Théol. Cath.* VI, 1 (1913), 204–22.

[7] I cannot agree with the opinion that only the second idea—the prayer for a fruitful communion—is present in the anaphora of Hippolytus, while the first is lacking. The text reads: "We ask you to send your Holy Spirit down upon the offerings of your holy Church. Gathering together all those who take part in your holy (mysteries to share in them) grant that they may be filled with the Holy Spirit" (See above, Texts, p. 27, and ed. Botte, 16–17). The first phrase is a request that God sanctify the gifts offered. Thus we have a consecratory epiclesis, even though expressed very concisely by the request to send (*mittere*, *pempo*: one of the verbs characteristic of the terminology used in epicleses) the Holy Spirit upon the offering of the holy Church. The phrase "upon the gifts" makes sense, it seems to me, only in terms of their being made holy by this very presence. This is the central idea of the consecration, even if rather vague compared with the later development of theology. A fruitful communion is seen in every epiclesis as the fruit of this previous sanctification of the gifts. God is asked to consecrate the gifts by the coming of the Holy Spirit, so that those who share in these gifts may receive the same Spirit and his graces. Nor must it be forgotten that the text of Hippolytus is only an outline anaphora, in which the single points could be or were to be developed more fully by the individual celebrant.

The anaphora tradition of the Antioch type expresses the two ideas by giving them an immediate connection after the institution narrative.[8] The early Egyptian tradition may have had the consecratory part of the epiclesis before the institution narrative and the request for a fruitful communion after it.[9] And this is the situation in our present Roman canon: the consecratory part of the epiclesis occurs before the institution (in the *Quam oblationem* at least), although there is no explicit mention of the Holy Spirit, as is fairly often the case in the history of the epiclesis; the request for a fruitful communion comes after it (*Supplices . . . iube . . . ut quotquot*).

(*c*) If the anaphora has a *Sanctus*—Hippolytus did not yet have it—it has to be linked with what follows, since the *Sanctus* tends to cut across the unity of the great eucharistic prayer.

(*d*) The prayers of intercession are prayers for those who are offering the sacrifice and for whom the sacrifice is being offered: the Church in general and the hierarchy; those present and possibly those remembered on particular occasions such as baptisms and so on; the dead; the ministers. They constitute an element that was introduced into the anaphora at a later date, and their precise position has always varied a great deal.

In the Gallican and Mozarabic traditions the intercessions, though included in the actual eucharistic prayer, always remained outside the canon; they were, in fact, included in the present offertory, between the placing of the *oblata* on the altar and the beginning of the preface dialogue.

In the tradition native to Alexandria the intercessions are all grouped in the canon, but before the *Sanctus*. In that of Antioch they are placed after the institution, anamnesis and epiclesis, while in the Edessa tradition they occur after the institution and anamnesis but before the epiclesis.

---

[8] As with Hippolytus, therefore, if one accepts the observations made in the previous note.

[9] See above, Texts, pp. 67–9 and below pp. 157 ff. (in the part of the documentation dealing with the epiclesis) for what is said about the anaphora of Dêr-Balizeh and the Louvain Coptic fragment.

In the Roman canon as it stands today one part of these intercessions comes after the *Sanctus* and before the institution, while the other part comes after the institution. They appear in the following order: intercession for the Church in general and for the hierarchy—*in primis quae tibi*; for those who are present and offering the Mass—the *Memento* of the living as it is called; for those on whose behalf the sacrifice is offered at certain times—*Hanc igitur*. After the institution come the intercessions for the dead—*Memento* of the dead—and for the ministers—*Nobis quoque*.

The value of an anaphora depends not only on the ideas expressed, but also on the simplicity and clarity of its structure; on the natural and logical sequence of its ideas; on an absence of useless repetition and on its theology. With these points in mind, we can make the following observations in our analysis of the Roman canon:

(1) *The impression given of an agglomeration of features with no apparent unity*

This is the first and most serious defect that is immediately evident when it is compared with the anaphoras of Hippolytus or the Eastern Churches, especially with those of the Antioch type. The modern canon stands out as a patchwork of a number of prayers put into some sort of order, but it is an order where unity and logical connections are not easily found, even by specialists. This impression is heightened by the four occurrences of *Per Christum Dominum nostrum. Amen*, not to mention that at the end of the *Nobis quoque*, which indicate the apparently independent character of the prayers they conclude.[10]

---

[10] "Although the fabric thus formed (i.e. a thanksgiving that extends into the words of consecration and the offering of the sacred gifts, terminating in a solemn hymn of praise) continues to survive unbroken in our present Mass, it is difficult for anyone not initiated into the history of the Mass to recognise the outlines of such a plan in the text of today. In the 'preface' the prayer of thanksgiving is presented as an isolated unit, a preparatory item to be followed by the canon. The canon itself, however, with the exception of the words of consecration (*la parte della consecrazione*) appears to be nothing more than a loosely arranged succession of oblations, prayers of intercession and a reverential citation of apostles and martyrs of early Christianity" (Jungmann, op. cit., 363).

(2) *The lack of a logical connection of ideas*

This follows from the first fault. The connection of the *Te igitur* with either what comes before or what follows is anything but clear. The *Sanctus* is finished by *Pleni sunt . . . Benedictus . . . Hosanna in excelsis*, and then follows *Te* IGITUR . . . *rogamus ac petimus ut accepta habeas et benedicas haec dona . . ..* For the ideas to follow logically it would be necessary for the *Sanctus*, or at least the preface, to make some mention of the offering of the gifts or of the fact that God blesses and sanctifies. This is what happens, giving a natural sequence, in the *Te igitur* of the consecration of chrism in the Gelasian Sacramentary, where there is no *Sanctus*, but in which immediately before the *Te igitur* mention is made of the fact that God sanctifies and blesses. So there is a natural continuity: "Therefore we ask you to bless and to sanctify. . . ."

In the anaphoras of other traditions the passage from the *Sanctus* to what follows is a great deal clearer. After the *Sanctus* they refer back to what has just been said and continue the idea: "Truly you are holy, who . . ."[11] or "Truly heaven and earth are full of your glory, since. . . ."[12]

The transition from the *Memento* of the living to the *Communicantes* presents another well-known difficulty in the Roman canon. In the present text the participle *Communicantes* is suspended in mid-air, since it is not at all clear to what it refers.

---

[11] Thus the Antiochene tradition, as well as the Gallican and Palaeo-Hispanic.

[12] Thus the Egyptian tradition. Jungmann, op. cit., 389–90, expresses the inconsistency of the *Te igitur* as follows: "The first prayer that we meet in the text of the canon after the *Sanctus* is an offering of the gifts in the solemn yet suppliant form of a plea for gracious acceptance. Such an offering, at least in this position, is not self-explanatory. It is on the same footing as the offertory, or more precisely the *oratio super oblata*, the offering up even of the earthly gifts, which is distinctive of the Roman Mass. In other liturgies such an offering, as well as the insertion of the intercessions after the *Sanctus*, is unknown. Instead, they build a short span from the *Sanctus* to the words of institution, either by developing the Christological theme of the prayer of thanks, as in the West Syrian and in the Byzantine formularies; or by continuing in a free fashion the words of praise, as often happens in the *Post Sanctus* of the Gallic liturgies; or, finally, by attaching an epiclesis to the *Pleni sunt caeli*, as the Egyptian liturgies do. The transition from the *Sanctus* to this offering in the *Te igitur* has been considered rather abrupt, and the word *igitur*, which seems to mark the connection externally, has been found unintelligible. Even up to the very present the word has been given various and varied interpretations."

In the text as we have it, the *igitur* of the *Hanc igitur* in no way forms any clear and logical link between this prayer and the one preceding it. Nor is the *igitur* of this prayer our only difficulty, for the prayer itself gives rise to a serious problem. Its origin is clear enough. It began as a prayer of special intercession on behalf of those for whom the Mass was being offered on some special occasion: the newly baptized at Easter and at Pentecost, for example. But the reason for the prayer's becoming a fixture in the canon is obscure.[13]

(3) *The unsatisfactory way in which the various prayers of intercession are assembled in the canon*

In the anaphoras of other traditions the prayers of intercession are grouped together. They may be before the beginning of the canon, when the gifts are placed on the altar—as happens in the Gallican liturgies—or, as at Alexandria, within the canon before the *Sanctus*. Or again, they may be placed within the canon, but after the prayer for a fruitful communion (Antioch tradition) or after the anamnesis (Edessa).

The Roman Church prays for the Church in general and for the hierarchy before the institution (*in primis quae tibi offerimus*); for those present offering the Mass (the first *Memento* and normally the *Hanc igitur* too, though this was once a prayer inserted only for special intentions. (It remains so today in certain circumstances, as at Easter and Pentecost.) After the institution there are further prayers for the dead (the second *Memento*) and for the ministers (*Nobis quoque*).

---

[13] "The only problem that seems to require further elucidation is why this prayer, in its present form, should have been inserted just here. Is the prayer nothing more than a plea for the acceptance of the sacrificial gifts, as it is captioned in some translations? But such a plea has already been made and is here simply repeated in different words. One would scarcely have inserted an independent prayer just for this purpose. Or maybe the stress is on the contents of the petitions appended? But then why are these petitions included precisely in this place? It is around this prayer that the various theories regarding the canon have been developed, and a summary consideration has forced the conclusion that in this prayer we have 'perhaps the most difficult prayer in the Mass'" (Jungmann, op. cit., 409).

Such a distribution is hardly a model of simplicity and clarity. It is as though the worst possible solution had been chosen: as if the choice had been made deliberately to split up the connection of ideas and so ruin the unity of this great prayer.

(4) *An exaggerated emphasis on the idea of the offering and acceptance of the gifts*

It has been stated above that this idea is in itself one of great value. But the Roman Mass, particularly the Roman canon, insists on it in an exaggerated and disorderly manner, with much useless repetition.

In the Roman Mass, the *Oratio super oblata* is the usual and most suitable place specified for the offering of the gifts and for asking God to accept them; we find that this is regularly the case in the Leonine Sacramentary. Further, in the Roman tradition this prayer is for the most part well constructed and rich in content.[14] It would be enough to remove from the Roman Missal those "Secrets" that make no mention of the offering of the gifts and to replace them with others that do. These could be taken from the older Roman tradition or possibly from the Gallican, Mozarabic or Ambrosian liturgies, or they could be composed afresh.

In the Middle Ages, however, the ideas that really belong to the *Oratio super oblata* were anticipated in the prayers *Suscipe sancte Pater*, *Offerimus tibi calicem*, *In spiritu humilitatis*, *Veni Sanctificator* and *Suscipe sancta Trinitas*, all of which were recited silently during the ceremony of laying the offerings on the altar.

In the canon, too, the same fundamental ideas are expressed: in the first part of the *Te igitur* (*ut accepta habeas et benedicas haec dona . . . illibata*); in the *Hanc igitur* (*Hanc . . . oblationem . . . placatus accipias*); in the *Quam oblationem* (*Quam oblationem . . . acceptabilemque facere digneris*), where there is clearly a repetition of the first part of the *Te igitur* and the *Hanc igitur*. Further repetition is again in evidence at the end of the *Unde et memores* (*offerimus . . . panem sanctum vitae aeternae et calicem salutis*

[14] See the fine observations of M. Righetti, *Storia Liturgica*, III, Milan, 1949, 288–90.

perpetuae), which at first sight obscures the fact that in the expressions *hostiam puram*, *hostiam sanctam*, *hostiam immaculatam* there is a direct reference to the living victim, that is, to Christ himself.

It is difficult to avoid the impression that this same idea of offering gifts underlies the first part of the *Supplices te rogamus* (*iube haec perferri per manus sancti angeli tui*). Here again there is the idea of *commercium*: we offer the gifts to God; he receives them by the ministry of the angels and restores them to us once again in the body and blood of Christ.

Finally, the idea is once more implied, at least in the present practice of the Roman rite, by the saying of the *Per quem haec omnia* at every Mass, even though there is no longer any food present to be blessed. The *haec omnia* that God creates, vivifies, sanctifies and gives us are obviously the *oblata* as well.

As the canon stands, therefore, a theme that in itself is excellent has been rendered clumsy and unwieldy; the result is anything but a model of liturgical composition.

If we consider the canon in its present state in isolation from the rest of the Mass, there is only one passage to be found after the institution narrative which clearly states that what we receive in communion is the body and blood of Christ. This is the second part of the *Supplices*, in the words *ut quotquot sacrosanctum Filii tui corpus et sanguinem sumpserimus* . . ..

The disordered insistence upon the idea of the offering of the oblata obscures the idea that what we offer above all in the Mass is Christ our Lord himself, and ourselves with him. We lose sight of the fact that the real and primary offering of the Mass takes place after the institution with the *Unde et memores*. I do not say that there is no such idea in the canon; on the contrary, it is an underlying one throughout, but it is given no prominence and is therefore not easily seen, notwithstanding its primary importance. Convincing proof of this lies in the well-known fact that our people have sadly lost the essential idea of the offertory.[15]

---

[15] See B. Capelle, *Il sacrificio della messa*, Rome, 1958, 37–63.

(5) *The number and disorder of epicletic-type prayers in the canon*

We have seen above[16] the wide variety of structures and literary forms that were assumed by epicleses as the anaphoras evolved. Lietzmann[17] has documented this not only for the Eastern tradition, but for the Gallican and Palaeo-Hispanic as well. Looking through these and then turning to the prayers of our present Roman canon, one notices there that a number of prayers have the characteristics of an epiclesis: not only the *Quam oblationem* and the second part of the *Supplices*, but also the *Te igitur* and the first part of the *Supplices*. It is difficult to escape the impression that even these last two prayers in their present state are fragments of epiclesis prayers. This makes them hybrid compositions which only duplicate what is contained in the *Quam oblationem.*

In order to realise that the formulas of the *Te igitur* and the first part of the *Supplices* are of an epicletic type let us look at the following obviously epicletic parallels:

(*a*) *For the* Te igitur:

The *Te igitur* in the consecration of chrism in the Gelasian Sacramentary first (in the part corresponding to the Roman preface) gives thanks to God for the creation of the trees from whose sap the chrism is made, and goes on to thank him for the Old Testament "sacraments" of anointing, and especially for the anointing that took place in Jesus Christ himself, the Anointed par excellence. The text then passes directly to an epicletic invocation:

Te igitur deprecamur, Domine, sancte Pater, omnipotens aeterne Deus, per Iesum Christum Filium tuum Dominum nostrum, ut huius creaturae pinguedinem sanctificare tua benedictione digneris et ei Sancti Spiritus immiscere virtutem . . . ut sit his qui renati fuerint ex aqua et Spiritu Sancto chrisma salutis . . .[18]

We therefore pray you Lord, holy Father, almighty and eternal God, through Jesus Christ your Son, our Lord, be pleased to sanctify with your blessing the fat of this creature. Pour into it the might of the Holy Spirit . . . in order that it may be, for those reborn by water and the Holy Spirit, the chrism of salvation.

[16] Pp. 91–3.

[17] *Messe und Herrenmahl*, Berlin, 3rd. ed., 1955, 93–122.

[18] See above, Texts, p. 41; Gelasian Sacramentary, n. 388.

Here the grafting of the epiclesis on to the preface is completely natural and takes place using the same words as the *Te igitur* of the Roman canon—until the Holy Spirit is mentioned. Now we can see why in the canon the first part of the *Te igitur* (*ut accepta habeas et benedicas haec dona, haec munera, haec sancta sacrificia illibata*) duplicates the meaning of the first part of the *Quam oblationem* (*Quam oblationem . . . benedictam, adscriptam, ratam, rationabilemque facere digneris*). In both cases we have the beginning of an epiclesis.

(*b*) *For the first part of the* Supplices:

Compare with the following two parallels from the Palaeo-Hispanic liturgy:[19]

Petimus ergo maiestatem tuam, (ascendant) preces humilitatis nostrae in conspectu tuae clementiae et descendat super hunc panem et super hunc calicem plenitudo tuae divinitatis. Descendat etiam, Domine, illa Sancti Spiritus tui incomprehensibilis maiestas, sicut quondam in patrum hostiis mirabiliter descendebat. Ac praesta, Domine, ut huius panis vinique substantia sanis custodiam adhibeat, languentibus medicinam infundat.[20]

We therefore beg your majesty, may our humble prayer be seen by you in your mercy and may the fullness of your divinity descend upon this bread and wine. May the majesty of your Holy Spirit, that Spirit who surpasses our understanding, come down as he once came down upon the victims of the fathers. Grant, too, Lord, that the substance of this bread and wine may give safekeeping to those who are well and healing to those who lie sick.

Hanc quoque oblationem ut acceptam habeas et benedicas supplices exoramus, sicut habuisti accepta munera Abel pueri tui iusti et sacrificium patriarchae patris nostri Abrahae et quod tibi obtulit summus sacerdos tuus Melchisedech. Descendat hic, quaeso, invisibiliter benedictio tua, sicut quondam in patrum hostias visibiliter descendebat. Ascendat odor suavitatis in conspectu divinae

We earnestly beg you to receive and bless this offering too, as you accepted the gifts of Abel your servant and the sacrifice of our father, the patriarch Abraham, and what was offered to you by your high priest Melchisedech. May your blessing descend invisibly on us here, I pray, as once it visibly descended upon the victims of the fathers. May a savour of sweetness rise before your majesty from this

[19] Cited also by Lietzmann, op. cit., 101–3.
[20] *Lib. Ord.*, *Post Pridie*, 265, 5.

maiestatis tuae ex hoc sublimi altario tuo per manus angeli tui: et deferatur in ista sollemnia Spiritus tuus Sanctus, qui tam adstantis quam offerentis populi et oblata pariter et vota sanctificet. Ut quicumque ex hoc Corpore cibaverimus, sumamus nobis medelam animae ad sananda cordium vulnera.[21]	altar through the hand of your angel, and may your Holy Spirit come down upon these solemn offerings; that same Spirit who sanctifies the offerings and prayers of your people who are present here and offering sacrifice to you. Let us who eat of this body take it as a spiritual remedy bringing healing to the wounds of our hearts.

If we compare these prayers with the *Supplices* of the Roman canon, we get an unmistakable impression that this text too as it now stands, in its first as well as its second part, is what remains of a complete epiclesis. It would have included at the same time a prayer for the acceptance of the offerings, for their sanctification and consecration, and for the fruitful communion of those who were to receive them. So we can see that the first part of the *Supplices* repeats in substance, even if employing other images, the idea of the acceptance and sanctification of the gifts that was already expressed in the first part of the *Te igitur* and the first part of the *Quam oblationem*, not to mention the *Hanc igitur*.

(6) *The lack of a theology of the part played by the Holy Spirit in the Eucharist*

In spite of the numerous fragments in the Roman canon that follow the pattern of an epiclesis, there is absolutely no theology of the part proper[22] to the Holy Spirit in the Eucharist. And this theology is of prime importance. One need only reflect on the biblical and traditional character of this doctrine[23] to realise immediately that this is a serious deficiency. Today we have quite rightly become very aware of this, not only for ecumenical reasons, but also because of the rediscovery of that aspect of the Trinity we call "economic", an aspect underlined by the Second Vatican

---

[21] *Lib. Sacr., Post pridie*, n. 627.

[22] I say simply "proper" in order not to involve myself with the question of appropriations, into which there is no need to go here.

[23] See below, in the part of the documentation dealing with the epiclesis, pp. 157 ff.

Council.[24] This means to think of the persons of the Trinity not so much in terms of their unity in the divine nature as in terms of their relative distinction, known to us principally through their manifestation in the history of salvation. It is in fact in the progressive revelation and enactment of man's salvation that the Persons of the Trinity have gradually revealed themselves and continue to reveal themselves to us.[25]

(7) *Deficiencies in the* Qui pridie *and the institution narrative*

In the liturgical tradition of the anaphora three phenomena are apparent in the institution narrative:[26]

(1) A considerable freedom as far as the data of scripture are concerned.

(2) The tendency to put together the various details that the four Gospels have passed on to us in order to form one single composite picture of the event: a synopsis or *diatessaron.*

(3) The tendency to create a well-nigh perfect parallel between the narration of the consecration of the bread and that of the wine.

In this respect the Roman canon falls down in three ways:

(*a*) The greatest defect is that *Hoc est enim corpus meum* stands alone; no attempt is made to follow it up with any of the phrases: *quod pro vobis tradetur*, given in I Cor. 11: 24 by the Vulgate; or *quod pro vobis datur*, as in Lk. 22: 19; or again, *quod pro vobis frangitur*, or *frangetur* or *confringetur* according to the variant readings of I Cor. 11: 24.

After *Hoc est corpus meum*, all the Eastern liturgies continue with the Pauline or Lucan sequel in one of the variant readings.

---

[24] See, for example, *Constitution on the Church*, arts. 2; 3; 4; 39, 5; 40, 2; 41, 1; 48, 2, 6 & 7; 49, 2; *Decree on Ecumenism*, arts. 3; 4; *Constitution on the Liturgy*, arts. 50, 1; 51, 4.

[25] See C. Vagaggini, *Il senso teologico della liturgia*, Ed. Paoline, 4th ed., 1965, 196–242.

[26] P. Cagin, *Eucharistia*, Tournai, 1912, 225–44, gives, in columns, the Latin versions of the institution narrative in 76 anaphoras and of the four New Testament texts. See, too, F. Hamm, *Die liturgischen Einsetzungberichte*, LQF 23, Münster, 1928; G. Lucchesi, *Mysterium Fidei—Il testo della consecrazione eucaristica nel canone romano*, Faenza, 1959.

This is done in the Palaeo-Hispanic rite too (*quod pro vobis tradetur*).[27] The *De Sacramentis* of the Milanese tradition has *quod pro multis confringetur*, while the Ambrosian canon for Holy Thursday is the same as the Roman. Hippolytus has *quod pro vobis confringetur* (according to the Latin translation) or *confringitur* (from the Greek).

The omission in the Roman canon, which at this point follows Mt. and Mk., is a serious one liturgically and theologically. In the first place, it lacks the parallelism with the wine (*qui pro vobis effundetur*), although in details of much less importance[28] parallels have been introduced. There is also the tradition of the *mysterium fidei*, a phrase which is not biblical and anything but clear. Secondly, considering the words of the eucharistic mystery under their aspect of *sign*, this omission considerably weakens the first part of the consecration in a point of capital importance, namely its sacrificial character. This sacrificial character is not in fact indicated simply by the words *Hoc est corpus meum*. Taken alone, they indicate the presence of the body and nothing more. In the Roman tradition the sacrificial character of the first consecration is retained only by the liturgical context, particularly in the *benedixit*, FREGIT, *deditque discipulis suis* . . . and, according to one explanation of medieval origin, by the separation of the two consecrations.

However, in actual fact the sign given by Christ in the Eucharist is not simply that the bread means his body and the wine his blood, but that the *broken* bread signifies his body *broken for us* for the remission of our sins, and the wine *poured out* means his blood *shed* for us.

So it can be seen how important the breaking of the bread is as a sign. All the New Testament sources refer to it (*eklasen*) and

---

[27] See above, Texts, p. 48. There is no text that gives us the exact words of institution in the Gallican tradition.

[28] This happens, for instance, in the details such as *in sanctas et venerabiles manus suas*, repeated for both consecrations, but not attested by the New Testament sources; (*accipite et manducate*) *ex hoc omnes* for the bread, added to parallel the *ex hoc omnes* given by Mt. and Mk. and preceding the consecration of the wine.

point to its importance. Not for nothing was the first name given to the Eucharist *klasis tou artou*, the breaking of bread.[29]

It can easily be understood, then, how important are the words that explicitly point to the relation between this breaking of the bread and the body given, or broken, for us.

(*b*) The second of the major faults of the Roman canon in its narration of the institution is that in the consecration of the wine it makes no mention, as do many liturgies, of Jesus taking the chalice, *pouring in wine and water*, and blessing it. There is no explicit reference to this detail in the New Testament, but it seems that the action of pouring wine and, according to the Jewish custom, water too into the cup must have taken place before Jesus blessed it. It was in fact the "cup of benediction". Moreover, the New Testament witnesses seem to affirm this when, corresponding to the gestures over the bread, they say *similiter et calicem* .... It is certain, however, that in the intention of Jesus the sign contained in the rite of the cup is not simply that the wine signifies his blood, but that the wine *poured* into the chalice signifies his blood *poured out* for the salvation of the world in the remission of sin. So the explicit mention made in almost all Eastern anaphoras[30] of the act of pouring the wine and water into the chalice conforms with a natural liturgical tendency to

---

[29] In various liturgies both ancient and modern, the breaking of the bread at the very moment of the narration of the institution, (a more perfect rite both historically, because Jesus did it, and liturgically, as a sign), is vouched for: (1) In the canons of St Basil of the sixth century (see A. Raes, *Introductio in liturgiam orientalem*, Rome, 1947, 59); (2) among the West Syrians (see Jungmann, op. cit., 423). For the West-Syrian Jacobites the rite was already attested by Moses Bar Kepha (d. 903 A.D.); (3) among the Copts (Jungmann, loc. cit.; according to Renaudot, *Liturgiarum orientalium collectio*, I, 14, the same rite appears in the Coptic anaphora of St Basil); (4) in the Abyssinian rite (see Brightman, 232). The Maronites do not break the bread, but make a sign at this point which signifies the breaking (see Hanssens, *Institutiones*, III, 2, 423). In the Roman rite the same custom is recorded in the thirteenth century, particularly in England and France, where, at the word *fregit* missals have the rubric *hic faciat signum fractionis*, or *fingat frangere panem*, or at least *hic tangit hostiam*.

[30] It is mentioned in neither the Dêr-Balizeh nor Nestorian rites, nor in the Byzantine rite of St John Chrysostom. Those of Addaï and Mari as we have them do not contain the institution narrative.

form a parallel between the two consecrations; more than this, it corresponds to the theological significance of the mystery of the Eucharist.

(*c*) The third important defect in the way it relates the instituting of the Eucharist is the insertion of the phrase *mysterium fidei* in the midst of the words said over the chalice. This has no parallel in any other liturgy, and within the Roman rite itself its origin is uncertain and its meaning debatable.[31] However, it is obvious that in its present form at least the insertion *mysterium fidei* serves to break up and interrupt the words of institution.

(8) *Difficulties raised by the* Supplices

The *Supra quae* and the *Supplices*, far from having an obvious and undisputed meaning, give rise to problems of such complexity that neither historical erudition nor theological subtlety alone will solve them.[32] As to the *Supplices*, specialists confess: "This prayer is difficult to interpret and has aroused numerous arguments."[33]

My own view is that the difficulty lies not in discovering the historical and literary origin of the various themes contained in the prayer, such as that of the angel of sacrifice or of the heavenly altar; it lies rather in discovering the meaning that such a prayer can and ought to have today, as it stands and in its present context, always bearing in mind the origin and historical and literary meaning of these themes.

As regards the thought content, the present-day *Supplices* contains two main ideas: in the first part we ask (*a*) "Lord, we pray that these gifts may be offered before your heavenly altar by your angel", then we continue: (*b*) "so that those who share

---

[31] See B. Botte, *Le canon de la messe romaine*, Louvain, 1935, 62. See, too, G. Lucchesi, *Mysterium Fidei: Il testo della consecrazione eucaristica nel canone romano*, Faenza, 1959.

[32] For the *Supra quae* see Jungmann, op. cit., 434–7.

[33] H. M. Denis-Boulet in A. G. Martimort (ed.), *L'Eglise en Prière*, Paris, 1961, 406. See, too, Jungmann, op. cit., 437–41. B. Botte, op. cit., 66–7.

in the body and blood of your Son may be filled with every heavenly grace". What link there is between these two ideas is far from clear.

Many authors believe that any acceptable connection between the two parts supposes a third intermediary; only if it were structured in this way would the prayer make sense. Then it would run: (*a*) "May these gifts be offered to you by your angel"; (*b*) "accept them, bless them" (and perhaps: "transform them, fill them with the Holy Spirit and make them into the body and blood of Christ"); (*c*) "so that those who share in the body and blood of your Son may be filled with every heavenly grace". In this case the text of the *Supplices* would be what remains of an ancient epiclesis, in one of the many forms that such a prayer has assumed in liturgical tradition; it matters little whether or not it was in its present state in the old Roman canon.

Perhaps the solution is not so simple, but this outline is enough to show that, in any case, the *Supplices* in our present canon can scarcely be called the ideal of clarity and liturgical simplicity.

What is the meaning of *iube haec perferri per manus sancti angeli tui in sublime altare tuum* in its present context? Does the *haec* refer to the bread and wine, that is, to the body and blood of Christ? Since to us today the *haec* cannot refer simply to the bread and wine, coming as it does after the institution narrative, still less can it refer to our prayers alone, and the point of having an angel[34] offer the body and blood of Christ to the Father is not altogether obvious.[35]

---

[34] The text of *De Sacramentis* (see above, Texts, p. 33) shows that in the early sense of the prayer the *angelus* really was an angel, the angel of sacrifice, and not yet Christ or the Holy Spirit. Nor is there any need in the prayer as it stands to understand by *angelus* anything other than an angel.

[35] What Lietzmann (op. cit., 86–93) has to say about the angel in the incensation prayer and about the transfer of this idea to the Eucharist can help in clarifying the historical development of a theme, but does little to resolve the problem of the meaning that we must give to these words today when we recite the prayer. Is it an ideal situation, when the priest and the faithful are obliged to recite a prayer, to give it a meaning other than that of the words they are saying or to which they are listening? Think too of the present offertory of the Mass for the dead.

(9) *The lists of saints in the present canon*

The lists of saints in the *Communicantes* and the *Nobis quoque* lend themselves to a great deal of criticism: the length of the lists; the historical difficulties involved in the lives of some of the saints mentioned; the limited representation of Catholic holiness. With regard to this last point: the lists mention only early saints whose cult was a local one in the Church of Rome, while today use of the Roman canon has spread to all parts of the world. It is not as if there have been no saints in the Church since the seventh century.[36]

(10) *The lack of an overall presentation of the history of salvation*

We have already shown[37] that this is a failing of the Roman canon and of the whole anaphora tradition in the West. Quite apart from the defects already mentioned, when looked at from this point of view the Roman canon inevitably appears at a disadvantage if compared with the anaphoras of the East. Certainly there are the movable prefaces, with all their merits, but when put side by side with the Eastern anaphoras (those of Antioch, for instance) the present canon is found wanting.

The problem to be faced, therefore, is whether there can be found a solution that would allow the Roman liturgy to have in its canon at the same time both the riches of the movable prefaces that it has enjoyed up to now, and the advantages of an overall presentation of salvation history.

There is a solution to this problem, and it is an easy one: introduce into the Roman liturgy one or more anaphoras with a fixed preface to be used alongside the anaphoras with a movable preface. The fixed-preface anaphora ought to have as its distinctive mark precisely this broad presentation of the entire history of salvation, and could be employed in Masses without a proper preface and in all Sunday Masses throughout the year, whether or not they have a proper preface.

---

[36] See Jungmann, op. cit., 404–7.

[37] See above, p. 86.

Conclusions

What follows is a brief *résumé* of the conclusions reached in our examination of the merits and failings of the present Roman canon:

(1) The merits of the Roman canon are very real. To choose one obvious example: there must be no thought of abandoning the tradition of Roman prefaces in favour of a more unified anaphora such as that of Hippolytus or of one of the Eastern liturgies. Such is the position occupied by this canon, even in its present form, in the liturgical, spiritual and religious tradition of the West, and such is the attachment to it, that any idea of suppressing it from the Roman liturgy is unthinkable.

(2) The defects and limitations of the Roman canon are, however, numerous and serious when looked at in the light of the general liturgical principles promulgated by the Second Vatican Council and of the findings of comparative study in this field. It is not a question of there being dogmatic or doctrinal errors;[38] they are rather defects and limitations of structure and liturgical expression. It is in this respect that they do not measure up to what an anaphora ought to be. Further, they are failings which make a difference to the clarity of the canon and so hinder its pastoral effectiveness as a source of spirituality for the clergy and Christian people alike.

It is no longer possible to close our eyes to these limitations. The more liturgical instruction there is, and the more people and priests come to understand the meaning of the liturgy, the more evident these failings become, and the problem of the Roman canon is raised with ever greater urgency. The general liturgical reform called for by the recent Council would be failing in one of its gravest tasks if its courage faltered in confronting this problem.

(3) How is this to be resolved? The first solution that springs to mind is that of "correcting" the present Roman canon. Can this be done?

---

[38] In this respect the defence of the Roman canon made by the Council of Trent to rebut Protestant accusations remains firm. See Denz, 1745 (942); 1756 (953).

CHAPTER III

Can the Defects of the Present Canon be Corrected?

Correction supposes a series of changes, of greater or lesser importance according to the case, which will be effective in removing at least the major defects, and yet leave unaltered the general structure and appearance of the present text.

If the changes were to leave the main defects standing, they would not solve the problem. If, on the other hand, they were such as to alter the structure and physiognomy of the canon, they would no longer be mere corrections, but would entail a revision or reshaping of the canon—equivalent in fact to producing a new text. Such a text might well preserve certain elements of the ancient Roman canon, but it would almost inevitably suffer from the great disadvantage of still being too closely tied down to the text which preceded it.

Attempts have been made to "correct" the present canon; let us now take a look at how these attempts have been made.

I. Abbreviation of the lists of saints
Elimination of the Amens
The question of the Hanc Igitur

Abbreviating the lists of saints in the *Communicantes* and in the *Nobis quoque*, or perhaps even combining them into one—and one far better adapted to the fact that the Roman canon is now in use throughout the world—would not alter the structure of the canon nor its general appearance. These lists, moreover, developed gradually between the sixth and seventh centuries and continued to vary even after that.[1] In addition, some of the saints named in them have posed more than a few problems for the hagiographer.

Nor would there be any difficulty in eliminating the Amen at the end of the *Communicantes*, *Hanc igitur*, *Supplices*, *Memento* for the dead, and *Nobis quoque*. These Amens—which accentuate even further the fragmentary character of the Roman canon, as if it were composed of a mosaic of prayers, each one complete in itself—began to appear in the ninth and tenth centuries, became widespread in the twelfth, were included in the missal printed at Milan in 1474, and were finally inserted into the missal of Pius V. For this reason Bernard Botte does not include them in his critical edition of the Roman canon.[2]

Would it be feasible to reserve the *Hanc igitur* for special occasions only, as it was before St Gregory, while perhaps increasing the number of these occasions to include marriages and similar cases? There can be no doubt that the *Hanc igitur* which is said every day in the present text duplicates the *Te igitur* and *Quam oblationem*. Reserving the *Hanc igitur* for special occasions only, but re-adopting the more numerous versions found in the ancient tradition would not affect the structure of the canon, but would reveal its shape more clearly. The intention for general peace, inserted by St Gregory in the modern formula of the *Hanc igitur*, has today reassumed its natural position in the Prayer of the Faithful.

These three corrections do not therefore give rise to serious difficulties and would doubtless bring about some measure of improvement.

II. Altering the position of the Memento of the living

Some authors[3] have suggested transferring the so-called *Memento* for the living to a position immediately before the

[1] See J. A. Jungmann, op. cit., 404–6, 449–51.

[2] *Le canon de la Messe*, Louvain, 1935.

[3] E.g., N. Antunes Vieira, in a short note, *Adnotationes anaphoram eucharistiam spectantes*, Rio di Janeiro, no date.

Memento for the dead. By so doing, they claim to give the canon a clearer and more logical sequence of thought. This proposal is almost certainly influenced by the well-known model of the Antioch family of anaphoras, in which the intercessions for the living and the dead are grouped together in the second part of the anaphora after the epiclesis.

Such a "correction" of the present Roman canon raises a difficulty which is much more serious than those examined in connection with the lists of saints, the Amens and the *Hanc igitur*. More specifically, transferring it in this way would involve not merely a correction, but an alteration of the structure; and what is more, it fails to solve the problem it sets out to solve. It neither achieves any greater clarity nor gives a more logical thought sequence.

At this point in fact the whole problem of the intercessions in the Roman canon comes up again. The *Memento* for the living, so-called, is one of the five prayers of intercession normally to be found in the anaphora: the prayer for those present and taking part in the offering.[4] The term *Memento* for the living is a misleading one.

We have already explained[5] how the solution adopted in the modern Roman canon of distributing the intercessions partly before and partly after the institution was anything but ideal. We have also observed[6] that the intercessions were introduced into the anaphoras only at the second stage of their development and arranged in the various anaphoras in different ways. But this does not mean that once admitted into the anaphora, the intercessions have not had their importance, or that they can be taken out or moved around at will. On the contrary, liturgists are agreed in affirming the importance of the position occupied by inter-

[4] The other intercessions are, as we noted above, pp. 92–3: for the universal Church and the hierarchy (the second part of the *Te igitur*, in the first place which we offer you . . .); for those who offer or for whom the Mass is offered on some special occasion (*Hanc igitur*); for the dead (*Memento* for the dead); for the ministers (*Nobis quoque*). In all, four prayers for the living.

[5] See p. 95.

[6] See p. 92.

cessions in the anaphoras; it is the key feature among those elements which characterize the different types of anaphora.[7]

For this reason, whatever the deficiencies of the Roman solution to the problem of arranging the intercessions in the canon, a change in this arrangement means a change in a characteristic element which is part of the very structure of the canon.

Worse still, the juxtaposition of the *Memento* for the living with the *Memento* for the dead conspicuously fails to obtain the end intended. The intercessions would still not be grouped as are anaphoras of the Antioch type: there would still remain, before the institution, those intercessions for the living which form the second part of the *Te igitur* and the *Hanc igitur*.

In other words, in order to obtain here the logicality and clarity desired for the Roman canon, it would be necessary to move all the intercessions, grouping them either before the anaphora as in the Gallican and Mozarabic traditions; or, following the Egyptian custom, within the anaphora itself before the institution; or again, after the institution, as in the tradition of Antioch or Edessa. But it is obvious that this would no longer constitute a correction of the Roman canon, but a rearrangement bordering on the complete reconstruction of a new canon. In the remainder of its text, however, this would still tend to preserve the defects of the present-day canon—which are far from negligible.

III. Eliminate the intercessions?

Some[8] insist on the straightforward elimination of the intercessions from the Roman canon. Their argument is as follows: now that the Prayer of the Faithful has come back into the

---

[7] See Botte in Martimort (ed.), *L'Eglise en prière*, p. 16.

[8] H. Küng, "Das Eucharistiegebet. Konzil und Erneurung der römischen Messliturgie", in *Wort und Wahrheit*, 18 (1963), 102–7. K. Amon, "Gratias agere. Zur Reform des Messcanons", in *Lit. Jahrb.*, 15 (1965), 79–98. P. Borella, "Unità e continuità del canone nei testi ambrosiani del Giovedì Santo e della Veglia Pasquale", in *Ambrosius*, 41 (1965), 79–110 comes out strongly in favour of this solution both for the Roman canon and for the Ambrosian too.

liturgy, the intercessions in the canon have become redundant. Leave out the intercessions and you will give the Roman anaphora that lucidity and clarity in the development of ideas which we so much admire in Hippolytus' anaphora.

But the claims that these intercessions duplicate those of the Prayer of the Faithful cannot, it seems to me, be accepted. The essential difference is that in the canon one prays for those who offer the sacrifice and for whom the sacrifice being celebrated is offered, whilst this is not the case in the Prayer of the Faithful.

The intercessions of the canon presuppose the idea of sacrifice, of the offering of the sacrifice and of offering it for someone; that is, they presuppose the idea of the propitiatory value of the eucharistic sacrifice. These ideas are developed in strict relation to the emphasis given to the ideas of the offering of the gifts and of the actual rites of the offering.

The intercessions in the canon are, of their nature, a eucharistic prayer; but this is not true of the *Oratio fidelium*, which among other things can form part of any liturgy of the word, and indeed, of any other rite. Even in the Gallican and Mozarabic tradition, where the intercessions remained outside the canon, they were nevertheless conceived as prayers of the eucharistic liturgy properly so called. They were closely connected with the offering of the faithful and with the prayer *Post nomina* which corresponds to the prayer *Super oblata* of the Roman tradition.

If the intercessions were completely eliminated, the idea of the Eucharist as a sacrifice that can be offered and offered for someone, and so the idea of the propitiatory nature of the sacrifice, would disappear from the canon.

That this is the fundamental concept underlying these intercessions in the anaphora is shown very clearly by St Cyril of Jerusalem in his Mystagogic Catecheses. These are, if I am not mistaken, among the first texts (perhaps even the first) to give an interpretation of the intercessory prayers of the anaphora:[9]

[9] About 350, there are some of Cyril himself; about 390 there are some of his successor John of Jerusalem. See J. Quasten, *Patrology*, Westminster, 1960, III, 366.

"After the spiritual sacrifice, the unbloody worship, has been carried out, *over that propitiatory victim we pray God* for the general peace of the world, for rulers, for soldiers and companions, for those who are sick, for those who are burdened by affliction and for those who are in need; *we all pray and we offer this victim* . . . finally for all the holy fathers and pastors who have died and for all those from among us that have departed this life (we pray), believing this to be the greatest help for those on whose behalf the prayer is offered, *while the holy and awesome victim lies there* . . .. In the same way, offering prayers to God for the dead, even if they were sinners, we do not fashion wreaths but *offer Christ sacrificed for our sins, begging the merciful God to forgive and have mercy both on them and on ourselves*."[10]

It must, however, be admitted that the actual way in which the intercessions within the canon have developed in some anaphoras[11] leads to a real duplication with the Prayer of the Faithful because the idea that the intercession is for those who offer or for whom the sacrifice is being offered is not expressed with sufficient clarity.

This is the phenomenon, frequently to be found in the liturgy, of a particular type of prayer being developed without proper regard for its individual character in relation to other types of prayer. For the anaphora intercessions to retain their own character and avoid duplication with other prayers in the Mass, it is sufficient that they clearly express a desire to pray for those who offer the sacrifice, or for whom the sacrifice is being offered. This the Roman canon does very effectively.[12]

---

[10] *Catech.* 23, *Mystag.* 5, 8–10; PG, 33, 1115–8.

[11] In some Syrian, Byzantine and Egyptian anaphoras, for example.

[12] . . . *haec munera, haec sancta sacrificia illibata, in primis quae tibi offerimus pro Ecclesia tua* . . . (*Te igitur*). *Qui tibi offerunt hoc sacrificium laudis pro se suisque omnibus, pro redemptione animarum suarum* . . . (*Memento Domine*). *Hanc igitur oblationem servitutis nostrae quam tibi offerimus pro iis* . . . (*Hanc igitur* of Easter and Pentecost). In this context the sense of the intercessions for the dead and the ministers is also clear.

The conclusion to be drawn from all that we have said is that the elimination of the intercessions would introduce an enormous change of structure and of theological significance into the Roman canon.

Küng considers that one of the greater advantages of the elimination of the intercessions from the canon would be a rapprochement with the Protestant position on this matter. But unless I am mistaken, it is not difficult to see at what price such a result would be obtained. Is this true ecumenism?

Finally, would it be enough merely to remove the intercessions from the canon in order to obtain that logical development and clarity which is so desired? An examination of the actual result obtained by Küng and by others working on similar lines leaves the reply to this question in very little doubt.

IV. Küng's attempt at a "correction" of the Roman canon

Küng's proposed correction of the Roman canon is a very straightforward one: completely to omit the intercessions, the commemoration of the saints and the *Mysterium fidei* added to the words of the institution.[13]

From one point of view this alteration is too great, implying a substantial change in the structure and the significance of the canon, as was stated above. From another point of view, however, this same alteration is utterly insufficient to remedy the radical defects of the present-day canon.

In fact, if the intercessions are omitted as Küng stipulates:

1. The text which immediately follows the *Sanctus-Hosanna in excelsis* can no longer consist—as does Küng's version—of the simple juxtaposition of the first part of the *Te igitur*, i.e. up to *haec sancta sacrificia illibata*, and *Quam* (*Hanc*) *oblationem*. The reasons for this are as follows:

(*a*) The *Quam oblationem*, in which God is asked to accept, bless, etc., these offerings, supposes that in the preceding text the

[13] See the text above, pp. 76–9.

idea of offering these same oblations has already been expressed. The connection between the ideas is: we offer you this oblation and may you, O God, accept it, bless it, etc.

This is precisely the form of the present Roman canon, even if the *Hanc igitur* is omitted. In fact it has

> *. . . haec dona, haec munera, haec sancta sacrificia . . . in primis quae tibi offerimus . . . qui tibi offerunt hoc sacrificium . . . Quam oblationem tu Deus . . . benedictam . . . acceptabilemque facere digneris . . .*

Küng's text has:

> *Te (igitur) clementissime Pater, per Iesum Christum, Filium tuum, Dominum nostrum, supplices rogamus ac petimus ut accepta habeas et benedicas haec dona, haec munera, haec sancta sacrificia illibata. Hanc oblationem, tu Deus, in omnibus quaesumus, benedictam, adscriptam, ratam rationabilemque facere digneris . . .*

In this text, it is not said that we offer, nor that we have offered, gifts to God, but it begins abruptly: here are gifts, bless them; and, O God, bless these offerings . . . Because of this, the idea of the acceptance of the oblation, coming immediately after the hymn of praise of the preface, is suspended in mid-air. In the Roman canon, on the other hand, there is: *ut accepta habeas . . . haec dona . . . imprimis quae tibi offerimus . . . Quam oblationem tu Deus . . .*.

(*b*) A more serious consideration. The first part of the *Te igitur* which Küng retains in his text, forms and obviously duplicates the *Quam* (*hanc*) *oblationem* which immediately follows it:

> *Supplices rogamus ac petimus ut accepta habeas et benedicas haec dona . . . Hanc oblationem, tu Deus . . . quaesumus benedictam . . . acceptabilemque facere digneris . . .*

This means that if the intercessions—and therefore the second part of the *Te igitur* from . . . *in primis quae tibi* . . .—are omitted, the first part of the *Te igitur* must then be joined with the *Quam* (*hanc*) *oblationem* to form a single prayer without repetitions, which would read something like this:

Vere dignum . . . Hosanna in excelsis. Te igitur clementissime Pater, supplices rogamus ac petimus ut hanc oblationem quam tibi offerimus, tu in omnibus benedictam, adscriptam, ratam rationabilemque facere digneris ut nobis corpus et sanguis fiat dilectissimi Filii tui Domini nostri Iesu Christi. Qui pridie . . .

That such should be the sequence of ideas in the canon is convincingly demonstrated, I think, in the preface of the consecration of the oils on Holy Thursday.[14] By joining, in the sense already mentioned, the first part of the *Te igitur* with the *Quam oblationem*, there spontaneously emerges the framework of a great eucharistic prayer centred on the consecration of an object. Its style is that of the ancient Roman eucology, as typified in the prayer of thanksgiving and of the consecration of the oils which has just been mentioned.

This shows how impossible it is to touch upon one part of the structure of the present canon without laying hands on some other parts which may well be of considerable importance. Thus we are driven to a thorough-going revision of the whole which takes us far beyond any simple correction.

It must also be evident that it is not sufficient merely to omit the intercessions in order to rediscover the primitive canon. Their omission compels a reworking of other important passages.

Moreover, Innocent I and Jerome testify[15] that in 416 the intercessions already held a place in the Roman canon. And while there is no positive argument to support the view that they were perhaps new in Rome about 416,[16] there are reasons for believing that the intercessions in the canon are in fact very old: the sentence in the *De Sacramentis* which precedes the passage which Küng quotes: "praises are offered to God, praying for the people, for kings and others . . ."; the fragment of the anonymous Arian

---

[14] See the text above, pp. 39–41.

[15] See above, p. 28.

[16] Decenzio's questioning of Innocent I, from which some have concluded that the habit of reciting intercessions in the canon was new in Rome in 416, shows only that Decenzio was acquainted with the habit of making intercessions before the canon, as in the Gallican and Hispanic traditions; nothing more.

which concludes with a passage of intercession; the Mozarabic *Post pridie* which begins like the anonymous Arian, and has a conclusion similar to the text of the canon quoted from the *De Sacramentis* (which in fact contains intercessions),[17] the crucial importance in the Roman canon of the idea of oblation and offering from which the intercession must spontaneously develop.

2. Besides leaving the intercessions out of the canon, Küng also omits the commemoration of the saints. This commemoration formed part of all anaphoras together with the intercessions, and existed in strict connection with them.

In omitting any such commemoration, Küng not only discards the idea of the invocation and intercession of the saints but, what is more important, he also rejects the idea of that intimate union which, in the most sublime act of the Church on earth—the very summit of the Church's life and activity[18]—binds the Church on earth with that of heaven and, in a special way, with the mother of God. The omission from the canon of every commemoration of the saints deprives it conclusively of its eschatological dimension and of its movement towards paradise.

Whatever the precise historical moment when this profound characteristic of the Church, realised above all in the action of the eucharist, found explicit expression in the anaphoras, it cannot be denied that with its adoption there took place an authentic theological enrichment of the Church's consciousness, and of the eucharistic action too.

I feel that the Church is today less inclined than ever to forsake this enrichment. The Second Vatican Council's *Constitution on the Church*, with Chapters 7 and 8 devoted to the eschatological character of the Church, its union with the heavenly Church, and in a special way with the Mother of the Saviour; the emphasis rightly laid upon the eschatological character of the whole of the liturgy;[19] the rediscovery of the eschatological nature of the

---

[17] See above pp. 31–2.

[18] See *Constitution on the Liturgy*, art. 10; 41.

[19] See *Constitution on the Liturgy*, art. 8.

Eucharist and of its movement towards paradise; all these make it impossible to accept the removal of this perspective from the great eucharistic prayer.

3. Finally, Küng's version leaves untouched many of the fundamental defects which mar the present canon. These we have outlined above: the lack of logical connection between the *Te igitur* and the prayer which precedes it due to the absence of a *Vere sanctus*; the over-emphasis given to the idea of the offering of the oblation; defects in the actual epiclesis; the failure to bring out the part played by the Holy Spirit; and all the defects of the *Qui pridie* and the *Supplices*. In particular, Küng's version does not make good the lack in the Roman canon of a synthetic exposition of the entire economy of salvation well-provided for in the eastern tradition, especially that of Antioch. The Eastern tradition, on the other hand, as is well exemplified in the Antioch system, undoubtedly gains from the inclusion of this particular aspect.

In conclusion: if from one point of view, Küng's version disrupts the modern canon, from another it is still too tightly bound to it, and thus leaves many of its numerous and even fundamental failings unaltered.

This means that the solution to the problem of the Roman canon cannot lie in its merely being corrected, however profound the correction might be.

V. Amon's version

In my opinion, Amon's version[20] lends itself to the following criticisms: even apart from the removal of the intercessions (regarding which what was said above still applies), Amon's version is not a simple correction of the present Roman canon, but for all practical purposes, a re-elaboration of its text, structure and spirit: the equivalent, that is, of a new canon—even if numerous elements of the present canon are still to be found. This new canon contains serious defects, some inherited directly from the

[20] See above, pp. 79–83.

modern canon, and others which Amon has in fact made worse.

(1) Amon discards the request contained in the second part of the *Quam oblationem*: that God, accepting the gifts which we offer him, make them the body and blood of Christ. In other words, he drops the consecratory epiclesis. He wants this idea to be transferred to the present offertory, adding it to the *Veni Sanctificator*.

It cannot be denied that in the Roman tradition—one might almost say, in all the Western tradition, and in the Eastern too—the epiclesis theme, as much in its consecratory element as in that of a request for a fruitful communion, is often included in the prayers which the priest says while preparing the offerings, and in the *Oratio super oblata*. The result of this is that some of the prayers constitute an anticipation and so a duplication of the epicletic concepts of the canon itself.[21]

---

[21] There are examples of authentic epicleses in the *Orationes super oblata* of the Western tradition. Leonine Sacramentary n. 578: "Send down, O Lord, the Holy Spirit, to make our present offerings your sacrament, and to purify our hearts, so that we may perceive this." This is a perfect pneumatological epiclesis, and can be found in other sacramentaries (see Mohlberg).

There can be found numerous other *Orationes super oblata* in Leonine Sacramentary, of a more general epicletic type: n. 228; 433; 457; 493; 511; 529; 546; 595; 667; 901; 908; 922; 934; 1027; 1177; 1196; 1296.

Note in the Ambrosian liturgy the *Orationes super oblata* following the Berg. Sacramentary: n. 757: "Touch our gifts by the power of the Holy Spirit, so that what he has dedicated with his name in solemnity, he may make intelligible and eternal for us"; n. 767: "May our gifts, Lord, be made holy by the advent of the Holy Spirit through whom . . ."; n. 794: "Sanctify the gifts that we offer, Lord, so that they may become for us the body and blood of your only-begotten . . ." Note also how in the prayers for the preparation for Mass in the Roman missal, there has been included an ancient epiclesis (authentic): Prayer for Fridays: ". . . I ask for your mercy, Lord, that the fullness of your blessing and the sanctification of your divinity come down upon the bread about to be sacrificed to you. And may the invisible and incomprehensible majesty of the Holy Spirit also descend, as formerly he descended on the victims of the fathers, so that he might make our oblations also your body and blood . . ." It is the very well-known type *Descendat* of the Gallican and Mozarabic epiclesis (see H. Lietzmann, *Messe und Herrenmahl*, 3rd ed. Berlin 1955, 102 ff). The preceding prayer is an adaptation of the Mozarabic epiclesis which can be found in the *Lib. Ord.*, 265: "We therefore ask of your majesty that our humble prayers may ascend in the sight of your mercy, and the fullness of your divinity descend on this bread and this wine. May the incomprehensible majesty of your Holy Spirit also descend, O Lord, as formerly he descended on the victim of the fathers: and grant, Lord, that . . ." See also Lietzmann, loc. cit., 102 ff.

The offertory rite has undergone, in fact, various stages of development. Someone as early as Justin—in his dialogue with Trypho—[22] gives us to understand that the eucharistic rite of which he speaks contains an offering (*prosphora*) of the bread and wine as types of the body and blood of Christ and of his passion. For Justin, this offering occurs in the great eucharistic prayer itself, because at that time the carrying of wine and water to the altar was not yet part of the liturgical rite, and even less was it accompanied by prayers proper to it.

In Hippolytus, the same state of affairs is apparent. For him, the offering of the bread and wine is one of the key points of the anaphora, and is expressed in immediate connection with the prayer that God send down his Spirit on the gifts offered, and grant that those about to share in these gifts be filled with the same Spirit. In other words, in Hippolytus the offering of gifts is quite naturally accepted as being in an epiclesis context, either in the consecratory aspect of epiclesis,[23] or in that of prayer for a fruitful communion.

In fact, the two ideas go together quite naturally. This explains why, when later the offertory of the faithful and the bringing of the bread and wine to the altar became a liturgical rite, properly so-called, with appropriate prayers to accompany it,[24] there emerged what to all intents and purposes was a second offertory of the oblations, anticipating that of the canon. Moreover, several of the accompanying prayers tended to become perfectly genuine epicleses, thus anticipating the epiclesis of the canon.

But all this does not alter the fact that the epiclesis has always remained one of the essential points of every anaphora[25] and that the desire to throw such an essential part out of the Roman canon under the pretext of "correcting" it means altering its structure

[22] 41 PG, 6, 564.

[23] At least, this is what I maintain. See above, p. 91, n. 7.

[24] Firstly the *Oratio super oblata*, and then in the Middle Ages, the present-day prayers which accompany the gestures with which the priest prepares the oblations and places them on the altar.

[25] See above, pp. 91–2.

profoundly and arbitrarily, in direct opposition to the whole of the anaphora tradition.

2. In Amon's scheme all the defects of the Roman *Qui pridie* remain.

3. The *Communicantes*, too, begins abruptly, as it does in the present Roman canon.

4. Amon preserves the commemoration of the saints but omits without a plausible motive the idea of their merits and intercessions pleading for us before God,[26] or of the part which we hope to obtain with them in paradise.[27]

There can be no doubt, however, that the essential motive for commemorating the saints was from the beginning to obtain their intercession at the precise moment of the offering of the holy sacrifice. Saint Cyril of Jerusalem states explicitly: "After which we bring to mind the memory of those who have gone to sleep in the Lord, and firstly the prophets, patriarchs, apostles and martyrs, so that God may accept our request for their prayers and intercession."[28]

5. The first part of the *Quam oblationem* which Amon puts after the institution, is not suited, as a prayer for acceptance of the sacrifice, to the function which Amon wishes it to perform here. Theologically speaking, it does not make sense to say: *quam oblationem . . . benedictam, adscriptam, ratam acceptabilemque facere digneris* . . . after the institution.

6. As a replacement for the *Quam oblationem* on ferial days, Amon puts forward a text consisting of the first part of the *Te igitur* and the *Supra quae* as a prayer asking God to accept the sacrifice. This is not conducive to clarity and simplicity, and among other things the first sentence expresses in other words and in a general way precisely the same idea as the second.

---

[26] *Quorum meritis precibusque concedas ut in omnibus protectionis tuae muniamur auxilo.*

[27] In the *Nobis quoque: Intra quorum nos consortium . . . admitte.*

[28] *Catech.* 23, *Myst* 5. 9; PG 33, 1116.

7. In the *Supplices*, the link between the prayer that God accept the sacrifice and the one asking for a fruitful communion is broken. In the *Supplices* of the Roman canon this link is quite clear.

8. Finally, Amon's solution does not provide for the lack in the present canon of a general and unified picture of the work of our salvation.

Conclusion

Any attempt to revise the present canon merely by way of rearranging it, cutting it, or simply patching it up, will inevitably lead to an awful mess. And what is more, this sort of approach does not solve the problem of its intrinsic shortcomings and defects, to which we are rightly becoming more and more sensitive today.

The time when the Roman canon was believed to be irreplaceable because "apostolic" or perfect is certainly over. But it is also true that it is impossible to lay hands on it with impunity under the pretext of improving it. We must, therefore, resolutely set out along another path. In the anaphora tradition of large liturgical groups, the Roman liturgy is almost alone in never having known the possibility of using simultaneously more than one anaphora.[29]

The solution to the problem of the canon in the Roman liturgy should be based, in my opinion, on the following three propositions:

1. That the present Roman canon be retained, but with those minor modifications already indicated as being possible and helpful, since they alter neither its structure nor its general lines.

---

[29] Of the Antiochian group of anaphoras: the West-Syrians have or have had about seventy anaphora formulae; the East-Syrian three; the Byzantines two; the Armenians four. In the Egyptian group: the Copts have three; the Abyssinians seventeen. And note that in the Gallican and Palaeo-Hispanic traditions every part of the anaphora was variable except for the *Qui pridie*. The present Ambrosian tradition has a special canon for Holy Thursday and the vigil of Easter, besides the Roman canon.

2. That the Roman liturgy be given another canon in place of the present canon, with a variable preface. This could be used *ad libitum* by the priest in place of the present canon, and would be an original composition which, with all due regard for the literary and liturgical style proper to an anaphora, would seek to come as close as possible to what biblical, traditional, liturgical and pastoral feeling suggests as the ideal for today in this field.

3. That, in addition to this, the Roman liturgy should have a third canon with a fixed preface. Prior to the *Qui pridie* this would give a synthetic exposition of salvation history, following the best Eastern tradition, and from the *Qui pridie* onwards would follow the text of the second canon. It would in fact be a variation of the same canon. This third anaphora could be used *ad libitum* in Masses without a proper preface, and so on the Sundays throughout the year, even if they were eventually to have their own preface.

Naturally this new canon would have to answer many needs, and the question which immediately arises is this: "Can we possibly do anything like this now?"—The various schemes I am about to present have as their sole ambition a desire to indicate a possible path to the much hoped for solution to this question.

CHAPTER IV

Project of a Second Roman Canon with a Movable Preface (Canon B) together with a Variant having a Fixed or Stable Preface (Canon C)

I. Project of a second Roman canon with a movable preface (canon B) to be used *ad libitum* in the Masses with a proper preface

I	I
Vere dignum . . .	It is good and fitting . . .
Sanctus . . . Hosanna in excelsis.	Holy . . . Hosanna in the heights of heaven.
II	**II**
1 Vere sanctus es Domine,	1 You are indeed holy, Lord,
2 et merito semper te laudat	2 and it is right that your creation
3 omnis a te condita creatura	3 gives you unending praise
4 ac iugiter profitetur te caelum terramque	4 with a voice proclaiming forever
5 tua gloria mirabiliter replevisse:	5 that the heavens and earth are filled with the wonders of your glory;
6 quia per Filium tuum, Dominum nostrum Iesum Christum,	6 for through your Son, Jesus Christ, our Lord,
7 in infusione Spiritus Sancti,	7 and through the life of the Spirit within us
8 vivificas et sanctificas universa.	8 you make all things live, all things holy.
III	**III**
9 Te igitur, clementissime Domine, supplices obsecramus	9 We ask, therefore, most merciful Lord,
10 ut haec munera, quae tibi sacranda detulimus,	10 be pleased to bless these gifts and make them holy,

11 sanctificare tua benedictione digneris.	11 gifts which we offer for you to sanctify.
12 Iubeas, quaesumus, Sancti tui Spiritus eis immisceri virtutem,	12 We pray you, bid your Spirit in his strength to enter them
13 per eiusdem Domini nostri, Christi tui, potentiam,	13 by the power of your Anointed, our Lord,
14 ut ipsius nobis fiant corpus et sanguis	14 so that they become, for us, his body and his blood,
15 in sacrificium tibi placitum	15 a sacrifice pleasing to you
16 quod nobis offerre mandavit.	16 such as he demanded we offer you.
IV	IV
17 Ipse enim pridie quam pateretur	17 For he, the day before his passion,
18 hoc magnum novi testamenti mysterium	18–19 gave us in trust this great mystery of the new covenant,
19 nobis voluit commendare,	
20 mirabilium suorum memoriale perpetuum:	20 an everlasting memorial of his marvellous works:
21 ut se in cruce misericors oblaturus	21–22 in his mercy he ordained before he offered himself on the cross that we too, his humble servants
22 a nobis quoque, tuis servis exiguis,	
23 in corporis sanguinisque mysteriis	23 should constantly offer this sacrifice
24 indesinenter offerretur.	24 in the mystery of his body and his blood.
25 Et ideo, cum seipsum erat traditurus in mortem,	25 So, when he was about to give himself to die,
26 accepit panem in beatas ac venerabiles manus suas	26 he took bread in his holy and blessed hands,
27 et aspiciens in caelum ad te, Deum, Patrem suum omnipotentem,	27 looking up to heaven, to you, God, his all-powerful Father,
28 tibi gratias agens, benedixit, fregit, deditque discipulis suis dicens:	28 he gave thanks, blessed and broke it and gave to his disciples saying:
29 Accipite et manducate ex hoc omnes:	29 take and eat, all of you:

30 Hoc est enim corpus meum quod pro vobis tradetur.	30 this is my body which shall be given for you.
31 Hoc facite in meam commemorationem.	31 Do this in memory of me.
32 Simili modo, postquam caenatum est,	32 In the same way when they had eaten,
33 accipiens calicem ex vino mixtum et aqua,	33 he took wine and water in a cup,
34 tibi gratias agens, benedixit deditque discipulis suis dicens:	34 gave thanks, blessed and gave it to his disciples saying:
35 Accipite et bibite ex eo omnes:	35 take and drink, all of you:
36 Hic est enim calix novi testamenti in sanguine meo	36 this is the cup of the new covenant in my blood
37 qui pro vobis et pro multis effundetur	37 which shall be poured out for you and for everyone
38 in remissionem peccatorum.	38 to take away all sins.
39 Hoc facite in meam commemorationem.	39 Do this in memory of me.
V	V
40 Unde et memores, Domine,	40–42 Therefore, Lord, we your servants, and your holy people, remember the glorious passion of your Son,
41 nos, servi tui, sed et plebs tua sancta,	
42 eiusdem Filii tui gloriosissimae passionis	
43 necnon mirabilis resurrectionis et ascensionis in caelum,	43 his wonderful resurrection and ascension into heaven;
44 sed et alterum adventum eius praestolantes:	44 thus, while we await his second coming,
45 adimus cum fiducia ad thronum misericordiae tuae	45 we confidently approach the throne of your loving mercy;
46 et gratias agentes offerimus tibi hoc sacrificium incruentum	46 we thank you, we offer you this gift which you yourself have given us,
47 de tuis donis ac datis:	47 this bloodless sacrifice:
48 Hostiam puram,	48 the pure Victim,
49 Hostiam sanctam,	49–50 the holy, blameless Victim, the Victim given that the world might live.
50 immaculatam hanc Hostiam pro saeculi vita.	
VI	VI
51 Supplices te rogamus, Domine sempiterne,	51 We beg you, eternal Lord,

52 ut agnoscens Victimam cuius voluisti intercessione placari, 53 in oblationem Ecclesiae tuae benignus aspicias, 54 tui Spiritus operatione sacratam. 55 Ipsam, quaesumus, acceptam habeas et concede propitius 56 ut quotquot Filii tui corpus et sanguinem sumpserimus, 57 eodem Spiritu sancto copiosius repleamur	52–57 receive this Victim, for you desired our salvation through his intercession. Look with kindness on the offering of your Church, an offering made holy by the work of your Spirit. Accept it, we pray; grant, in your goodness, that as many of us as receive the body and blood of your Son, may be filled with this Holy Spirit;
58 et unum corpus et unus spiritus efficiamur in eo.	58 may we become in him one body, one spirit.
59 Ita tibi munus aeternum nos ille perficiat	59 May he make us an eternal offering to you,
60 ut cum electis tuis hereditatem consequamur.	60 that we may come to the lasting inheritance the saints enjoy;
VII	VII
61 In primis cum beata, gloriosa, semperque virgine Maria,	61 above all in company with the blessed, glorious, and ever-virgin Mary,
62 Genitrice Dei et Domini nostri Iesu Christi:	62 mother of our God and Lord, Jesus Christ;
63 sed et cum beatis Ioseph et Ioanne Baptista,	63 with blessed Joseph and John the Baptist,
64 cum sanctis Apostolis tuis Petro et Paulo,	64 your holy apostles Peter and Paul,
65 cum sancto N. (*patrono dioeceseos*), cum beato N. (*cuius festum agitur*) *—in missis quae non sunt de sanctis liceat singulis aut sacerdotibus aut coetibus—v. g. religiosis—nomen facere unius sancti ad libitum—* et omnibus sanctis	65 saint N. (patron of the diocese), saint N. (saint of the day), and all your saints; [*in Masses which are not* de sanctis *the individual priest—or community—may here insert a saint's name of his own choice*]
66 quorum meritis et intercessione perpetuo apud te confidimus adiuvari.	66 we trust that through their merits and prayers we shall receive your help, as they plead on our behalf.

VIII	VIII
67 Memento, Domine, Ecclesiae tuae sanctae toto orbe diffusae,	67 Remember, Lord, your holy Church throughout the entire world,
68 pro qua tibi offerimus hanc Hostiam salutarem.	68 for which we offer this saving Victim.
69 Illam undique congregare et custodire digneris	69 Be pleased to gather your people from every place on earth and protect them,
70 una cum famulo tuo Papa nostro N. et episcoporum ordine universo,	70 with your servant our Pope N., and all the bishops of the world,
71 cum antistite nostro N. et omni populo acquisitionis sanctae tuae.	71 our own bishop N., and the holy people you have redeemed.

IX	IX
72 Votis supplicibus, quaesumus Domine,	72–73 We pray, Lord, accept the petitions and prayers of those who have made this offering and all those here present,
73 offerentium et adstantium adesto propitius,	
74 qui tibi deferunt hoc sacrificium placationis et laudis	74 who offer this sacrifice of praise to make amends.
75 eosque ita sacris tuis mysteriis efficias expiatos	75 Wipe away their sins through these holy mysteries,
76 ut ad tuam magnificentiam capiendam	76 and, in your kindness, cleanse them
77 tuis semper miserationibus instaurentur.	77 that they may receive forever the gifts of your faithful love.

X	X
78 Nos etiam peccatores, altaris tui ministros,	78–79 Look on us, ministers at your altar, with mercy, Lord, for we too are sinners.
79 in tua miseratione respicias	
80 et famulatum nostrum tibi faciens dignanter acceptum	80 Accept our service kindly,
81 concede nos sedulo quod tractamus imitari.	81 grant that our lives may be true to the mystery we celebrate.

XI	XI
82 Memento quoque, Domine, famulorum famularumque tuarum	82–84 Remember also, Lord, those men and women, your servants, who have died marked with the sign of faith,
83 qui nos cum signo fidei praecesserunt	

84 et in pace Christi requiescunt.	and rest in the peace of Christ.
85 Eis, quaesumus, locum refrigerii et lucis indulgeas	85 Let them enter, we pray, that place of eternal joy and light,
86 quo speramus simul gloria tua perenniter satiari.	86 where we hope one day to enjoy with them the everlasting vision of your glory.
XII	XII
87 Per Christum Dominum nostrum,	87 Through Christ, our Lord,
88 per quem mundo omnia dona largiris:	88 through whom you give all gifts to the world,
—*quando hic cibi benedicuntur, dicitur:* . . . per quem haec omnia, Domine, semper bona creas, sanctificas, vivificas, benedicis et praestas nobis . . . —	[*when food is blessed here, there is said:* . . . through whom you ever create all things, and they are good, you make them holy, you endow them with life, you bless them, and you offer them to us.]
89 per ipsum,	89 through him,
90 et cum ipso	90 with him,
91 et in ipso	91 and in him
92 est tibi, Deo Patri omnipotenti,	92 be all honour and glory,
93 in unitate Spiritus Sancti,	93 to you, God the almighty Father,
94 omnis honor et gloria,	94 one with the Holy Spirit,
95 per omnia saecula saeculorum.	95 for ever and ever.
℟. Amen.	Amen.

II. Project of a variant on this canon with a fixed preface (canon C) to be used *ad libitum* on Sundays of the year, and in those Masses which do not have a proper preface

The basic aim of introducing an anaphora of this type into the Roman liturgy is to give it the possibility, at least on certain occasions, of presenting in the canon itself a general view of the whole history of salvation. This would be the primary object of that hymn of joy and thanksgiving which is the first part of the anaphora. As was pointed out earlier, it is this type of synthetic presentation of salvation history that is the great advantage of the oriental anaphora tradition, and especially that of Antioch, as compared with the Western tradition. One would think that in this way the Roman liturgy would acquire an inestimable wealth of thought and religious depth from the universal Church, without having to forsake any of the no less valuable qualities of its own tradition.

An anaphora with a fixed preface, like this one, would not be able to be used in Masses with a preface of their own. A preface, in fact, which is proper to the feast of the day is by its very nature not so much a hymn of rejoicing and thanks for the whole history of salvation, but rather for that particular aspect or feature which is brought out by the feast of the day. An anaphora having a preface proper to the day could not, without tiresome repetitions, also contain a full exposition of the course of redemption. To do so would be to repeat what was already said in the proper preface.

However, an anaphora with a fixed preface, giving in synthesis the history of salvation, could well be used *ad libitum* on the Sundays *per annum*, even if the Roman Missal were to adopt in the future a certain number of proper prefaces for the Sundays. Such proper prefaces would necessarily require a general character, referring in fact ultimately to the paschal mystery. Therefore an anaphora with a fixed preface, in the first part of which there is presented a synthesis of the history of salvation—basically, as the paschal mystery—would be admirably suited to any Sunday *per annum*.

I	I
1 Vere dignum est iustum est	1–5 It is good and fitting
2 aequum et salutare	and for our salvation,
3 nos tibi semper et ubique	to give glory to you;
4 gratias agere,	to offer thanks
5 Domine,	at all times,
	in every place,
	to you, Lord,
6 sancte Pater,	6 holy Father,
7 omnipotens, aeterne Deus,	7 almighty and eternal God,

8 per Christum Dominum nostrum.
9 Per quem nobis agnitio tuae veritatis est indita
10 ut te, Patrem gloriae sempiternae,
11 cum ipso Filio tuo et Spiritu Sancto
12 excelsum super omnia humiliter adoremus
13 et te ineffabilem caritatem confitentes
14 exultantibus semper animis diligamus.

15 In quo unigenito Filio tuo
16 visibilia et invisibilia condidisti
17 ut ipse esset ante omnes
18 et omnia constarent in ipso
19 ac nomen tuum per ipsum in aeternum collaudarent.

20 Et ideo per eum tuam aeternam maiestatem
21 omnes laudant ordines angelorum,
22 sanctorum tuorum catervae innumerae venerantur
23 et in circuitu throni magnitudinis tuae
24 perenni iubilatione proclamant:
25 Sanctus,
26 Sanctus,
27 Sanctus,
28 Dominus Deus Sabaoth.
29 Pleni sunt caeli et terra gloria tua.
30 Hosanna in excelsis.
31 Benedictus qui venit in nomine Domine,

8 through Christ our Lord.
9 Through him
you have enabled us
to acknowledge the truth
10–12 that we might humbly adore you
above all things,
Father of eternal glory,
with your Son
and the Holy Spirit;
13 that in proclaiming you,
Love itself beyond all telling,
14 we might love you
with undying gladness of heart.
15 It is in him, your only Son,
16 that you have made all things,
visible and invisible,
17 in order that he be
first among all men;
18 and all creation is in him;
19 and through him
all forever
praise your name.
20–21 Through him, therefore,
all the choirs of angels
adore your eternal glory.
22 the countless saints of heaven
worship your eternal majesty.
23 Gathered around your throne
24 with unending joy they sing:
25 Holy,
26 Holy,
27 Holy,
28 Lord,
God of all.
29 The heavens and the earth
are filled with your glory.
30 Hosanna
in the heights of heaven.
31 Blessed is he who comes
in the name of the Lord.

32 Hosanna in excelsis.	32 Hosanna in the heights of heaven.
II	II
33 Vere sanctus es Domine,	33 You are indeed, Lord, holy:
34 vere caelum et terram	34 truly you have filled heaven and earth
35 gloria tua mirabiliter replevisti:	35 with the wonder of your glory.
36 qui ab initio hominem formasti de terra	36 In the beginning you made man out of earth,
37 ad imaginem et similitudinem tuam:	37 made him in your image, like to yourself;
38 ut universa 39 simul animantia 40 rerumque miracula 41 sibi subiciens, 42 dominaretur, vicario munere, omnibus quae creasti, 43 et in operum tuorum magnaliis iugiter te laudaret.	38–43 so that, having subjected all living things to him, the wonders of your world are his to rule; all that you have made is a gift in trust, and at all times he adores you in the wonders of your works.
44 Quem deiectum de gratia paradisi	44 After his fall from the life of grace
45 tuis beneficiis cumulare non desisti	45 you did not cease to favour him
46 ut te quaerere non cessaret;	46 so that he still searched for you:
47 sed et eum manu ad Salvatorem duxisti per legem et prophetas.	47 in your goodness, through the Law and the prophets, you led him by the hand to the Saviour.
48 Et sic mundum, Pater sancte, dilexisti	48 You loved the world so much, holy Father,
49 ut Unigenitum tuum nobis mitteres Redemptorem	49 that you sent your only Son to be our Saviour,
50 unde amares in nobis quod in Filio diligebas.	50 that you might love in us what you have always loved in the Son.
51 Qui de Spiritu Sancto et virgine Maria conceptus	51 Conceived through the Holy Spirit in the virgin Mary,
52 superabundanter nos ad tua dona reparavit	52 he has brought back to us, in abundance,

53 quae in priore amiseramus Adamo.	53 the gifts we lost in the first Adam.
54 Quin et nos in finem usque dilexit;	54 He loved us to the end;
55 et ideo tibi, per Spiritum Sanctum,	55–56 thus, through the Holy Spirit
56 immaculatam Hostiam obtulit semetipsum	he offered himself to you, a blameless Victim,
57 veterum sacrificiorum implens in veritate figuras	57 fulfilling in himself what the sacrifices of old prefigured,
58 aeterna redemptione semel inventa.	58 and once for all gained our eternal redemption.
59 Qui gloriose ab inferis resurrexit	59 He arose from the dead in glory,
60 et ascendit ad dexteram tuam Pontifex in aeternum	60 ascended to his place at your right hand,
61 semper vivens ad interpellandum pro nobis.	61 the eternal High Priest, living forever to intercede for us.
62 Qui venturus vivos et mortuos iudicare,	62 He will come to judge the living and the dead,
63 se tamen cuncta per saecula 64 nobis est pollicitus adfuturum.	63–64 and we have his promise he will be with us forever.
65 Unde et alium, Pater, at te misit Paraclitum,	65 And so, from you, Father, he has sent another Paraclete,
66 Spiritum veritatis, qui nos cuncta doceret	66 the Spirit of truth, to teach us all things
67 et omnem sanctificationem compleret in mundo.	67 and fill the world with all holiness.
III	III
68 Te igitur, clementissime Pater, supplices obsecramus	68 We ask, therefore, most merciful Lord,
69 ut haec munera, quae tibi sacranda detulimus, 70 idem Spiritus Sanctus 71 praesentia suae maiestatis implere dignetur,	69–71 that the Holy Spirit be pleased to fill with the presence of his glory these gifts we offer for you to sanctify;
72 qua corpus et sanguis fiant	72 through him may they become the body and the blood

73 dilectissimi Filii tui, Domini nostri Iesu Christi,	73 of your beloved Son, Jesus Christ, our Lord,
74 in sacrificium tibi placitum,	74 to be a sacrifice pleasing to you,
75 quod nobis offerre mandavit.	75 the sacrifice he demanded we offer you.
IV	IV
76 Ipse enim pridie quam pateretur,	76 For he, the day before his passion,
77 hoc magnum novi testamenti mysterium	77–78 gave us in trust this great mystery of the new covenant,
78 nobis voluit commendare,	
79 mirabilium suorum memoriale perpetuum:	79 an everlasting memorial of his marvellous works:
80 ut se in cruce misericors oblaturus	80 in his mercy he ordained before he offered himself on the cross
81 a nobis quoque, tuis servis exiguis,	81 that we too, his humble servants
82 in corporis sanguinisque mysteriis	82 should constantly offer this sacrifice
83 indesinenter offerretur.	83 in the mystery of his body and his blood.
84 Et ideo, cum seipsum erat traditurus in mortem,	84 So when he was about to give himself to die,
85 accepit panem in beatas ac venerabiles manus suas	85 he took bread in his holy and blessed hands,
86 et aspiciens in caelum ad te, Deum, Patrem suum omnipotentem,	86 looking up to heaven, to you, God, his all-powerful Father,
87 tibi gratias agens benedixit, fregit, deditque discipulis suis dicens:	87 he gave thanks, blessed and broke it and gave to his disciples saying:
88 Accipite et manducate ex hoc omnes:	88 take and eat, all of you:
89 Hoc est enim corpus meum quod pro vobis tradetur.	89 this is my body which shall be given for you.
90 Hoc facite in meam commemorationem.	90 Do this in memory of me.
91 Simili modo, postquam caenatum est,	91 In the same way when they had eaten,

92 accipiens calicem ex vino mixtum et aqua,	92 he took wine and water in a cup,
93 tibi gratias agens, benedixit deditque discipulis suis dicens:	93 gave thanks, blessed and gave it to his disciples saying:
94 Accipite et bibite ex eo omnes:	94 take and drink, all of you:
95 Hic est enim calix Novi Testamenti in sanguine meo	95 this is the cup of the new covenant in my blood
96 qui pro vobis et pro multis effundetur	96 which shall be poured out for you and for everyone
97 in remissionem peccatorum.	97 to take away all sins.
98 Hoc facite in meam commemorationem.	98 Do this in memory of me.
V	V
99 Unde et memores, Domine,	99 Therefore, Lord,
100 nos, servi tui, sed et plebs tua sancta,	100 we your servants, and your holy people,
101 eiusdem Filii tui gloriosissimae passionis	101 remember the glorious passion of your Son,
102 necnon mirabilis resurrectionis et ascensionis in caelum,	102 his wonderful resurrection and ascension into heaven;
103 sed et alterum adventum eius praestolantes:	103 thus, while we await his second coming,
104 adimus cum fiducia ad thronum misericordiae tuae	104 we confidently approach the throne of your loving mercy;
105 et gratias agentes offerimus tibi hoc sacrificium incruentum 106 de tuis donis ac datis:	105–106 we thank you, we offer you this bloodless sacrifice, the gift which you yourself have given us:
107 Hostiam puram,	107 the pure Victim,
108 Hostiam sanctam,	108 the holy, blameless Victim,
109 immaculatam hanc Hostiam pro saeculi vita.	109 the Victim given that the world might live.
VI	VI
110 Supplices te rogamus, Domine sempiterne,	110 We beg you, eternal Lord,
111 ut agnoscens Victimam cuius voluisti intercessione placari,	111 receive this Victim, for you desired our salvation through his intercession.
112 in oblationem Ecclesiae tuae benignus aspicias,	112 Look with kindness on the offering of your Church,

113 tui Spiritus operatione sacratam.	113 an offering made holy by the work of your Spirit.
114 Ipsam, quaesumus, acceptam habeas et concede propitius	114 Accept it, we pray;
115 ut quotquot Filii tui corpus et sanguinem sumpserimus,	115 grant, in your goodness, that as many of us as receive the body and blood of your Son,
116 eodem Spiritu Sancto copiosius repleamur	116 may be filled with this Holy Spirit;
117 et unum corpus et unus spiritus efficiamur in eo.	117 may we become in him one body, one spirit.
118 Ita tibi munus aeternum nos ille perficiat	118 May he make us an eternal offering to you,
119 ut cum electis tuis hereditatem consequamur.	119 that we may come to the lasting inheritance the saints enjoy.
VII	VII
120 In primis cum beata, gloriosa, semperque virgine Maria,	120 Above all in company with the blessed, glorious, and ever-virgin Mary,
121 genitrice Dei et Domini nostri Iesu Christi:	121 mother of our God and Lord, Jesus Christ;
122 sed et cum beatis Ioseph et Ioanne Baptista,	122 with blessed Joseph and John the Baptist,
123 cum sanctis Apostolis tuis Petro et Paulo,	123 your holy apostles Peter and Paul,
124 cum sancto N. (*patrono dioeceseos*), cum beato N. (*cuius festum agitur*) —*in missis, quae non sunt de sanctis, liceat singulis aut sacerdotibus aut coetibus—v. g. religiosis—nomen facere unius sancti ad libitum*— et omnibus sanctis	124 saint N. (patron of the diocese), saint N. (saint of the day), and all your saints; [*in Masses which are not* de sanctis *the individual priest—or community—may here insert a saint's name of his own choice.*]
125 quorum meritis et intercessione perpetuo apud te confidimus adiuvari.	125 we trust that through their merits and prayers we shall receive your help, as they plead on our behalf.

VIII	VIII
126 Memento, Domine, Ecclesiae tuae sanctae toto orbe diffusae,	126 Remember, Lord, your holy Church throughout the entire world,
127 pro qua tibi offerimus hanc Hostiam salutarem.	127 for which we offer this saving Victim.
128 Illam undique congregare et custodire digneris	128 Be pleased to gather your people from every place on earth and protect them,
129 una cum famulo tuo Papa nostro N. et episcoporum ordine universo,	129 with your servant our Pope N., and all the bishops of the world,
130 cum antistite nostro N. et omni populo acquisitionis sanctae tuae.	130 our own bishop N., and the holy people you have redeemed.

IX	IX
131 Votis supplicibus, quaesumus, Domine,	131 We pray, Lord, accept
132 offerentium et adstantium adesto propitius,	132 the petitions and prayers of those who have made this offering
133 qui tibi deferunt hoc sacrificium placationis et laudis,	133 and all those here present, who offer this sacrifice of praise to make amends.
134 eosque ita sacris tuis mysteriis efficias expiatos	134 Wipe away their sins through these holy mysteries,
135 ut ad tuam magnificentiam capiendam	135 and, in your kindness, cleanse them
136 tuis semper miserationibus instaurentur.	136 that they may receive forever the gifts of your faithful love.

X	X
137 Nos etiam peccatores, altaris tui ministros, 138 in tua miseratione respicias	137–8 Look on us, ministers at your altar, with mercy, Lord, for we too are sinners.
139 et famulatum nostrum tibi faciens dignanter acceptum	139 Accept our service kindly,
140 concede nos sedulo quod tractamus imitari.	140 grant that our lives may be true to the mystery we celebrate.

XI

141 Memento quoque, Domine, famulorum famularumque tuarum

142 qui nos cum signo fidei praecesserunt

143 et in pace Christi requiescunt.

144 Eis, quaesumus, locum refrigerii et lucis indulgeas

145 quo speramus simul gloria tua perenniter satiari.

XI

141 Remember also, Lord,
those men and women, your servants,
who have died

142 marked with the sign of faith,

143 and rest in the peace of Christ.

144 Let them enter, we pray,
that place of eternal joy and light,

145 where we hope one day
to enjoy with them
the everlasting vision
of your glory.

XII

146 Per Christum Dominum nostrum,

147 per quem mundo omnia dona largiris:

—*quando hic cibi benedicuntur, dicitur:* . . . per quem haec omnia, Domine, semper bona creas, sanctificas, vivificas, benedicis et praestas nobis . . .—

148 per ipsum,

149 et cum ipso

150 et in ipso

151 est tibi, Deo Patri omnipotenti,

152 in unitate Spiritus Sancti,

153 omnis honor et gloria,

154 per omnia saecula saeculorum.

℟. Amen.

XII

146 Through Christ, our Lord,

147 through whom you give all gifts to the world,

[*when food is blessed here, there is said:* . . . through whom you ever create all things,
and they are good, you make them holy,
you endow them with life,
you bless them,
and you offer them to us.]

148 through him,

149 with him,

150 and in him

151–3 be all honour and glory,
to you, God the almighty Father,
one with the Holy Spirit,

154 forever and ever.

℟. Amen.

III. The structure of projects B and C

The structure of the projects proposed here is as follows:

A. The hymn of exaltation and thanksgiving for the economy of salvation

I. Preface and *Sanctus*

II. Connecting passage leading to the sacrifice proper: *Vere Sanctus*

B. The sacrifice proper

III. Consecratory epiclesis: *Te igitur*

IV. Institution: *Ipse enim pridie quam pateretur*

V. Anamnesis and offering of the sacrifice: *Unde et memores*

VI. Prayer for the acceptance of the sacrifice and for a fruitful communion: *Supplices te rogamus*

VII. Commemoration of the saints: *In primis*

VIII. Prayer of intercession for the Church in general and for the bishop: *Memento Domine*

IX. Prayer of intercession for those present and offering the sacrifice: *Votis supplicibus*

X. Prayer of intercession for the ministers at the altar: *Nos etiam peccatores*

XI. Prayer of intercession for the dead: *Memento quoque*

C. The conclusion

XII. Final doxology

This structure seems to have the clarity and logic of the best Eastern anaphoras, namely those of the Antioch type: the Alexandrine anaphora of St Basil, for example.

The proposals put forward here particularly resemble the Antioch anaphoras in grouping together the prayers of intercession after the institution and the prayer for a fruitful communion, but the commemoration of the saints comes before the actual prayers of intercession, as in the Byzantine anaphora of St Basil. In the Basilian anaphora the commemoration is not introduced within the framework of a prayer *per*, *huper*, as is often the case with other Antiochene anaphoras. Instead, it occurs in connection with the prayer for a fruitful communion, which is undoubtedly due to a more accurate theological perspective: we pray that we may find mercy with God along with Mary and his other saints.

The consecratory epiclesis, on the other hand, is in the position characteristic of the Roman canon, immediately after the *Qui pridie* (*Quam oblationem*), and afterwards the anamnesis has the prayer for God's acceptance of the sacrifice and another for a fruitful communion (*Supplices*). In other words, the anamnesis of the Roman canon contains only the last theme present in the Antiochene type of epiclesis. The Roman tradition probably agrees with the Egyptian in placing the consecratory epiclesis before the institution with the request for a fruitful communion after the anamnesis.[1]

The place kept in the projects for the consecratory epiclesis before the *Qui pridie* serves, in my opinion, to distinguish their structure from that of the Antiochene anaphoras. So too, the place given in them to the prayers of intercession—which are all grouped after the anamnesis and the prayer requesting a fruitful communion—is sufficient to mark them off from the Egyptian type, in which the intercessions all occur before the *Sanctus*. The proposed anaphoras are therefore more than simply a transfer of an Eastern anaphora into the Roman liturgy.

The proposed canons differ in structure from the present Roman canon in two essential features: (*a*) The presence of the *Vere sanctus*, which occurs in all Gallican and Palaeo-Hispanic anaphoras as well as in all the Eastern rites, and which must be present to connect the *Sanctus* to what follows; (*b*) the grouping together of the prayers of intercession after the institution, as happens in the Antioch tradition.

Project B differs from its variant C only in that it is a canon with a movable preface referring to the feast of the day, which

[1] See above, pp. 67–9.

means that its *Vere sanctus* is necessarily very short and alludes to the history of salvation only in a general way. In contrast to this, the *Vere sanctus* of project C is highly developed and, continuing the themes of the fixed preface—revelation in general, the creation of the world—it recalls in a synthesis the chief phases of the economy of salvation on the model of the Syrian tradition, particularly true of the Alexandrine anaphora of St Basil.

In this synthesis of project C there is only one feature which is really new. Other anaphoras, in recalling the economy of God in our life and in the work of Christ for us, all conclude with mention of the ascension and the future glorious coming of the Lord. In project C, however, following scripture itself, there is an explicit reference to the promise of Christ to be with us always and to his sending of the Holy Spirit to complete his work of sanctifying the world. Such mention of the Holy Spirit's work of sanctification at the end of the *Vere Sanctus* is, it seems to me, the only logical way of introducing immediately afterwards the prayer by which we ask God to send this same Holy Spirit to sanctify the holy gifts and make them into the body and blood of Christ. For the same reason, so that the epicletic prayer will lead smoothly into the *Qui pridie* which immediately follows, marking the start of the sacrificial part of the Eucharist, neither project B nor project C ends in the usual way, with the prayer that the gifts may become the body and blood of Christ. Instead there is added: may they become the body and blood of Christ *in sacrificium tibi placitum quod nobis offerre mandavit. Ipse enim pridie quam pateretur . . .*

IV. Notes on the general theology of project B and its variant C

(1) *A canon of an archaic type can no longer be used today*

There is a temptation today, since an anaphora is bound to express certain theological ideas, to consider as the ideal the most archaic type of anaphora possible, one in which the theological concepts are extremely simple or even undifferentiated. From this point of view the anaphora of Hippolytus or the East Syrian anaphora of Addaï and Mari would serve as the best model. There are those, in fact, who would like to replace the Roman canon with that of Hippolytus.

Various reasons can lead to this position: it may be a diffidence towards any sort of "theologising", an outlook widespread today in some circles, or it may be the taste for history and archaeology that is frequently very strong with those liturgists who are in fact simply philologists and liturgical historians. Or, again, it may be due to a certain way—certainly a superficial one—of understanding the ecumenical spirit, a way which sees our duty to come closer to our separated Protestant brothers as being furthered by our acceptance of a position regarding the Eucharist that is, so to speak, undifferentiated.

I think, however, that to take this path would be unrealistic: a giving way to a learned archaism that today is anti-historical. An attentive consideration of the development of the anaphora in the history of the liturgy clearly shows that although conforming to a rigorous pattern determined by scripture and tradition, as their literary *genre* demands, and though there are sections which, from a theological point of view, are archaic, at the same time each anaphora was an expression— if fairly subdued in tone, in accordance with the style—of the state of theological reflection, of the interests and of the doctrinal preoccupations of its time, and sometimes of its author. We have come to realise that even in the outline anaphora of Hippolytus,[2] rudimentary and jealously traditional though it is, there are sections that clearly show the theological preoccupations of both its age and its author.[3]

The heavy emphasis given to the offering of the gifts in the Roman canon must be seen, then, in the light of the doctrinal

[2] I deliberately call it an "outline anaphora" and not simply an anaphora. In doing so I am following the intention of Hippolytus himself, who naturally presumes that the themes he does no more than mention will be expanded by anyone using the scheme he suggests.

[3] See B. Capelle, "Le Logos, Fils de Dieu, dans la théologie d'Hippolyte", in *Rech. de Théol. Ancienne et Médiev.*, 9 (1937), 109–24. While on this point, it is worth noting that Hippolytus includes the Church in his final doxology; in fact, this is general in the doxologies of his prayers.

interest of the time in which it was written. It was undoubtedly further stimulated, at least at its origin, by a preoccupation with dualism, which is to be seen, for example, in the eucharistic texts of Irenaeus.[4]

The stress put on the doctrine of the equality between Father, Son and Holy Spirit in many anaphoras, even that of Addaï and Mari (at least as it has come down to us), is an obvious reflection of the preoccupation with Arianism.

The development of the theology of the Holy Spirit, particularly as reflected in the epiclesis, originated in the fourth century difficulties over the concept of *pneuma.*

But the best example of the insertion of a theological outlook (though here it is a sound theology, deeply biblical and traditional) is to be found in the Byzantine anaphora of St Basil. It is now certain that it was edited by St Basil the Great himself on the basis of the Alexandrine anaphora previously attributed to him. Capelle has demonstrated[5] how St Basil's rewriting, while never ceasing to be thoroughly biblical in its mode of expression, is directed by the interests of precision and theological depth that closely reflect the preoccupations of both the Church and the author in this area. The result of his work was certainly not an impoverishment but an enrichment of the Alexandrine anaphora. Though the original enjoyed a considerable clarity by reason of its coherence, it is undoubtedly inferior to its Byzantine redaction. As Capelle writes: "The doctrinal transformation of the earlier watery outline shows in every line the firmness of the theologian and the ardour of the saint."[6] If the Byzantine anaphora of St Basil has a fault in comparison with the Alexandrine or the Byzantine anaphora of St John Chrysostom, it lies in its length, not in its being more theological.

Recent studies, sometimes even a simple reading of the text,

[4] See for example G. Joppich, *Salus Carnis. Eine Untersuchung in der Theologie des hl. Irenäus von Lyon*, Münsterschwarzach, 1965, 69–78.

[5] In "Les Liturgies 'Basiliennes' et Saint Basile" appended to J. Doresse and E. Lanne, *Un Témoin archaïque de la liturgie copte de St Basile* (Publications du Muséon, No. 47) Louvain, 1960, 45–74.

[6] Loc. cit., 74.

show that theological preoccupations are only too evident in anaphoras such as those contained in Book VIII of the *Apostolic Constitutions* or that of Serapion,[7] in the Syrian anaphora of Theodore of Mopsuestia, in the Alexandrine anaphora said to be by St Gregory, or in the fragments of that attributed to St Epiphanius.[8] The theological character, often strongly emphasized, in the abundant material of the variable parts of the Palaeo-Hispanic anaphora tradition is no less evident. And if this tradition was for a long period overshadowed by the Roman, it was not due to its variety and theological depth, in which it was greatly superior to the Roman. (Here we limit ourselves to a consideration of the values that formed part of the liturgy itself, taking no account of external factors.) Its subjection was due rather to its lack of sobriety and austerity in expression and to the length of its texts, which by comparison with the Roman liturgy appear overgrown and disordered.

My own opinion is that one of the major tasks in reinvigorating the Roman liturgy, which now extends to every region of the world, lies precisely in its assimilating in an organic way the many theological—and therefore spiritual and pastoral as well—attributes of the Palaeo-Hispanic liturgy while safeguarding the sobriety and austerity of expression which is the glory of the authentic tradition of Rome. I do not therefore consider it in any respect legitimate to yield to the temptation of archaism or archaeologism in the composition of new anaphoras for the Roman liturgy. To give just one example: I do not believe it is an acceptable solution to the problem of the epiclesis simply to reproduce that of Hippolytus, and my reason for holding this view is that Hippolytus' text is too vague and indistinct if we take account of subsequent theological development. After him the theology of the Holy Spirit and the formulation of the epiclesis

---

[7] See B. Capelle, "L'anaphore de Sérapion, essai d'exégèse", in *Le Muséon*, 59 (1946), 425–43. B. Botte: "L'Euchologe de Sérapion est-il authentique?" in *Oriens Christianus*, 48 (1964), 50–6.

[8] See B. Botte, "Fragments d'une anaphore inconnue attribuée à St Epiphane", in *Le Muséon*, 73 (1960), 311–15.

developed a great deal and there arose, and still exist, the well-known controversies between East and West; they cannot now be ignored.

In fact there must be accepted right from the start the principle that any new anaphora has the right and the obligation not only to be deeply theological but also to reflect, in its own particular way, the theological interests of the Church of our day. I say, of course, "in its own particular way", that is, taking into account its own literary *genre*. For we must remember that not only is it a prayer, it is a prayer of a well determined type, profoundly traditional and biblical in character. It is traditional with the tradition that expresses itself in the fixed or movable anaphoras or in the prayers closely linked to them: in the *orationes super oblata* and the prayers after the communion of the Roman sacramentaries, for example, or in the prayers which correspond to these in the Ambrosian, Gallican and Palaeo-Hispanic traditions. In fact, I would go so far as to say that an anaphora, precisely because it is a prayer meant to be frequently repeated and listened to, calls for a certain theological compactness, though this is presuming, naturally, that at the same time it satisfies the numerous other requirements of an anaphora.

(2) *Some general aspects of a theological nature in projects B and C*

In the documentation for the two projects B and C (given in Chapter V) it will be shown how the various theological themes brought out are drawn from scripture; here it is enough to call attention to three general aspects which are reflected in various places within the texts themselves:

(*a*) The emphasis given to the part, or rather the parts, played by the Holy Spirit in the work of salvation and, in particular, in the eucharistic mystery. This part is shown in the conclusion of the *Vere sanctus* (B6–8; C65–7, and already in C55 and C56 with respect to the sacrifice of Christ on the cross); in the epiclesis (B12–16; C69–75); in the *Supplices* where we pray for a fruitful communion (B51–60; C110–19).

(*b*) The emphasis given to the fact that in the Mass the Church offers above all Christ himself and his sacrifice and consequently offers herself in sacrifice. It is in fact true that the Church could not offer Christ in sacrifice did she not offer herself. But it is no less true that she could not offer herself in a sacrifice pleasing to God unless the offering took place in union with and along with the acceptance of the offering which Christ, as head of mankind and our pledge and substitute, makes of himself and us to God: in other words, if it did not take place in the shadow of the offering which the Church too makes of Christ in sacrifice to God. These ideas are the background for understanding lines B15–16; 21–4; 45–50; 53; 59–60; 80–1; 89–95; C74–5; 80–3; 104–9; 112; 118–19; 139–40; 148–54. The idea of the offering of the gifts is recalled as an action performed in the offertory and the *Oratio super oblata* (B45; C69; and it is included in B47; C106). In contrast with the emphasis which it receives at present in the Roman canon, however, it is relegated to a subordinate position.

(*c*) In variant C the following points should be especially noticed:

(i) the stress laid on the theme of creation in general, although, in accordance with the New Testament (Col. 1: 15–20), creation is seen in its general Christocentric framework: C15–24;

(ii) that given to man's task as God's regent in the world: C36–43.

(*d*) The sobriety that is necessary in the commemorations of the saints and the prayers of intercession: B61–86; C120–45.

V. Some observations on the style of projects B and C

(1) *The length of the texts*

An essential practical point is that the length of the texts proposed should not exceed that of the present Roman canon. This is how they compare:

(*a*) The present Roman canon, excluding the preface, contains 719 words; with the shortest of the prefaces (the ferial) it has 782; with the longest (those of Christ the King and St Joseph) it has 827.

(*b*) Project B without the preface contains 564 words, which is 155 less than the Roman canon without a preface.

(*c*) Project C with the preface has 849 words, which is 67 more than the Roman canon with its shortest preface, and 22 more than the Roman canon with its longest preface.

Project B is therefore considerably shorter than the Roman canon and project C somewhat longer, but by so little that I think it would be unreasonable to cut down its theological content on the pretext of shortening it.

(2) *The language and style*

(*a*) *Any eventual new canon in the Roman liturgy must be thought out and written in Latin, even if it is afterwards to be translated.*

The anaphora is a particular literary *genre*. To endow the Roman liturgy with a new canon it is essential that it should first be written in Latin. The question of translation and of possible adaptations of such texts to suit different modern languages is a very real problem, but one that must be left to a later stage.

This is not to claim that among peoples now using the Latin rite we should rule out for all eternity the direct composition of new texts, of new anaphoras even, in the vernacular, according to the capabilities of each language, a factor which would make each text proper to its own language group.

All I am saying is that when that happens, according to the measure in which it happens and wherever it happens, such an event will bring about something of a loosening of the bond between those peoples and the Roman liturgy. It will introduce a more or less rapid evolution towards a different type of liturgy. And if this process were to go on without respite it would lead firstly to the establishment, probably according to linguistic areas, of various groups each with its own character, within the Roman liturgy, and then even to what would in fact be new rites, differing from the Roman rite though derived from it.

Liturgists have always been agreed that among the elements which make up the unity of a liturgical rite the primary factor is the use of the same anaphora or anaphoras, even though perhaps in different languages, and that to abandon this is to abandon the unity of a rite in one of its substantial elements. This means, therefore, that if we wish to retain at least a substantial degree of unity among those who now use the Roman rite, we cannot abandon our unity in the same canon (or canons), though these may make use of different languages and allow sufficient flexibility for the needs of each tradition.

If we wish, then, to enrich the anaphora tradition of the Roman liturgy, the new texts must be thought out and written in Latin, leaving to the future the possibility of their being used in modern languages too with such adaptation to individual needs as this may entail.[9]

(*b*) *New compositions must observe the stylistic rules of the best Roman and Latin traditions of prayer.*

Not all Latin liturgical compositions are in this authentic prayer tradition: far from it. One need only think of many of the Gallican and Palaeo-Hispanic anaphoras, or even some of the later additions to the Roman tradition, particularly those from more recent times.

Every people is rightly concerned today that the vernacular liturgical language which is being created should be one which reflects its highest aspirations, traditional and actual, in the choice of words and in its periods and cadences. Similarly, if new

---

[9] The same equally applies to the prefaces, which are an integral part of the anaphora. On the other hand, it is obvious that where hymns are concerned much greater scope must be allowed for rewriting and for original composition in the language of the people. It is practically impossible to translate poetic compositions as hymns in such a way that they can be used in a vernacular liturgy.

compositions are called for in the Latin liturgy, first of all in the Mass, and especially in the canon, the heart of the entire liturgy, they must be modelled upon the style of the best Roman euchological tradition.[10] To do otherwise would lead to patchwork compositions unacceptable to anyone with a feeling for the style of Roman liturgical prayer and would be tantamount to a corruption of the Roman liturgy in a feature of some importance. All this goes for the prefaces too, of course; in fact, especially for the prefaces.[11]

The stylistic characteristics of the cadences of classical Roman euchology are now known, particularly as the result of the work of di Capua on the *cursus oratorio postclassico*, with its special reference to St Leo and the Roman sacramentaries.[12]

In order to absorb completely the style and mode of expression of the anaphora, it would appear essential to acquire a close familiarity not only with scripture and the general anaphora tradition of the Church, but also with the modern Roman canon, with the fragments, more or less probable, of early anaphoras, and with related texts,[13] especially the prefaces of the Roman tradition: those of the Leonine Sacramentary in the first place, and the *orationes super oblata* of the same tradition. Valuable elements can be gleaned for the same purpose from reading the texts of the Palaeo-Hispanic tradition—which retains notable

[10] For a general treatment of the Roman euchology see P. Alfonso, *L'eucologia romana antica*, Subiaco, 1931.

[11] The question of the observance of the Roman Latin style of formal prayer in new compositions coming into the Roman liturgy can be applied to other texts, starting with the *orationes* of the Mass. But it is undeniable that as regards the *orationes* of the Mass (and even more for certain texts of the Ritual and the Pontifical), the Roman liturgical tradition itself has been more flexible, frequently including texts which, while in Latin, have differed considerably in form from the authentic Roman euchological tradition. I am thinking not so much of certain medieval texts Gallican in origin as of some modern compositions, put together without any feeling for biblical or liturgical tradition and with no attention paid to the Roman prayer style, since all sense for it had been lost. See, for example, the *orationes* of the Mass of the Holy Name of Jesus.

[12] See di Capua, art. "Cursus", in *Enciclopedia cattolica italiana*, IV (1950), 1083–92, which gives a *résumé* of the results of enquiries made in this field, and the bibliography dealing with the question.

[13] See above, Texts, pp. 28–34.

traces of the early Roman tradition as well as those of Gaul and Milan.

From the documentation which concludes this study it can be seen how near to these liturgical traditions come the schemes proposed here; how close they are in similarity of thought and terminology.

The *cursus* in projects B and C

The scheme which follows indicates the observance of the *cursus* in the projects put forward here, showing the proportion of the whole taken up by each of the four possibilities in the liturgical *cursus*, namely:

(1) Metrical phrases in one of the four classical forms:

1. The *planus*, with its two variants:
   (*a*) –́ ⏑ / – –́ ⏓
   (*b*) –́ ⏑ – / –́ ⏓

2. The *tardus*, with its two variants:
   (*a*) –́ ⏑ / – ⏓́ ⏑ ⏓
   (*b*) –́ ⏑ – / ⏓́ ⏑ ⏓

3. The *velox*, with two variants in the second part
   ⏓́ ⏑ ⏓ / – ⏓ –́ ⏓
   or ⏓́ ⏑ ⏓ / ⏑ – –́ ⏓

4. The *trispondaicus*: –́ ⏑ / ⏑ ⏑ –́ ⏓ . The so-called *quarta forma*, the *spondaicus dachtylicus*, being considered a poorer form, is for the most part avoided:
   (⏓ ⏑ ⏓) –́ ⏑ / –́ ⏑ ⏓. or – ⏑ –́ ⏑ ⏓.

(2) *Clausole accentative*, exactly the same in form as the metrical phrases except that for particular reasons the strict rules of syllabic quantity have not been observed.

(3) Sticles or continuous commatic phrases, paired members, assonances, etc.

(4) Stiches or phrases composed of scriptural or traditional expressions that have become more or less fixed and in which there is no particular necessity for either *clausola* or commatic style.

The cursus in project B

Metrical phrases:

planus:	a	15	
	b	1	
tardus:	a	13	
	b	1	
velox		18	
trispondaicus		1	
quarta forma		—	
Total of metrical phrases			49

Clausole accentative:

planus:	a	2	
	b	2	
tardus:	a	5	
	b	—	
velox		4	
trispondaicus		1	
quarta forma		—	
Total of *clausole accentative*			14

TOTAL OF CLAUSOLE	63	
Commatic stiches	6	
Total of stiches with *cursus*		69
Stiches with scriptural quotations and traditional expressions		26
		—
TOTAL OF STICHES		95

The cursus in the proper parts of project C

Metrical phrases:

planus: a	7		
b	6		
tardus: a	4		
b	—		
velox	19		
trispondaicus	1		
quarta forma	—		
Total of metrical phrases	37		

Clausole accentative:

planus: a	5		
b	1		
tardus: a	1		
b	—		
velox	1		
trispondaicus	5		
quarta forma	1		
Total of *clausole accentative*	14		
TOTAL OF CLAUSOLE		51	
Commatic stiches		22	
Total of stiches with *cursus*			73
Stiches with non-commatic scriptural quotations			2
			—
TOTAL OF STICHES			75

CHAPTER V

The Documentation of Projects B and C from Scripture, the Fathers and Liturgy

The purpose of this chapter will be to indicate the various sources—biblical, patristic and liturgical—used in the preparation of projects B and C.

No liturgical text, least of all an anaphora, should give the impression of piecemeal construction. Preferably, it should be a homogeneous composition issuing almost spontaneously from a living familiarity with the Church's traditional language and thought.

In fact, any study of the anaphoras that have been used in the Church's worship will show quite clearly that their authors have made extensive use of the traditional expressions and ideas already familiar to them from earlier liturgies, and that they have often used one of these earlier texts as a model. A superficial reader might indeed gain the impression that these compositions have been put together rather like a mosaic.

For example, when we examine the parallel texts noted by Doresse and Lanne in their edition of the Coptic anaphora of St Basil, or when we read in the same volume the study of Dom B. Capelle on the "Basilian" liturgies and on St Basil; if we were to compare the Byzantine anaphoras of St Basil and of St John Chrysostum, or the Chaldean anaphora of Addaï and Mari with that of Theodore of Mopsuestia or with the Maronite anaphora of St Peter; when we place the text of the canon from the *De Sacramentis* alongside that of the present Roman canon, or compare the Gallican anaphora formulae with the Roman, Ambrosian and Hispanic ones; the immediate impression is of moving within a closed circle of the same ideas and expressions.

Nevertheless, we cannot deny that these compositions often possess originality, unity and depth. In the more fortunate cases, the authors have known how to make the traditional expressions their own, and how to enrich them with new meanings, in such a way that they have produced works which are perfectly and harmoniously constructed.

These observations apply equally to the prefaces and prayers of the Latin liturgy.

Moreover, this method of composition corresponds exactly to the rule laid down by the Second Vatican Council in its *Constitution on the Liturgy*, where we are told that "the new forms should to a certain extent be developed in an organic way from those already in existence" (art. 23).

I. The documentation of project B

II

1. Vere Sanctus. The various liturgical traditions have different ways of joining the *Sanctus* to the prayers that follow it in the canon.

The Roman liturgy follows the *Sanctus* with the *Te igitur*: a prayer which asks God to accept and to bless the offerings. Basically, this prayer is almost an epiclesis in form, although the epiclesis proper only appears later, in the *Quam oblationem.* The disadvantages of such a mode of procedure have already been mentioned above (p. 94): the words of the *Te igitur*, "we therefore ask you . . . to accept and bless these gifts", presuppose that the prayer immediately before has already mentioned the fact that gifts are being offered or, at least, the fact that God blesses and hallows; but this in fact is not the case. Does the *Te igitur*, then, date from a period when there was no *Sanctus*, and when there was a reference to the offering of gifts or to God's blessing in the first part of the canon, the preface? We might well be led to believe so, were we to study the structure of the solemn prayer of consecration from the Blessing of the Holy Oils in the Roman liturgy: a prayer preserved for us in the Gelasian Sacramentary, but which is in fact much more ancient. (See above, pp. 41, 98.)

In the Gallican liturgy, the transition from the *Sanctus* to the *Qui pridie* is made by means of a short prayer called the *Post Sanctus*, which begins with the words *Vere sanctus, vere benedictus* and which alludes in broad terms to the events in the life of the Lord, thus leading directly into the *Qui pridie*. This, at any rate, seems to have been the original character of the Gallican *Post Sanctus*, even though its purpose came to be changed later on. A good example of this Gallican *Vere sanctus* prayer is the *Post Sanctus* for Christmas Eve: "Truly holy and truly blessed is your Son, our Lord Jesus Christ, who manifested himself on earth while still remaining in heaven. On the eve of his passion, he . . ." (*Missale Gothicum*, n. 4). Occasionally, the *Post Sanctus* itself seems to develop into a consecratory epiclesis (cf. *Missale Gothicum*, nn. 271, 281, 423, 430). Typical examples of the Gallican *Vere sanctus* will be found in the *Missale Gothicum*, nn. 210, 482, 537; and in the *Missale Gothicum Vetus*, nn. 6, 44—these latter much influenced by the Roman canon.

In the Eastern liturgies, the canon continues after the *Sanctus* with "*Sanctus es . . .*", or with "*Vere sanctus es . . .*"; and then there follows an account of the whole history of salvation, from Adam to Christ. The passage from the account of Christ's life to the institution is made with the words: "And he, the night he was betrayed . . ."

The Egyptian liturgy has an original way of dealing with the problem. The *Sanctus* ends with the words: "Heaven and earth are full of your glory", there being no *Hosanna*. The text then continues to the effect that: truly heaven and earth are full of your glory; "therefore, Lord, fill this sacrifice also with your Holy Spirit" (and here there follows the consecratory epiclesis); "For the same Lord Jesus Christ, the night he was betrayed, . . ." (and then there follows the account of the institution). This arrangement also can be observed in the Greek anaphora of St Mark (cf. above p. 69), in the Coptic anaphora of St Cyril (Renaudot, I, 45), in the papyrus of Dêr-Balizeh (Roberts, 24), and in the Louvain Coptic fragment, n. 27 (Roberts, 25). It may also be found partially verified in the anaphora of Serapion, despite that anaphora's rather suspect peculiarities (cf. Funk, 174).

1–8. Cf. the Mozarabic *Post Sanctus* given in the *Liber Moz. Sacram.* at n. 178: "You are holy in a truly incomparable way, Lord; this is what every creature you have made declares about you, you who create and sanctify all things."

6–8. In order to show the traditional nature of the idea expressed in the words ... *quia per Filium tuum* ... *in infusione Spiritus Sancti vivificas et sanctificas universa,* we have only to recall to mind the common teaching of the Fathers that God always acts through his Son, the incarnate Word, in the presence of the Holy Spirit. (For the biblical, patristic and liturgical foundations of this idea cf. C. Vagaggini, *Il senso teologico della liturgia*, 4th ed., Rome, 1965, 202–42). Here are some typical examples:

"The Father does everything through the Word in the Holy Spirit" (St Athanasius, *Ad Serap.* I, 28; PG, 26, 596). "The Holy Spirit is the oil and the seal with which the Word anoints and signs all things ... Thus signed, we naturally become, as Peter says, sharers in the divine nature; in this way a created being can become a sharer of the Word in the Holy Spirit, and thus, through the Spirit, a sharer in God ... Now that we are called sharers in Christ and in God, we realise that our anointing and our sealing comes, not from our own created nature, but from the Son who, through the Spirit present in him, joins us to the Father" (St Athanasius, *Ad Serap.* I, 23; PG, 26, 585).

"Everything that God does for his creatures, whatever this action may be called, originates from the Father, passes through the Son, and is accomplished in the Holy Spirit" (St Gregory of Nyssa, *Ep. ad Ablavium*, PG, 45, 125 C).

"There can be no complete blessing except through the pouring out of the Holy Spirit" (St Ambrose, *De Spir. Sancto*, I, 7, 89; PL, 16, 755).

"Every grace and every perfect gift comes down on us from the Father, through the Son, in the Holy Spirit ... God the Father gives life to everything through the Son in the Holy Spirit" (St Cyril of Alexandria, *In Luc.*, 21, 19; PG, 72, 908 B D). "Our return to God, made through Christ our Saviour, can only take place with the help and the blessing of the Holy Spirit. For in receiving him who joins and, as it were, unites us to God, we become sharers and partners in the divine nature; we receive him through the Son, and in the Son we receive the Father" (St Cyril of Alexandria, *In Jo.*, VI, 10; PG, 74, 544 D ff.).

In the hymn of thanksgiving from the anaphora of Theodore of Mopsuestia, we have this text: "... for you are Lord and creator of all things, seen and unseen: who through your only Son, God and Word, who is the reflection of your glory, the splendour which radiates from you, and the image of your substance, have created and established heaven and earth with all they contain. And through your Holy Spirit of truth, who comes from you, Father, all rational natures, seen and unseen, are strengthened, sanctified and made worthy to offer praise to your adorable Godhead" (cf. above, p. 60).

There is also this prayer from the Mozarabic liturgy: "We pray you ... almighty Father ... to deign to bring to perfection by means of the Holy Spirit, those whom you created and redeemed through your Son" (*Liber Moz. Sacram.*, n. 785, 338).

This teaching has been endorsed by the Second Vatican Council. In connection with the celebration of the Eucharist among the Eastern Churches, it declares: "Through this celebration, the faithful united with their bishop gain access to God the Father; through the Son, the Word made flesh, who died and was glorified; and in the outpouring of the Holy Spirit. They thus attain communion with the Holy Trinity, and become 'sharers in the divine nature' (2 Peter 1:4)" (*Decree on Ecumenism*, art. 15. Cf. also *Constitution on the Church*, art. 2–4).

III

9–16. Cf. the Preface for the Consecration of the Oils in the Gelasian Sacramentary (above p. 41): "We therefore pray you, Lord, holy Father, almighty and eternal God, through Jesus Christ your Son, our Lord, be pleased to sanctify with your blessing the fat of this creature. Pour into it the might of the Holy Spirit through the power of your Son the Christ, from whose holy name this chrism has taken its name, this chrism with which you have appointed the priests, kings, prophets and martyrs, in order that it may be, for those reborn by water and the Holy Spirit, the chrism of salvation, making them sharers in eternal life and co-heirs of heavenly glory. Through Jesus Christ, your Son, our Lord."

In project B, the consecratory epiclesis has been placed immediately before the *Qui pridie*, the position which is occupied by the *Quam oblationem* in the Roman canon. The similarity between the Roman and the Egyptian liturgies on this point has already been mentioned (p. 140).

The formula used in the project is, in substance, that of the *Quam oblationem*. The principal difference lies in the explicit mention of the Holy Spirit, and also in the fact that the prayer ends with a reference to the Lord's command, thus allowing a natural transition to the *Qui pridie* (on this last point cf. the Byzantine anaphora of St Basil, Brightman, 327, lines 22–3). The explicit mention of the Holy Spirit at this point, far from being arbitrary, is in fact particularly fitting, even within the historical perspective of the *Quam oblationem*. Indeed, it was the general conviction from the fourth to the seventh century that the change of the bread and wine into the body and blood of Christ took place through the presence and the action of the Holy Spirit. This was in accord with the regular teaching of the Fathers, that any sanctification, whether of things or of persons, is achieved by God through the presence and the action of the Holy Spirit (cf. above, in the commentary on nn. 6–8; and also S. Salaville, "Epiclèse Eucharistique", in *Dict. de Théol. Cath.*, VI, 1 (1913), 234–47). There is also this testimony of Gelasius in his letter to

Elpidius of Volterra: "How will the heavenly Spirit, who is invoked for the consecration of the divine mystery, be able to come, when the priest who is asking for his presence is himself guilty of criminal deeds?" (Thiel, *Epist. Rom. Pont.*, I, 486). This text bears witness to the conviction that the "consecration of the divine mystery" only takes place through the coming of the Holy Spirit.

There is a further point to consider. In an anaphora, the various elements—thanksgiving, praise and prayer directed to God, blessing of the oblations—all inter-penetrate each other, and cannot really be separated. Even though, in a given passage, one element may predominate over the others, yet these other aspects are never completely absent. It is thus important, for a proper understanding of the nature of the epiclesis and of its proper place in the anaphora, to be aware that the whole anaphora, including its more strictly laudatory parts and the account of the institution, is basically a single prayer, and a prayer of a Trinitarian character: it is addressed to the Father, to him in whom all things originate; and it views the sanctification of all things as being achieved through the Son, in the outpouring of the Holy Spirit.

An instructive text in this regard is the following quotation from St Cyril of Alexandria. Commenting on the account of the institution, he writes: "Jesus gives thanks—that is, he addresses the Father in prayer, thus showing himself to be a recipient, as well as a donor, of the life-giving blessing that is about to be granted us. For every grace and every perfect gift comes to us from the Father through the Son in the Holy Spirit. This action (of Christ's) was therefore an example for us of the prayer we also should make when we are offering up the mystery of the holy and life-giving oblation. And this in fact is what we always do: we approach the holy altars giving thanks and praise to the Father, the Son and the Holy Spirit . . . God the Father gives life to everything through the Son in the Holy Spirit" (*In Luc.*, 22, 19; PG, 72, 908. Cf. also *In Matt.*, 26, 27; PG, 72, 452–3).

St Augustine writes: "How is it that both the Lord and Moses impart the blessing? Moses is not blessing on behalf of the

Lord, but it is the Lord himself who blesses by means of visible sacraments through his minister. As well as this, however, the Lord blesses by means of invisible grace through the Holy Spirit, in whom is the fruit also of the invisible sacraments. For, indeed, what would be the use of visible sacraments without the blessing of invisible grace?" (*Quaest in Hept.*, III, 84; PL, 34, 712).

St Isidore of Seville, writing about the sacraments, states: "If they produce fruit in the Church it is because of the Holy Spirit who remains within her, accomplishing the effect of the sacraments in a hidden way" (*Etym.*, VI, 19, 41; PL, 82, 255). Cf. the texts cited below at n. 54.

IV

17. Ipse enim, pridie quam pateretur, following the Western liturgical tradition. The Eastern liturgy has "*in qua nocte tradebatur*" ("the night he was betrayed"). In the composition of the project, it did not seem necessary to depart from the Roman tradition on this point, despite the latest theories concerning the precise date of the Last Supper. It must be conceded, however, that this is not an important question, and that one would not be changing the nature of the project by adopting the formula "the night he was betrayed".

18–19. Hoc magnum novi testamenti mysterium nobis voluit commendare. Cf. the Alexandrine anaphoras of St Basil, both Coptic and Greek: "Ascending into heaven . . . he left us this great mystery of love" (cf. above p. 52). The words "great mystery of love" are taken from I Tim. 3: 16, where, however, they refer to the incarnation. Their application to the Eucharist is nevertheless quite justified; cf. *Apostolic Constitution*, VIII, 12: "He broke it and gave it to his disciples saying, This is the mystery of the new covenant; take and eat" (Brightman, 20).

Cf. also the anaphora of Nestorius: ". . . he left us a memorial of our salvation, this mystery which we offer before you. For when the time had come when he was to be betrayed . . ." (Renaudot, II, 623).

And there is this text from the Abyssinian anaphoras: ". . . he showed them (the disciples) the covenant of the oblation of the mystery (*testamentum mysterii oblationis*)" (E. Hammerschmidt, *Studies in the Ethiopic Anaphoras*, Berlin, 1961, 119).

20. Mirabilium suorum memoriale perpetuum. The Eucharist, from the immediate significance of the words and signs used, is a memorial of the passion: the broken bread is the bruised body, the wine that is poured out is the blood that is shed. This is the meaning of the Byzantine anaphora of St Basil when it states: "He left us this memorial of his saving passion, which we now offer before you. For, at the moment when he was going to his freely-chosen death . . ." (Brightman, 327).

But, from the fact of concomitance, the Eucharist is also the memorial of the resurrection—there is now only one Christ, risen and glorious—and the memorial also of the incarnation, since the same Christ who suffered and rose again is the incarnate Word of God. Moreover, Christ's whole life was a movement towards his passion, death and resurrection; a movement also towards passing on to us the saving value of that passage of his through death to resurrection and glory: and that communication of salvation takes place primarily in the sacraments, and especially in the Eucharist. All the other sacraments, including baptism, are orientated towards the Eucharist. This truth is recalled by the Second Vatican Council in its *Decree on the Ministry and Life of Priests*: "The sacraments, as well as all the Church's ministries and apostolic undertakings, are all of them linked with the Holy Eucharist and are directed towards it. For the Eucharist contains the whole spiritual wealth of the Church: namely, Christ himself, our Pasch and our living bread. It is he who, through his flesh, now quickened and quickening by means of the Holy Spirit, gives life to men, inviting and leading them to offer, together with him, their own lives, their work, and indeed the whole of creation. We see, therefore, how the Eucharist is both the source and the goal of all evangelization: the catechumens are gradually introduced to a full participation, while the faithful, sealed through baptism and confirmation, are themselves fully inserted into the body of Christ through their reception of the Eucharist" (art. 5).

Cf. also, the Council's *Decree on Ecumenism*, art. 15. quoted above, p. 156.

Against this background, it is easy to see how the Eucharist may well be called the "perpetual memorial" of the marvels accomplished for us by Christ.

21–24. In support of this passage, we have the following texts: "He (Christ) not only offered himself for our sakes, but he also wishes to be offered up by us in the mysteries of his body and blood, so that where we find life, there we may also find forgiveness, and that in offering him, we may ever offer ourselves" (*Liber Moz. Sacram.*, ed. Ferotin, n. 367, 172).

"On the cross . . . he offered himself as a spotless victim to you, and he commanded that, in his memory, we his humble servants should unceasingly offer him up" (Ibid., n. 744: *Post pridie*).

"On the eve of his passion, he instituted the form of a perpetual sacrifice": this formula is conserved for us by Hincmar of Rheims (PL, 125, 610), though G. Morin considers it to be of African origin (*Rev. Bénédictine*, 41 (1929), 70–3). Cf. also the following preface from the Missale Gothicum: "It is right and proper . . . Father of our Lord Jesus Christ, who instituted the form of a perpetual sacrifice by first offering himself as victim and commanding that this victim should be offered up" (n. 514).

"Being present around your altar, O Lord of divine power, we glory in acknowledging the spotless Lamb, who offered himself for sacrifice on our account. Through the heavenly sacraments of his body and blood, which have redeemed us from our sins, we nourish ourselves for eternal life" (Gelasian Sacramentary, n. 482).

". . . He left in our hands the pledge of his holy body, in order to be with us through his body, and to be always within us through his power" (Fragment from a Chaldaic anaphora, given in Brightman, 515, 23 ff.).

"... Your Son, Jesus Christ, promised to be with his faithful ones to the end of time: let him not then deprive us, whom he has redeemed, of the sacraments of his corporeal presence, nor take away the blessings of his majesty" (Missale Francorum, n. 145. Cf. PL, 78, 187).

28. Tibi gratias agens, benedixit, fregit... Another possible formula would have been "*Tibi gratias agens, te benedixit* ..."; but, according to the whole of liturgical tradition, the "giving of thanks" is at the same time a praising of God pronounced over the bread and the wine, and thus a blessing of those elements (cf. P. Audet, "Esquisse Historique...", in *Rev. Bibl.*, 65 (1958), 372–99): St Justin calls it "eucharistic bread" (*Apol.*, I, 65, n. 5; PG, 6, 824 B). This is why St Paul can call the cup the object of the blessing: "The cup of blessing which we bless, is it not a communion in the blood of Christ? The bread which we break, is it not a communion in the body of Christ?" (I Cor. 10: 16).

30. Quod pro vobis tradetur, according to the Vulgate text of I Cor. 11: 24. The Greek text reads "which is for you". The three variations of this insert either "broken", "bruised", or "given". The Greek text of Lk. 22: 19 has "given", the Vulgate rendering being: *Quod pro vobis datur*. Mark and Matthew have only "This is my body".

The various anaphoras adopt one or the other of the scriptural readings.

(1) "*Bruised*" (Greek *thruptomenon*, Latin *quod confringetur*) is found in Hippolytus, in the Apostolic Constitutions, and in the *De Sacramentis* of St Ambrose.

(2) "*Broken*" (Greek *klômenon*, Latin *quod frangitur*) is found in the Byzantine anaphora of St Basil, in the Greek and Syriac anaphoras of St James, in the anaphora of Serapion, in the Coptic anaphora of St Basil (Renaudot), in an Abyssinian anaphora (Brightman, 232: "which is broken for you in forgiveness of sins"),

in the Syriac Jacobite anaphora (Brightman, 87), in the anaphora of Theodore of Mopsuestia, and in the fragment attributed to Epiphanius (*Le Muséon*, 75 (1960), 299).

(3) "*Which is for you*", from 1 Cor. 11: 24, is found in the Byzantine anaphora of St John Chrysostom.

(4) "*Given*", from Lk. 22: 19, is found in the Dêr-Balizeh papyrus, and in the Mozarabic *Qui pridie* (but there in the Vulgate form of 1 Cor. 11: 24: "*quod pro vobis tradetur*").

(5) "*Broken and distributed for you and for many in remission of sins*" is found in the Greek Alexandrine anaphora of St Basil, in the Greek anaphora of St Mark, in the Coptic anaphora of St Cyril, and in the Syriac anaphora of the Twelve Apostles.

(6) The Coptic anaphora of St Basil (according to Doresse-Lanne) has the same text as the one immediately above, but without the word "broken".

(7) "*This is my body*", from the Gospels of Matthew and Mark, is found in the present Roman canon, as well as in the Ambrosian canon for Maundy Thursday. The formula used by the Gallican liturgy is not known. It is therefore evident that the Roman canon holds a solitary position among the various anaphoras. The drawbacks of such a situation have already been pointed out above (p. 101 ff.).

31–39. Hoc facite in meam commemorationem. This phrase has been inserted after each of the two consecrations, for a number of reasons. Primarily, because this is the arrangement we find in 1 Cor. 11: 24–25; in addition, for the sake of parallelism, since liturgical tradition has always tended to a symmetrical arrangement of the actions and words of the two consecrations; and finally, because this arrangement adds more force to the Lord's command.

On this point, liturgical tradition does, in fact, vary.

(1) *The Egyptian liturgy*. The papyrus of Dêr-Balizeh does not contain the Lord's command, but instead, after the second

consecration, it continues: "Whenever you eat this bread and drink this cup you announce my death and you commemorate me. We announce your death, and we proclaim your resurrection . . .". The other anaphoras in use in the Egyptian Church place the Lord's command after each of the two consecrations, the second one continuing with: "Whenever you . . .".

(2) *The Antiochene liturgy*. The Lord's command comes after the second consecration only, and it continues with: "Whenever you . . .". The Byzantine anaphora of St John Chrysostom has neither the Lord's command nor the subsequent formula. The Syriac anaphora of the Twelve Apostles has the command, but not the formula.

(3) *The Western liturgy*. The anaphora of Hippolytus does not have the Lord's command as such, but it does have, after the second consecration: "When you do this, do it in memory of me" (cf. above p. 27; ed. Botte, 16–17). The *De Sacramentis* does not have the command either but, after the second consecration, it has: "Each time you do this, you will do it in memory of me until I return" (cf. above p. 33; ed. Botte, p. 116). The present Roman canon, of course, does not have the command but, after the second consecration, it has: "As often as you do these things, you will do them in memory of me." The normal Ambrosian canon, as well as that for Maundy Thursday, has this formula: ". . . also commanding them and saying to them: Whenever you do this, you will be doing it in my commemoration: you will be proclaiming my death, announcing my resurrection, and hoping for my coming until I come to you again from heaven". The Mozarabic canon repeats the Lord's command after each of the two consecrations, and at the end adds: "Every time you eat this bread or drink this cup, you will be proclaiming the death of the Lord until he comes from heaven in glory" (cf. above p. 48, and Lietzmann, *Messe und Herrenmahl*, 3rd edition, Berlin, 1955, 48–9).

In this suggested project, the Lord's command having been repeated after each of the two consecrations, it was not considered necessary to add also the text from 1 Cor. 11: 26: "Whenever you eat this bread, etc." These words are obviously a comment by Paul, and not the Lord's own words; also, the basic idea will be taken up by the anamnesis, nn. 40–44.

In order to add more force to the Lord's command, the project uses the imperative form, following the text of 1 Cor. 11: 24–25, and not the future form, as in the present Roman canon, which has: *Haec quotiescumque feceritis in mei memoriam facietis*. The only advantage of the wording used in the Roman canon is that of the *cursus* (a sentence split into two parallel parts, the first part ending with the metrical clause of the *tardus*, the second with that of the *velox*). Indeed, it must be admitted that the particular ending used in the suggested project: . . . *meam commemorationem*, having a final word of seven syllables, would never be found in the better Roman prose.

Nevertheless, it should be recognised that in the present case we are dealing with a biblical text which contains the very words of Christ, and the particular word in question does in fact indicate the underlying theological idea far better than others. Besides, even in Latin, this word does have a certain solemnity about it. All things considered, therefore, it did not seem necessary to sacrifice this Pauline expression merely to suit the rules of the *cursus*. And anyhow, *commemorationem* will be found at the end of the sentence in the Hispanic anaphora.

33. . . . Ex vino mixtum et aqua. As a parallel to: "He took bread, blessed it, and broke it", a large number of anaphoras, at the second consecration, state that Jesus "poured wine and water into the cup, blessed it", etc. (cf. F. Hamm, *Die liturgischen Einsetzungsberichte*, Münster i. W., 1928, 52–5). The only exceptions to this among the better-known anaphoras are those of Dêr-Balizeh, of Serapion, of Nestorius, and the Byzantine anaphora of St John Chrysostom; besides, surely, that of Addaï and Mari, although in its present state this does not contain the account of the institution.

The expression normally used in the anaphoras is this: "Having taken the cup, and when he had poured wine and water into it, he blessed it", etc. Some anaphoras (that of Dêr-Balizeh, the Coptic and Greek Alexandrine anaphoras of St Basil, that of St Cyril, and the Syriac anaphora of the Twelve Apostles) continue to the effect that Christ, having blessed the cup, tasted it or drank from it himself before giving it to the apostles.

St Irenaeus relates a similar tradition: "The Lord . . . after having given thanks with the cup in his hands, and when he had drunk from it . . ." (*Adv. Haer.*, V, 33, 1; PG 7, 1212).

The liturgical and theological value of the tradition that explicitly mentions Christ pouring wine and water into the cup resides not only in the familiar tendency to present the two consecrations in a parallel manner but, more importantly, in the way that the sacrificial value of the eucharistic sign is thus emphasised. Just as the *broken* bread signifies the bruised body, so does the wine that is *poured out* signify the blood that is shed. This is undoubtedly the meaning of Jesus' actions and words concerning the cup and the blood "shed for you and for many in remission of sins".

However, it is impossible to prove historically that Jesus would have himself filled the cup before passing it around the company. And it is for this reason that it has seemed preferable to use the words: "taking the cup filled with wine and water", rather than: "taking the cup, he filled it with wine and water".

V

42. Gloriosissimae passionis. Cf. the *De Sacramentis* (IV, 6, 27): "Calling to mind therefore his most glorious passion". This concept is particularly stressed by St John's Gospel, which insists on the fact that Christ manifested his glory in a special way through his passion. Cf. also, what Paul has to say about the folly and the glory of the cross (1 Cor. 1: 18–2: 3).

43. Mirabilis resurrectionis et ascensionis in caelum. Cf. the Leonine Sacramentary, n. 1137: ". . . through his wonderful resurrection there passed away death for the redeemed and there sprang up life for believers". The Litany of the Saints also contains the phrase: "Through your marvellous ascension."

44. Sed et alterum adventum eius praestolantes. This phrase underlines the eschatological character of the Eucharist, which, in 1 Cor. 11:26, is expressed in the words "until he comes".

The explicit mention in the anamnesis of the Lord's glorious return at the end of time is found very frequently among the various anaphoras: that of the Apostolic Constitutions, the Byzantine anaphora of St Basil, the Byzantine anaphora of St John Chrysostom, the Greek anaphora of St Mark, the Greek and Coptic Alexandrine anaphoras of St Basil, the Coptic anaphora of St Cyril, and the Syriac anaphora of the Twelve Apostles. Many of these anaphoras also contain, immediately after the consecration of the cup, the formula: "Whenever . . . until I come", in addition to this later mention in the anamnesis.

Let us now turn to the Western liturgies. We find only rare allusions to the Second Coming in the anamnesis of the Hispanic liturgy, although this rite does in fact point out very clearly the eschatological aspect of the celebration of the Eucharist by having, after the consecration of the cup, the formula: "Whenever . . . until he comes from heaven in glory." The same is substantially true concerning the Ambrosian anaphora for Maundy Thursday.

The present Roman canon appears to be the anaphora least marked with an eschatological spirit, since it has neither the formula "Whenever you . . . until I come" after the consecration of the cup, nor any mention of the Second Coming in the anamnesis. Our suggested project seeks to enrich the Roman liturgy in this matter.

45. Adimus cum fiducia ad thronum misericordiae tuae. Cf. Heb. 4:14–16: "Having therefore a great high priest who has passed through the heavens, Jesus the Son of God, let us hold fast to our profession of faith . . . Let us approach with confidence therefore the throne of grace, so that we may obtain mercy and find grace to help us in our need."

46. Gratias agentes offerimus tibi hoc sacrificium incruentum. The words *gratias agentes* underline once more, even at this particularly sacrificial part of the Mass, the sacrifice's thanksgiving, or "eucharistic" aspect.

"*Unbloody sacrifice*": this expression is quite common in anaphoras: cf. *anaimakton thusian* in the Greek anaphora of St James (Brightman, 53; ibid., 87–9 and 437 for the Syriac Jacobite liturgy and for the Armenian liturgy).

47. De tuis donis ac datis. This idea is biblical in origin: "Everything comes from you, and what we have given you is what we have already received from your hand" (1 Chron. 29: 14). In the Greek anaphoras, the formula *ta se ek tôn sôn* is frequently found at this point in the anamnesis, e.g. the Byzantine anaphoras of St Basil and of St John Chrysostom; the Greek and Coptic Alexandrine anaphoras of St Basil; and the Greek anaphora of St Mark, preserved for us in the Coptic anaphora of St Cyril.

The meaning of the formula is this. The bread and wine are taken as a symbol and, as it were, a sample of everything that the creator has given us, and which we are now spontaneously offering back to him in grateful recognition of his goodness and of his sovereign dominion.

By the use of this formula, therefore, we are joining on to the theology of sacrifice the whole idea of the cosmic value of the Eucharist, a theme magnificently developed by St Irenaeus in the course of his polemic against the Gnostics. The following texts from St Irenaeus' writings imply a whole theology on the offering of gifts, a theology which already contains the seeds of those great themes which the different liturgies, especially the Roman one, were later to develop:

"He gave directions to his disciples to offer to God the first-fruits of his own created things—not as though he needed them, but so that they might not be sterile or ungrateful. Thus he took bread, which comes from creation, and he gave thanks, saying: 'This is my body.' The cup of wine, too, which comes from the creation to which we belong, he declared to be his blood; and he taught that this was the new offering of the new covenant. It is this offering that the Church has received from the apostles, and which she now offers throughout the world to God—to him who gives us our very food as the first-fruits of the gifts he makes to us under the new covenant.

"All this was foretold by Malachi, one of the Twelve Prophets, in these terms: 'I do not take pleasure in you, says the Lord Almighty, and I will not accept sacrifice from your hands. But from the rising of the sun to its setting-place my name is glorified among the nations, and in every place incense and a pure sacrifice is offered to my name: for my name is great among the nations, says the Lord, the Almighty.' This obviously meant that the former people would cease to make offerings to God, and that instead a pure sacrifice would be offered to him everywhere, and his name would be glorified among the nations" (*Adv. Haer.*, IV, 17, n. 5; SC, 100, 590 ff.).

"Since the Church makes her offering with single-mindedness, her gift is properly reckoned as a pure sacrifice before God . . . For it is fitting that we should present an offering to God, and always witness to our gratitude to our creator, by offering him the first fruits of his creation, with a pure mind and with a faith without hypocrisy, with a firm hope and with a burning charity. And it is the Church alone who offers this pure oblation to the creator, by offering to him with thanksgiving, things taken from his own creation . . . But how can they (the Gnostic heretics) possibly claim that the eucharistic bread is the body of their Lord, and the cup his blood, if at the same time they deny that he is the Son of the world's creator, that is his Word—through whom trees bear fruit, springs flow, and through whom 'the earth gives first the blade, next the ear, and then the full corn in the ear'?

"Again, how can they possibly say that our flesh goes to corruption and does not receive life, when it is nourished by the body and blood of the Lord? Therefore, let them either change their way of thinking or let them abstain from offering these things. As for our way of thinking—it agrees with the nature of the

Eucharist, and it is in turn confirmed by the Eucharist. For in the Eucharist, we offer to God what is his own, congruously proclaiming the communion and unity between flesh and Spirit. For just as the bread, produced from the earth, is no longer ordinary bread after it has received the invocation of God, but is the Eucharist—made up of two realities, one earthly and the other heavenly; in the same way, our bodies are no longer corruptible after they have received the Eucharist, but now possess the hope of resurrection.

"In fact, we offer to God, not as though he needed anything, but in order to give him thanks for his gifts and in this way to sanctify the whole of creation. For although God does not need anything from us, yet we do need to offer something to God. For although he does not need anything, yet he does accept our good works—and for a purpose: so as to be able to give us in return his very own goods . . . Therefore, although he stands in no need of these things, yet he does ask them of us, and for our own sakes—so that we may not be unfruitful. This was why the Word himself commanded the people to make offerings: he himself did not need them, but it was so that they might learn in this way to serve God. In the same way, therefore, he wants us to offer our gifts at the altar regularly and often.

"There is then an altar in heaven, to which our prayers and offerings are directed; and there is also a temple there, as John says in the Apocalypse: 'The temple of God was opened', as well as a tabernacle: 'Behold, he says, the tabernacle of God with men' " (*Adv. Haer.*, IV, 18, nn. 4–6; SC, 100, 606 ff.) (PG, 7, 1023–4; 1029 ff.).

As we have already had occasion to remark (above, p. 87), we find this particular way of regarding the offering of the oblations quite strongly marked in the present Roman canon. It is also closely connected, in the Roman liturgy, with the theme of the "commercium", or the exchange. In the eucharistic celebration, by the presentation of our offerings, we are offering God something that in fact comes to us from God, but which he has given us as our own. In a kind of sacred exchange, God accepts our gift, and then returns it to us, in an infinitely more precious form, because now it has been changed into the body and blood of Christ—and through receiving this, we are filled with every heavenly blessing. For the eucharistic application of this theme of the exchange cf. the Leonine Sacramentary, nn. 88, 228, 433, 551, 560, 908; and the Gelasian Sacramentary, nn. 165, 251.

In the context of our project, the *de tuis donis ac datis* applies not only to the material goods, as in Irenaeus' cosmic perspective, but also to Christ himself, inasmuch as he is the greatest of the *dona ac data* given us by God. The twelfth century Armenian author, Nerses Lampron, was thus quite justified when, in commenting on the offertory formula *tua ex tuis offerimus per omnia et pro omnibus*, he wrote: "Then the priest adds, This gift which I offer you, Lord, as though it were a man taken from among us and of our own nature, this gift is your Son, whom you gave birth to in an inexpressible way. And although we, your servants, count him as one of ourselves, we also confess that he is God, and equal to you. And now we offer him again to you, this Son whom you have given us, as an oblation for everyone and as a gift of reconciliation" (quoted by S. Salaville, under "Epiclèse" in *Dict. de Théol. Cath.*, VI, 1 (1913), 255, which refers to Avechian, *Sulle Correzioni dei Libri Ecclesiastici Armeni*, Venice, 1868, 343).

48–50. Hostiam puram, hostiam sanctam, immaculatam hanc hostiam pro saeculi vita. This *hostia* is of course the Victim, that is to say, Christ himself. Cf. n. 52, which would remove any possibility of doubt in the interpretation of this particular passage, nn. 48–50.

The idea that the principal object of the sacrificial offering is Christ himself and his sacrifice will be found affirmed quite clearly in the patristic writings of the fourth and fifth centuries. We have already quoted (p. 113) the perfectly explicit text of St Cyril of Jerusalem in this regard, contained in his Fifth Mystagogical Catechesis (n. 8). The following passage from St Ambrose is equally confirmative: "We have seen the prince of priests coming to us; we have seen him and heard him offering his blood for us. We priests follow him as well as we can so that we may offer the sacrifice for the people, we who are of scanty merit, but who take on dignity through the sacrifice. For although we cannot now see Christ offering, nevertheless it is he himself who is being offered here on earth whenever the Body of Christ is offered. Indeed, it is obvious that it is he who is offering through us, since it is by his word that that which is offered is sanctified" (*En. In Ps.*, 38, n. 25; PL, 14, 1102).

St John Chrysostom is no less clear: "We do indeed make an offering, although in fact what we are doing is recalling to mind his death. For there is always a single victim—not many. Why one, and not many? Because the victim has been offered once and for all—since it was taken up into the holy of holies. That sacrifice was a figure of ours, just as ours is a figure of that one.

"For it is always the same thing that we offer—not one sheep today, and a different one tomorrow, but always the same. This is the reason why our sacrifice is one. But does it not follow that, since Christ is offered in many places, there are many Christs? By no means—it is the one and the same Christ who is offered everywhere, who is complete both in this place and in that, always the one and the same body. Since, therefore, it is the one body which is being offered in many different places, and not many bodies, then our sacrifice is also a single one. He who offered that victim which purifies us is our high priest: we also offer that same victim which he offered then, for it can never be exhausted. And what we do now, we do in memory of what was done then—'Do this in memory of me', he said. We do not offer a victim other than that of our high priest, but always the very same, or rather we commemorate his sacrifice" (*Hom.* 17 *in Heb.*, IX, 3; PG, 63, 131).

To go into the historical question of the progressive clarification of this idea in the anaphoras would be out of place here.

Certainly, it has to be admitted that that which is referred to in the anamnesis of most anaphoras as being offered, is in fact the bread and wine, over which the invocation of the Holy Spirit is going to be made immediately afterwards in the consecratory epiclesis, so that he might change them into the body and blood of Christ. Whereas, on the other hand, any reference to the idea that Christ's body and blood are being offered is very much rarer —despite the fact that, according to these same anaphoras, they are certainly present on the altar, at least after the consecratory epiclesis.

We find this state of affairs for example, in the Apostolic Constitutions (Brightman, 20–1); in the Byzantine anaphoras of St Basil and of St John Chrysostom, with their formula: "offering you these things which are yours and which come from you, in all and for all", which comes immediately before the consecratory epiclesis (ibid., 329); in the Alexandrine anaphoras of St Basil, both Greek (above, p. 54; and Renaudot, II, 67) and Coptic (Doresse-Lanne, 18–21); in the Greek anaphora of St Mark (Renaudot, I, 141); in the Coptic (Brightman, 178) and Ethiopian Jacobite (ibid., 233) anaphoras.

Nevertheless, the idea that the body and blood of Christ are being offered in sacrifice is reasonably explicit in a good number of anaphoras. We find it very clearly expressed, for example, in the anaphora of Theodore of Mopsuestia:

"In the presence of your glorious Trinity, and with a humble heart and penitent spirit, we offer this living and holy sacrifice, which is the mystery of the Lamb of God who takes away the sins of the world, asking and praying in your presence, Lord, that your adorable divinity may find it pleasing and that through your mercy this pure and holy oblation, by which you are appeased and reconciled, may be accepted for the sins of the world" (Cf. above, p. 64, and Renaudot, 11, 613).

In several other anaphoras, this same idea is expressed in perhaps a less explicit, but still quite real, way. This is surely the case when an anamnesis refers to the offering of "the fearsome and unbloody sacrifice", as in the Greek anaphora of St James (Brightman, 53), in a Syrian Jacobite anaphora (ibid., 87–9), and in an Armenian anaphora (ibid., 437). The same is true in those cases where an anamnesis will speak of the offering of the "antitypes" of Christ's body and blood, as in the Byzantine anaphora of St Basil (Brightman, 329), and in the *De Sacramentis*: "Grant us that this oblation be approved, and be counted as fitting and acceptable, since it is the figure of the body and blood of our Lord Jesus Christ. Who, on the eve of his passion . . ." (IV, 21; B. Botte, 115).

In the present Roman canon, we have the following text: "And so, calling to mind . . . we offer you, from the gifts which you yourself have given us, the perfect victim, the holy victim, the unblemished victim, the holy bread and the cup of everlasting salvation." These words would seem to be applicable both to the offering of the bread and wine, and to that of the body and blood of Christ.

And, to sum up, this indeed seems to have been the outlook in this matter of the earlier writers, in conformity with the idea of the *commercium*, or sacred exchange (already explained above, pp. 87 ff.): what is being offered in sacrifice to God is the bread and wine—taken from among the gifts he has given us, and considered as symbols of ourselves and of all things—but also, and at the same time, it is Christ in person.

In our project, this basic idea will be found expressed in nn. 46–60, nn. 59 and 60 being direct references to the offering of ourselves.

Profound reflection on the theology of the *commercium* will show that, for us, offering Christ and his sacrifice to God means consciously uniting ourselves to the offering which Christ, our head, makes of himself, of us, and of the whole world to God (cf. above, p. 88). Such an offering cannot therefore take place without our offering ourselves; and inversely, we cannot offer ourselves in sacrifice without offering Christ—which we do by uniting ourselves in heart and mind to the offering which he made, and never ceases to make, of himself, of us, and of the whole world. Indeed, no offering is acceptable to God unless it is made part of the offering which Christ makes of himself and of us to the Father.

This would not be the appropriate place to demonstrate how, in the ancient liturgies, one often finds, even outside the anaphoras themselves, this basic idea that in the Mass, Christ himself and his sacrifice are being offered (on this point, one can still consult with profit Muratori, *Dissertationes de Rebus Liturgicis*, PL, 74, 989 ff).

VI

52. Ut agnoscens victimam cuius voluisti intercessione placari. The following two texts from the Mozarabic liturgy are pertinent here: "Almighty God, acknowledge this victim through whose intercession you have been appeased" (*Lib. Moz. Sacr.*, n. 645, *Post pridie*); "We offer you, O God, this spotless victim which was brought into the world by the maternal womb of an undefiled virgin, which was given birth to by purity, engendered by sanctity, and begotten by integrity. For this spotless victim still lives, and living, is continually sacrificed. This is the only victim which could appease God, since it itself is God. It is this which we offer you, almighty Father, on behalf of your holy Church, for pardon of a sinful world, for the betterment of our souls, for the healing of all those who are sick, and for the peace and forgiveness of the departed faithful" (ibid., n. 112, *Post nomina*).

53. In oblationem ecclesiae tuae benignus aspicias. Cf. Hippolytus: "We ask you to send your Holy Spirit down upon the offerings of your holy Church" (*Trad. Apostol.*, n. 4, above, p. 27, and B. Botte, 16). Cf. also, the Leonine Sacramentary: "This oblation of the whole Church which rejoices with me . . ." (n. 959, for the anniversary of a bishop); "May this oblation of your Church, Lord, be commended by the apostolic prayers of John the Evangelist, by whose glorious preaching she has been instructed" (n. 1280, *Super oblata*).

54. Tui spiritus operatione sacratam. Cf. what was said above concerning nn. 6–8 and nn. 9–16. It will be sufficient here to quote the following texts: "Look with mercy upon the offering of your people, Lord, for it is not immersed in a fire alien to your altars, nor in the blood of brute beasts, but our sacrifice is now, through the working of the Holy Spirit, the body and blood of the priest himself" (Leonine Sacramentary, n. 1246, *Super oblata*). St Augustine says that the bread of the Eucharist "is not sanctified so as to become such a great sacrament, without the working of the Holy Spirit" (*De Trin.*, 1, 7, 87). St Thomas Aquinas also says that the Eucharist "is consecrated through the Holy Spirit" (*In* 1 *Cor.* 12, *Lect.* 3; Marietti n. 734).

56–58. Ut quotquot Filii tui corpus et sanguinem sumpserimus, eodem Spiritu Sancto copiosius repleamur et unum corpus et unus spiritus efficiamur in eo. This is the customary request for a fruitful communion, which is contained in every eucharistic epiclesis. In the present Roman canon, and perhaps also in the Egyptian anaphoras (cf. above, p. 69), this request has become separated from the consecratory epiclesis and is placed instead after the account of the institution.

The fruit hoped for from communion in the body and blood of Christ is generally described as being a sharing in the Holy Spirit, present and active in the consecrated oblations.

Hippolytus expresses the idea in this way: "We ask you to send your Holy Spirit down upon the offerings of your Holy Church. Gathering together all those who receive these mysteries, grant that they may be filled with the Holy Spirit, and that their faith may thus be strengthened in your truth. So may we praise and glorify you . . ." (*Trad.*, n. 4., cf. above, p. 27, and Botte, p. 17).

In the Coptic Alexandrine anaphora of St Basil (as given in Doresse-Lanne, 20–2), we have the following text: "We pray you, our God, . . . that your Holy Spirit might come down on us, and on these offerings which you have given us, in order to sanctify them and make them into the holy nourishment destined for your holy people. Make us all worthy of sharing in these holy mysteries of yours, so that our bodies and souls may be sanctified, thus being formed into but a single body and a single spirit, that we may find a place among the company of all your saints whom from the beginning you have found pleasing."

From among the Mozarabic and Gallican epicleses, we have selected the following: ". . . May they be changed into the likeness of the body and the blood of our Lord Jesus Christ, so that they may be beneficial for everyone: may they sanctify with a heavenly blessing those who share in these living and life-giving sacraments, and may they unite with the perfection of the power of their head those who have been made members of your only Son" (*Liber. Moz. Sacram.*, n. 441, *Inlatio*, 197, 23 ff.).

"May an odour of sweetness go up before your divine majesty from this heavenly altar of yours, through the ministry of your Angel: and may your Holy Spirit come down on those holy sacrifices and sanctify the offerings and the prayers of those who are present and who are offering . . . so that when we partake of this body, we may be receiving a goodly medicine . . ." (ibid., n. 627, *Post pridie*, 262, 14 ff.).

"Recalling to mind the Lord's glorious passion and his resurrection from the regions of death, we offer you, Lord, this spotless, perfect and unbloody victim, this holy bread and this saving cup, beseeching you to pour out your Holy Spirit upon us—we who eat and drink of that which is to give us eternal life and your kingdom" (*Missale Gothicum*, *Missa Dominicalis* V, *Post secreta*, n. 527).

59. Ita tibi munus aeternum nos ille perficiat. Cf. this *Oratio super oblata* from the Leonine Sacramentary: "In your goodness, Lord, sanctify these gifts; accept the spiritual offering of this Eucharist, and make of ourselves an eternal offering to you" (n. 216). This prayer will be found in many sacramentaries and also in the Roman Missal, in the Mass for Whit Monday.

VII

66. Quorum meritis et intercessione perpetuo apud te confidimus adiuvari. Cf. the text from St Cyril of Jerusalem, *Catech.* 23, *Mystag.* 5, 9; PG, 33, 1116 A–B, quoted above on

p. 113. The Roman canon has: "Through their prayers and merits, give us always the help of your protection."

The Greek Alexandrine anaphora of St Basil has: "Through their prayers and intercession, have mercy on us also and save us, because of your name which is invoked upon us" (Renaudot 1, 70). The Coptic Alexandrine anaphora of St Basil has: ". . . and especially of the holy and glorious ever-virgin Mary, mother of God; have mercy on us because of her prayers, and save us because of your holy name which is invoked upon us" (Doresse-Lanne, 26). The Byzantine anaphoras of St Basil and of St John Chrysostom have: "Above all, for the all-holy, spotless and highly blessed ever-virgin Mary, our Lady and mother of God . . . and for all the saints, through whose prayers do you protect us, O God" (Brightman, 330–2). The Greek anaphora of St James has: "All your saints who have been since the world began: not that we are worthy to make remembrance of those blessed people, but we do it so that they, for their part, will remember us wretched people before your terrible and frightening tribunal, and that we may thus find mercy before you, Lord" (ibid., 57).

VIII

67. Ecclesiae tuae toto orbe diffusae. Cf. the documentation given in B. Botte, *Le canon* . . ., 33 ad n. 111: Optatus of Milevis (VII, 2, 12; CSEL, 26, 47): "You declare that you are offering to God on behalf of the one Church which is spread throughout the whole world." From the Leonine Sacramentary: "Grant that your Church, spread throughout the whole world, be always directed by their teaching" (n. 280, on the feast of Sts Peter and Paul). From the Gelasian Sacramentary: ". . . . so that your Church, spread throughout the whole world, may persevere in the profession of an unwavering faith" (n. 401). Then there is this *Post pridie* prayer from the Mozarabic liturgy: "We offer them to you in the first place for your holy Catholic Church, which is spread throughout the whole world: may she be preserved in peace" (*Liber. Moz. Sacram.*, n. 1440). Finally, from the Ambrosian liturgy: "For your holy Church, which is spread both here and throughout the world" (Cf. *Rev. Bénédictine*, 46 (1934), 131).

71. Et omni populo acquisitionis sanctae tuae. Cf. 1 Peter 2:9: "But you are a chosen race, a royal priesthood, a holy nation, God's own people."

IX

74. Hoc sacrificium placationis et laudis. These words express the propitiatory value of the Mass. Cf. these three *Super oblata* prayers from the Leonine Sacramentary: "Lord, receive this sacrifice of appeasement and praise; through the intercession of your saints, may it bring us forgiveness, and may it cause us to render thanks to you without ceasing" (n. 33); "We place on your altar, Lord, our peace-offerings, extolling your power which is made manifest in the sufferings of the saints, and pleading through them for the forgiveness of our sins" (n. 270); "Lord, receive this sacrifice, through the offering of which you rightly wished to be appeased; grant that, having been purified by it, we may offer you those dispositions of heart which are pleasing to you" (n. 1302).

75. Eosque ita sacris tuis mysteriis efficias expiatos. These words express, in addition, the expiatory value of the sacrifice of the Mass: it is through the Mass that the expiatory value of the sacrifice of the cross is applied to us. This is an aspect of the Mass which nowadays needs to be brought once more into relief.

Here are some prayers from the Leonine Sacramentary which express this important aspect: "Almighty God, we pray that we who are burdened by our sins, may have these debts repaid by means of these sacred mysteries; so that we who are suffering because of our sins may be protected through the merits of your apostles" (n. 363, postcommunion). "Having been cleansed of our sins by means of these sacred mysteries, may we attain both pardon and grace" (n. 1023, *Super oblata*). "We humbly beseech your majesty, Lord, that we may be both cleansed of our sins by these heavenly mysteries, and constantly helped by your support" (n. 1089, postcommunion). The value of thc Eucharist as purification and expiation will be found expressed also in other prayers from the Leonine Sacramentary: nn. 222, 421, 427, 470, 500, 606, 656, 672, 810, 876, 1017, 1023, 1037, 1041, 1076, 1089, 1093, 1129.

76–77. Ut ad tuam magnificentiam capiendam, tuis semper miserationibus instaurentur. Cf. this *Super oblata* prayer from the Leonine Sacramentary: "May the celebration of this heavenly sacrament purify us, Lord, and may it so renew us with its divine power that we attain your glory" (n. 1042).

X

81. Concede nos sedulo quod tractamus imitari. Cf. the rite of priestly ordination in the Roman Pontifical—the *Admonitio*: "Be aware of what you are doing: imitate what you handle; as a celebrant of the mystery of the Lord's death, you should take care to mortify your body, keeping clear of sin and evil desires. Let your teaching be a spiritual tonic for the people of God, and let your way of life be a delight to the Church of Christ. Thus, through your preaching and your example, may you build up the house of God, that is to say, his family. In this way, neither of us will incur God's condemnation—myself, for raising you to such a high office; yourself, for taking it on—but rather we shall both earn God's reward." The whole text of this *Admonitio* reflects the ideas, the preoccupations and the style of St Gregory the Great. In particular:

(1) The way that the *Admonitio* explains the Lord's sending the seventy disciples before him, two by two—"because he wished to show by word and by deed that the ministers of his Church

should be perfect in both faith and works, rooted in the twin virtues of love of God and love of man." This is a theme dear to St Gregory. Cf. *Hom. in Ev.*, 17, n. 1; PL, 76, 1139.

(2) The *Admonitio*'s concern with instruction, with the duty of preaching and with the harmony between one's life and one's teaching is found again throughout the Fourth Part of the *Regula Pastoralis*, PL, 77, 125 ff.

(3) The formula *Agnosce quod agis: imitare quod tractas*, meaning the duty of the priest to sacrifice himself, is very similar to this passage from the *Dialogues*, where St Gregory is speaking about St Cassius, bishop of Narni: "That venerable man of God, Bishop Cassius of Narni, who used to offer God's sacrifice daily, also sacrificed himself in tears between the celebrations of the mysteries, in this way following the Lord's command which one of his priests had received in a vision: '*age quod agis, operare quod operaris*' " (IV, 58, ed. Moricca, 320). Cf. also, in the same work: "Since we celebrate the mysteries, we should also sacrifice ourselves to God in heartfelt repentance, for we who celebrate the mysteries of the Lord's passion should imitate what we are doing. Then indeed will the victim offered to God really benefit us, when he has made us also into victims . . . It is with full confidence that I tell you, we shall not be in need of the saving victim after our death (Masses for the dead) if we have become ourselves his victims while we were still alive" (IV, nn. 61–2, ed. Moricca, 323–5).

II. Documentation of those parts proper to project C

I

9. Per quem nobis agnitio tuae veritatis est indita. The hymn of thanksgiving and jubilation contained in nn. 9–24 embodies two themes: one concerned with the gift of revelation and of faith, which allows us to know, praise and love God; and the other concerned with creation.

The expression *agnitio tuae veritatis* (knowledge of your truth) contains the idea of revelation and faith familiar to us from the bible, the Fathers and the liturgy. This theme, expressed in Greek by the words *epignosis* and *gnosis*, forms an integral part of that hymn of thanksgiving, jubilation and praise which we call the Eucharist.

In fact, *agnitio* (knowledge) is one of the words used by the Vulgate to translate the Greek terms *gnosis* and *epignosis*. The other Latin words used are *scientia*, *cognitio* and *notitia*.

In a religious context, the term *epignosis* or *agnitio* normally means a knowledge and a living grasp of the things of God—of his will, of his interventions in the world, and so also of the real, deepest meaning of man's life and of world history. This knowledge and insight is given to us by means of divine revelation, found chiefly in the bible, and accepted through the gift of faith. It is precisely because this is not a purely intellectual reality that we have used the terms "knowledge and a living grasp" to describe it. The intelligence does indeed have its role to play, but there must also be the cooperation of the will, of the affections, and in fact, the involvement of the whole of a man's life. This is the full meaning of the biblical term "to know".

In the New Testament, *agnitio* is applied to the whole of Christian faith and the Christian way of life, often with a particular emphasis on the beginnings of this faith—and thus we have *agnitio veritatis* (cf. 1 Tim. 2: 4; 4: 3; 2 Tim. 2: 25, 3: 7; Tit. 1: 1; Heb. 10: 26; 2 Pet. 2: 20). At other times, however, it is rather a matter of the further deepening of that initial faith (cf. Col. 1: 9–10; 2: 2; 3: 10; Eph. 1: 17; 4: 13). But such a distinction indicates different emphases rather than entirely different meanings for the term.

This concept of "knowledge" has its origins in the Old Testament, in the idea of "the knowledge of God". This idea is found especially among the later prophets, and was subsequently considerably developed by later Judaism—for example, in the Qumran writings.

In the Old Testament, the object of the "knowledge" of God

is, above all, his creative and providential activity in the world. This includes therefore the designs of his wisdom manifested in the creation of the world, and in its history, especially in the history of Israel: election, liberation from Egypt, covenant, miracles in the desert, entry into the promised land, interventions by God through the means of prophets and good kings, the presence of God in the midst of his people and in the temple, his ways of acting with the pious and the impious, and finally his promises for the messianic age. All this is recorded in a pre-eminent way in the law and the prophets, and so the scriptures are the primary object of *gnosis* or knowledge. To "know" all this means the possession also of "wisdom", "understanding" and "learning"—all closely connected with each other. The possession of these gifts is the peculiar prerogative of Israel, and especially of the "pious Israelites", and of "those who fear God".

Now, since this "knowledge" of God and of his ways is God's own gift, then it should form the object of our prayer to him. The Tefilah of the Eighteen Blessings, Judaism's greatest prayer, makes the following request: "Teach us, O Lord our God, the knowledge of your ways, and circumcise our hearts that they may possess the fear of you."

"Knowledge" has, as one of its most important fruits, thanksgiving and the praise of God—expressed in the form of a hymn which is called the "blessing" of God, or the *berakah*. This hymn is, at one and the same time, a thanksgiving, a song of praise, and a prayer—a prayer which, when pronounced over an object such as bread and wine, becomes also a blessing of that object. The *berakah* is primarily concerned with the marvels accomplished by God, especially in his dealings with Israel. The "understanding" of these marvels (*magnalia Dei*) can only come from the knowledge of God and of his ways.

"The *berakah* is first of all an act of faith in God the creator and saviour, whose presence and redeeming action are discovered by faith to be shining through all things and every event. But this act of faith is already a prayer: a prayer in which we give ourselves up to the divine goodness in abandoning ourselves to the will of God made known through his word. We can say, consequently, that in the *berakah* is summed up the whole content of *gnosis* as we have described it, or again that the purest Jewish *gnosis* is its central object" (L. Bouyer, *The Spirituality of the New Testament and the Fathers*, London, 1963, 24. Cf. P. Audet, "Esquisse Historiquc etc." in *Rev. Bibl.*, 65 (1958), 371–99).

This same religious idea of "knowledge" is found in the New Testament also, although there it receives a new modality—the marvellous works of God, which man understands by means of this "knowledge", are now all centred on the person of Christ the Lord.

These same ideas were to take on great importance in early patristic literature, despite the polemic against the "false gnosis" which was soon found to be necessary (cf. L. Bouyer, op. cit., 211–55).

It is no surprise, therefore, that this idea of the gift of *gnosis* or knowledge also appears in the eucharistic anaphoras.

Already with Clement of Rome, in the great prayer which is contained in chapters fifty-nine to sixty-one, and which doubtless re-echoes the words of a very ancient anaphora indeed, right at the dawn of Christian liturgical development, we find thanksgiving being made for Christ's gift of "knowledge" to mankind: "through your beloved Son, Jesus Christ, who has called us from darkness into light, from ignorance (*agnosia*) to knowledge (*epignosin*) of the glory of his name . . . You have opened the eyes of our hearts so that we may know (*ginoskein*) you, who alone are the Most-High in the heights of heaven, you who alone are the Holy-One living among the holy ones" (1 Clement 59: 2–3).

In the Didache we have a strong confirmation that in the early period of Christianity, one of the normal objects of thanksgiving in the great eucharistic prayer was precisely this "knowledge". Here are the "eucharistic" prayers to be said over the cup and the bread: "Firstly over the cup: We thank you, our Father, for the holy vine of David, your servant, which you have made known to us through Jesus, your servant. Then over the broken bread: We thank you, our Father, for the life and knowledge which you have made known to us through Jesus, your servant. To you be glory for ever" (Didache 9: 2–3).

The hymn of jubilation from the anaphora of Serapion centres on the idea of *gnosis* or knowledge, and it is followed by the proclamation of those things that are "known", and by the subsequent hymn of praise (1: 3–7; Funk, 172). The same idea is found again in the Byzantine anaphora of St Basil: "You are he who has given us the knowledge of your truth" (Brightman, 322). The anaphora of Addaï and Mari has: "You have illuminated our knowing" (Brightman, 285), or "You have illuminated our understanding" (Renaudot, II, 584).

10–14. This passage points out the effects produced in us by "the knowledge of the truth": it enables us to know God's transcendence, the Trinity of persons, and the innermost nature of God—which is love. God's transcendence calls for our adoration; the knowledge of God as limitless love makes us respond joyfully with an undying love. These few lines therefore sum up the "theological" aspect of the thanksgiving.

15–16. Cf. Col. 1: 15–17: "He is the image of the invisible God, the first-born of all creation, for it is in him that everything has been created—everything in heaven and on earth, things visible and invisible, whether Thrones, or Lordships, or Rulers, or Authorities; everything has been created through him and for him. He is before everything, and everything is held together in him." We are not dealing directly with the christological theme in this project, but with the general idea of the creation of the world. Nevertheless, just as in the New Testament, creation is always regarded in its relationship to Christ. Indeed, it would be quite impossible to understand the meaning of creation outside of this perspective.

St Maximus the Confessor has this acute observation: "Following the economy, the creator of the universe became, by nature, that which he was not before . . . This is the great and veiled mystery. This is the happy end in view of which everything has been created. This is the divine plan which was known and willed even before the creation of finite beings. And the purpose known and willed beforehand is this: that thing for the sake of which everything else is made, while it itself is not willed for the sake of anything else. And it is with his gaze fixed on this end that God calls everything into being. The Word of God made man according to nature ... will show the end for the sake of which all creatures have received the principle of their being. Since it is in view of Christ that all ages, and that which fills every age, have received in Christ the principle and purpose of their being" (*Quaest. ad Thal.*, 60; PG, 90, 621).

The general theme of creation is common to all the Eastern anaphoras. Here we find a continuation of the Jewish tradition according to which the two leading ideas of the *berakah* are precisely God's creation and his special providence for Israel.

These two themes were to remain present in the Christian "Eucharist". Except that here, the Church is now regarded as the new and true Israel, and that both creation and providence are seen to be centred on Christ and on his work of salvation. St Justin bears clear witness to the fact that these two ideas remained the fundamental themes of the Christian anaphora when he says that Christ left us the eucharistic bread "so that we might give thanks to God for having created the world and all that is in it for man, and at the same time for having freed us from our former evil state, and for destroying once and for all the principalities and powers through him who obeyed the Father's will by submitting himself to suffering" (*Dialogue with Trypho*, 41: 1). St Justin alludes to this theme of creation also when he says, in connection with the anaphora, that he who is presiding takes bread and a cup "to praise and glorify the Father of the universe through the name of the Son and of the Holy Spirit" (1 *Apol.*, 65).

In the anaphora of Hippolytus, there is only a single allusion to the idea of creation: "We give you thanks through your beloved Son, Jesus Christ ... through whom everything was made" (cf. above, p. 26; ed. Botte, 12–13).

In the Roman canon, including its various prefaces, the general theme of creation, as well as the more particular theme of the creation of man, "has almost entirely disappeared" (H. Lietzmann, *Messe und Herrenmahl*, 173). The present Roman canon and the common preface do not mention it at all, and even in the more ancient prefaces we find only a few brief allusions (cf. Leonine Sacramentary, n. 94; Gelasian Sacramentary, nn. 386–390, the Blessing of the Chrism; Gregorian Sacramentary, n. 77). This then is another of those points on which the Roman liturgy is evidently poorer than the Eastern liturgy. Our project is an attempt to remedy such a state of affairs.

19. Ac nomen tuum per ipsum in perpetuum collaudarent. This thought is implicit in Col. 1: 16–18: if everything has been made in relation to Christ, and in subordination to him, then the reason for this must be that everything existing in this relation and subordination to Christ might praise God. The purpose of creation is in fact the glory of God. This idea is explicitly stated in the common preface of the Roman liturgy: "It is through him that the angels praise your majesty . . ."

22. Sanctorum tuorum catervae innumerae venerantur. This idea—that it is not only the angels, but also the saints, who join in singing the heavenly *Sanctus*—finds only rare expression in the anaphoras. Here are two examples from the Gallican and from the Palaeo-Hispanic liturgies: "All the angels, together with the great throng of the saints, praise him without ceasing, saying 'Holy . . .' " (*Missale gothicum vetus*, n. 282; 78, 33 ff.). "The golden voices of the saints hymn to you; the choirs of virgins and the ranks of confessors sing to you; everything in heaven, on earth, and in hell bows down before you, praising you as the eternal king. Hosanna in excelsis" (*Lit. Moz.*, Missale Mixtum; PL, 85, 484–5).

The idea is, however, implied in Rev. 5: 6–14.

23. . . . In circuitu throni magnitudinis tuae. This passage is based on Rev. 5: 9–13: "They sing a new song, saying: You are worthy to take the scroll and to open its seals, because you were slain, and at the price of your own blood you have ransomed for God men from every tribe and tongue and people and nation, and you have made them into a kingdom of priests for our God, and they will rule over the earth. And I saw, and I heard the sound of many angels around the throne, and the living creatures and the elders, and their number was myriads of myriads, and thousands of thousands. And they were crying out: Worthy is the Lamb who was slain to receive power and riches, wisdom and strength, honour, glory and praise. And every creature on heaven and on earth, those under the earth and in the sea, and all things, I heard them saying: To him who sits on the throne, and to the Lamb, praise and honour, glory and power for ever and ever."

Cf. also Heb. 8: 1: ". . . at the right of the throne of Majesty" (i.e. the divine majesty).

24. Perenni jubilatione proclamant. Cf. the Mozarabic liturgy: "The Cherubim and Seraphim . . . without rest and without cease, add their voices to that of the heavenly army and sing out with unending joy, adoring and glorifying you by saying: Holy . . ." (*Liber. Moz. Sacram.*, n. 788; ed. Ferotin, 341).

Cf. also the formula from the Roman preface: "incessabili voce proclamant . . .."

II

36–47. The themes of creation, of man's elevation to grace (implicit in the Genesis account of the earthly paradise), of man's fall from grace, and of God's providence for man throughout the Old Testament, are all present in the Eastern anaphoras.

Here, for example, is a fragment of a Nestorian anaphora as published by Brightman, 513–14: "You made us, from earth, into your own likeness, into your own image; you granted us, from dust, your own likeness. And, through your grace, you granted power to this image of yours, so that everything might be in subjection to your image, and serve your likeness. And behold, you have placed him over all things, for you desired mortal man to have dominion, and to have all creatures obey his rule. For, through your adorable grace, he was made so that he might be a ruler . . ."

In the Gallican and Palaeo-Hispanic anaphoras, these same ideas are occasionally found in the non-festive Masses. For example, here is an example from the so-called Mass of Mone: "You created man in the image and likeness of the Blessed Trinity, and placed him within the delights of paradise, so that he might both serve his creator, and be served by his fellow creatures . . . But when he became a sinner, he lost the life of paradise and became subject to death . . . But you, our merciful creator, having pity on sinful man, you came down to him with unabated power, to raise up him who had fallen" (ed. Mohlberg, *Missale gallicanum vetus*, 85, 26 ff.). Cf. also, in the same edition of Mohlberg, 87, 29 ff. In the *Missale gothicum*, cf. nn. 270, 492.

In the Bobbio Missal (ed. Bannister) cf. n. 488. In the *Lib. Moz. Sacram.*, cf. nn. 32, 1109, 1119, 1144, 1153, 1375, 1447.

In the Ambrosian liturgy, cf. the Bergamese Sacramentary, n. 648: ". . . and having created man to your own image, you subjected to him all living creatures and all the wonderful things in the world" (preface for the Second Sunday after Easter).

Among the prefaces which Alcuin collected together in his edition of the Gregorian Sacramentary, there are a good number of passages concerned with the creation of man. Cf. the Second Sunday after Christmas (Wilson, 257), the Second Sunday after Epiphany (ibid., 259), the Saturday of the first week in Lent (ibid., 263), the Thursday of the fourth week in Lent (267): ". . . whose goodness created man, whose justice condemned him, and whose mercy redeemed him." Cf. also the Bergamese Sacramentary, n. 410.

In the Roman liturgy itself, there is only this text from the Leonine Sacramentary, n. 90: "Your gifts to human nature at the beginning were abundant indeed: you created man from nothing, and you gave him knowledge of yourself; you placed him over all living things by giving him a share in your own rational nature, and you gave him the whole world as his own: but even more wonderful than these were your deeds when you not only gave life again to earthly mortality, but you also made it divine."

43. Et in operum tuorum magnaliis iugiter te laudaret. Cf. Ecclus. 17: 1–10: "The Lord created man out of earth, whither he must return. He granted them a set time of so many days, but gave them authority over everything on earth. He endowed them with strength like his own, and made them in his own image. He filled all living things with fear of men, and made them masters over birds and beasts. He made for them a tongue and eyes, he gave them ears and a heart to think with. He filled them with knowledge and understanding, and showed them good and evil. He put his own eye into their hearts, to show them the greatness of his deeds. And they will praise his holy name, proclaiming his marvellous works."

45. Tuis beneficiis cumulare non desisti. Cf. Acts 14: 17: "He did not leave us without evidence of himself in the good things he does, giving us rain from heaven and fruitful seasons, filling our hearts with food and gladness."

46. Ut te quaerere non cessaret. Cf. Acts 17: 26–27: "From one stock, he made all the nations of men to live over the face of the earth, fixing determined seasons and the boundaries of their dwelling-places, so that they should seek God, and by groping for him, might find him."

47. Sed et eum manu ad salvatorem duxisti per legem et prophetas. Cf. Gal. 3: 24–25: "So the law had the function of leading us to Christ, that we might be justified through faith. But now that faith has come, we are no longer under a leader." This idea is common in the oriental anaphoras, especially those of the Antiochene group.

48–49. Et sic, mundum, Pater sancte dilexisti, ut Unigenitum tuum nobis mitteres redemptorem. Cf. Jn. 3: 16–17: "God so loved the world, that he gave his only Son, that everyone who believes in him may not perish, but possess eternal life. For God did not send his Son into the world to judge the world, but that the world might be saved through him,"

50. Unde amares in nobis quod in Filio diligebas. Cf. this text from the Mozarabic liturgy: "You sent your Son into the world in the form of a man, so that you might love in us that which you always loved in your Son" (*Liber. Moz. Sacram.*, n. 725, *Inlatio*; ed. Ferotin, 312).

52. Superabundanter nos ad tua dona reparavit. Cf. Rom. 5: 15–20, especially vv. 15 and 20: "But the gift is a different matter from the offence. For if many died through the offence of one man, how much more has the grace of God and the gracious gift of one man, Jesus Christ, abounded to many . . . But where sin abounded, grace has abounded the more."

Cf. also, this fragment from a Catholic anaphora of the fourth century, attested to by an anonymous Arian author, and published by Mohlberg in his edition of the Leonine Sacramentary, 202: "In your incomparable goodness, you were pleased to make light shine in darkness when you sent Jesus Christ to us as protector of our souls. For our salvation, he humbled himself, and subjected himself to death, so as to restore to us that immortality which Adam had lost, and to make us God's heirs and sons" (cf. above, p. 31).

53. Quae in priore amiseramus Adamo. Cf. Rom. 5: 12–21 for what St Paul says about the sin of the first Adam, and the parallelism between the two Adams. Cf. 1 Cor. 15: 45: "The first man, Adam, became a living soul; the last Adam has become a life-giving spirit."

54. Quin et nos in finem usque dilexit. Cf. Jn. 13: 1: "Loving his own who were in the world, he loved them to the end."

55–56. Et ideo tibi per Spiritum Sanctum immaculatam hostiam obtulit semetipsum. Cf. Heb. 9: 14: ". . . who through the Holy Spirit offered himself without spot to God." The Greek text has "through the eternal Spirit", but the meaning is the same. The anaphora of Theodore of Mopsuestia uses this text in a context similar to that of our project: "He offered himself without spot to God, through the eternal Spirit, and sanctified us through the oblation of his body, made once and for all. Through the blood of his cross he has brought peace to heaven and earth" (cf. above, p. 62; Renaudot, 11, 612–13). Cf. also the "*Aliis Diebus de Resurrectione*" preface, given in Muratori's edition of the Gregorian Sacramentary: "Who brought to an end all fleshly sacrifices, when he offered himself through the Holy Spirit by the oblation of his body, presenting himself as both priest and sacred Lamb" (*Liturgia Vetus* II, 277–8).

57. Veterum sacrificiorum implens in veritate figuras. This text gathers together in one sweep all those sacrifices which had been offered to God and accepted by him before Christ's coming—those of Abel, Noah, Abraham, Melchisedech, etc., as well as those pagan sacrifices which were acceptable to God. Cf. Leonine Sacramentary: "... immolating without cease the victim of praise; that which was prefigured by Abel the just, foreshadowed also by the lamb of the Law, celebrated by Abraham, revealed by the priest Melchisedech but fulfilled only in the true Lamb and eternal High Priest, Christ, who this day is born" (n. 1250); "Having passed over the foreshadowings of fleshly victims, we humbly offer you, heavenly Father, this spiritual victim, which in a wonderful and mysterious way is forever immolated and also forever offered, being both the gift offered by the faithful and the reward granted them by you" (n. 253, *Oratio super oblata*).

From the Roman Missal: "O God, you who have brought to their fulfilment the various sacrifices of the old law in the single and perfect sacrifice of the cross; accept this sacrifice from the hands of your faithful servants, and sanctify it in the same way as you blessed the gifts of Abel; so that what is offered by each one to your glory, may serve to the salvation of all" (Seventh Sunday after Pentecost, *Oratio super oblata*).

From the Gallican liturgy: "O God, we offer you now this

unique victim, there being no longer a variety of different sacrifices . . ." (*Missale francorum*, n. 152).

From the Ambrosian liturgy: ". . . who brought to an end the sacrifices of fleshly victims when he offered himself to you for our salvation" (Bergamese Sacramentary, n. 614, preface). Cf. Gelasian Sacramentary, n. 476.

58. Aeterna redemptione semel inventa. Cf. Heb. 9: 12: "(Christ) has entered once and for all into the sanctuary, not with the blood of goats or of calves, but with his own blood, having won an eternal redemption for us"; ibid. 9: 28: "Christ was offered once for the sins of many"; ibid. 10: 10: "And this will was for us to be sanctified through the offering of the body of Jesus Christ, made once and for all"; ibid. 10: 14: "For through a single offering, he has perfected for ever those he is sanctifying."

60–61. Et ascendit ad dexteram tuam Pontifex in aeternum semper vivens ad interpellandum pro nobis. Cf. Heb. 7: 24–7: "Because he remains forever, his priesthood cannot be transferred. So that he is perfectly able to save those who approach God through him, since he lives on for ever to intercede for them. Such a high priest indeed suited us well—he was holy, innocent and undefiled, separated from sinners, and raised up above the heavens; he does not need to offer up daily sacrifices for his own sins, and then for those of the people, as the other high priests did—for he did this once and for all by offering himself." Cf. Heb. 6: 18–20; 8: 1–2; 9: 11–15; 10: 12: "He, on the contrary, having offered a single sacrifice for sins, now sits for ever at God's right hand."

63–64. Se tamen cuncta per saecula nobis est pollicitus adfuturum. Cf. Mt. 28: 20: "And behold I am with you through all days until the end of the world." Cf. also this Preface from the Gregorian Sacramentary: "We humbly pray that your Son, our Lord Jesus Christ, who promised to be with us to the end of time, might not deprive us, whom he has redeemed, of his bodily presence in the sacraments, nor remove his divine blessings from us" (Twenty-Third Sunday after Pentecost; PL, 78, 187). Here, the bodily presence of Christ which is preserved for us "in the sacraments" is probably a reference to the Eucharist.

65–66. Unde et alium, Pater, a te misit Paraclitum Spiritum veritatis qui nos cuncta doceret. Cf. Jn. 14: 15–21, where Christ's promise to remain with us even after his departure from this world ("I will not leave you orphans, I shall come to you") is quite clearly related to the coming of the Holy Spirit, the other Paraclete who will take Christ's place for us. Cf. also, this text from the Mozarabic liturgy: "This is that gift of the Father's help, similar to himself, which the Son promised would be given when, returning to his Father, he told us that he would not leave us orphans. In this way, he taught us that the Spirit contained his own and his Father's majesty" (*Liber. Moz. Sacram.*, n. 789; ed. Ferotin, 342).

In connection with the words *qui nos cuncta doceret*, cf. Jn. 16: 13: "When he comes, the Spirit of truth, he will lead you into the complete truth."

67. Et omnem sanctificationem compleret in mundo. Cf. above, p. 155, the documentation for nn. 6–8 of Project B.

71. Praesentia suae maiestatis implere dignetur. In liturgical terminology, "majesty" is equivalent, in practice, to "divinity". Cf. this prayer from the Leonine Sacramentary, which has the form of an epiclesis: "Heed our prayers, O Lord, and fill these gifts with the presence of your majesty, so that what is performed through our ministry may become effective through your action" (n. 565, *Oratio super oblata*). Cf. also this *Communicantes* prayer for Whit Sunday: "In communion with each other, we celebrate the holy feast of Pentecost, the day when the Holy Spirit filled the apostles and the gathering of believers with the majesty of his presence" (n. 204).

Index